THE AUTHEN

THE AUTHENTIC ANIMAL

Inside the Odd and Obsessive World of Taxidermy

DAVE MADDEN

St. Martin's Press ⚘ New York

Grateful acknowledgment is made to Travis Morrison for permission to reprint an
excerpt from his "Song for the Orca," copyright © 2004 by Travis Morrison.

www.stmartins.com

ISBN 978-0-312-64371-3

First Edition: August 2011

10 9 8 7 6 5 4 3 2 1

3 9547 00360 3938

For Jonis Agee

How can a people who do not mean to understand death hope to understand love, and who will sound the alarm?

—*John Cheever*

THE AUTHENTIC ANIMAL

INTRODUCTION

To skin an animal, you start with a single cut somewhere around the throat and draw the knife downward in a thin, straight line to the nethers. It's a lot like unzipping a fly. The thrush. The tom-cat. The tusker. The beginning is always the same: a single cut. After this beginning, every animal presents its own challenges, the idiosyncrasies of its own terrain. The wings. The antlers. The gills. The fatty haunches. The only way to get good is to practice, to skin animal after animal after animal, because what you want, ideally, is that skin not just intact, but flawlessly intact. A skin like the artful helix of an orange rind peeled off in one go. Thin, pliable, but strong. A skin clean and full of potential. It's hard at first to think about disembodied skins as nonetheless clean. Because we're animals, too, and we have skins, the idea of the removal of which makes us rightfully uncomfortable. Skin is both our largest organ and our most erotic—there's a whole line of mags promising nothing but the exposure thereof. It is also the oily soil out of which our hair grows, the place that seeps our sweats and sebums, the part that burns and wrinkles and flakes off from us like birch bark. Skin removed from our bodies becomes dust to be swept and tossed and forgotten. Skin removed from animals' bodies becomes any number of things. Coats, shawls, stoles, and shrugs. Rugs and mats.

Shoes, handbags, briefcases, and jackets. Footballs. Chew toys. Pork rinds.

And taxidermy. From the Greek *taxis,* meaning "arrangement," and *derma,* meaning "skin," *taxidermy* refers generally to any such arrangement (a bearskin rug, an expensive fur coat) and more specifically to the practice of re-creating the animal. In taxidermy, the empty becomes whole and what was dead becomes lifelike, and this is what interests me in the art form. For years now I've been obsessed with taxidermy, with the public and private spaces it fills, with the processes by which animal skins get converted to lifelike sculpture, despite the fact that I've never once in my life been on a hunt. I've never had a relationship to an animal other than the everyday owner-pet relationship and have in some sense always understood animals as outside the world, not a part of it. Kept in some separate space from my own. In other words, I'm not the typical person to fall in love with taxidermy, if such a person exists, and yet that's exactly what's happened. I've fallen in a kind of obsessive, curious love with this thing, and as a result I've begun to feel if not closer to animals then at least as though animals have begun at last to feel closer to me. How this all happened is what I've written this book to find out.

All the same, I've never personally wanted to go about mounting an animal. (And here we first arrive at the unfortunate middle-school pun that lies at the heart of taxidermy: "mounting," *har har.* It's a goofball double-entendre this book will by needs be lousy with, a regrettable outcome of the otherwise not regrettable shift in taxidermy from stuffing hides to draping them over sculpted forms, about which much, much more to come.) Taxidermy can be a brutal endeavor, but this isn't what deters me. I don't get green around the gills. I could stomach the skinning of a hide from an animal's carcass, the scraping of excess flesh from that hide, the chemical tans, the fitting over a bodyform, the sewing, the tucking in of eyelids. All of it. And it's not for any ethical reasons, either. A practicing taxidermist need never do the actual killing of an animal. Even still, I'm not interested. This obsession isn't so much participatory as spectatorial, much like an armchair quarterback or the theatergoer who'd rather *see* a show than have to be in one. I like very much to look at a mounted animal. I like very much its stillness, and the fact that I can touch it. I appreciate the work that goes into creating the illusion that it is alive, and I like very much this illusion. But why? Why does this illusion produce in me the nerves and giddiness of some preteen about to land his first slowdance? Why am I drawn toward this thing that repels so many others? It's not, please believe, a goth thing. I have no other inclinations toward the morbid—I collect yarn art, for Christ's sake. In other words: it wasn't me. I didn't push myself toward taxidermy. Taxidermy, somehow, drew me to it.

But I'm talking about more than the morbid dissection and reconstitution of animal parts. I'm talking about taxidermy as you know it, the end product hanging on your uncle's den wall. The "family" of brown bears you've seen behind glass in a museum. Taxidermy is a way to measure and characterize the relationship between humans and animals, a relationship that extends back to the beginning of time. It is an umbrella term covering a whole array of activities, from cataloging a bird skin for a scientific collection to dyeing a rabbit's paw for sale at a tourist trap. Taxidermy is beautiful and horrible. It is something about which everyone has an opinion or at least a reaction—usually negative. And taxidermy as a field includes a whole host of experts and scholars none of us has likely ever heard of. One of the first people I talked with about taxidermy was Dr. Trish Freeman, who works on the top floor of Nebraska Hall at the University of Nebraska-Lincoln, a floor with long fluorescent-lit hallways lined with dozens and dozens of game heads taken from Asia, from Africa, from all over the planet. These, Dr. Freeman explained, were part of the Elgin Gates Collection of the Nebraska State Museum on UNL's campus. Comprising more than 150 specimens, the taxidermy on all of them was done by a man in Denver who studied,

Dr. Freeman explained, under "the father of modern taxidermy"—
Carl Akeley.

A distinction, I imagine, is being made here from classical taxidermy, when skins were stuffed so full of straw you'd think we'd
meant to sleep on them. Modern taxidermy—an era we might be at
the tail end of—has brought what once amounted to little more than
spooky upholstery into the realm of sculpture; animal skins are now
draped and glued to premade bodyforms sculpted to precise dimensions based on each specimen's anatomy. Whatever lifelikeness we
imagine we see in a taxidermized animal we owe to these modern
developments. Whether we owe them specifically to Carl Akeley is
unclear. Certainly we're meant to; the moniker "father of modern
taxidermy" implies no less. In truth, he's like all fathers—the father
of modern science, the father of modern art, the father of modern
you—creating something new not from a void but from certain inherited traits. Presculpted forms were in use well before Akeley ever
skinned an animal, but without question he took these previous innovations and improved on them. What resulted was a technique
that came, in the early twentieth century, to be known as the Akeley
method. And thus the title, the implied siring of an entire art form—
if, that is, we can call taxidermy an art form, and thanks to Carl
Akeley we can.

It helps with these things to be a bit of a character. Cézanne, considered to be the father of modern art, was a depressive and a draft
dodger. The father of modern science, Galileo Galileii pissed off the
whole Roman Catholic Church. Freud, the father of modern psychology, was Sigmund Freud. Clarence Ethan Akeley had his share
of idiosyncrasies that makes him fit for the title, father of modern
taxidermy. He had a predilection for younger women, having met
his first wife when he was twenty-six and she was just fifteen—and
already married to his good friend and hunting companion. They
divorced after Carl met (and by some accounts was living with) his
second wife: a mountain climber. In a dry creek bed in Somalia he

choked an attacking leopard to death with his bare hands. He lived for a time with a monkey named J. T. Jr. He once sculpted a figure of a man bursting out of the skin of an ape and called it *The Chrysalis*. He had a dinner table made from an elephant's ear and tusks and fell head over heels in a manly, platonic (but what seems mostly unrequited) love for Teddy Roosevelt. He died at the top of a mountain. That was in 1926. Carl Akeley's life interests me the way a classical hero's might and for the story it can tell of a boy growing up on a farm in tiny Clarendon, New York, who through taxidermy ends up dying in the Belgian Congo. He interests me for the history his life represents, but taxidermy, let me be clear, isn't historic. Maybe because the age of the safari is over (though safaris still go on throughout Africa and are available to anyone with a couple thousand dollars and a tolerance for international hide-shipping regulations), or maybe because museum mammal collections go back sometimes to the wee morning hours of the nineteenth century, taxidermy has an otherworldly feel. It comes to us from some other lost time. But taxidermists live on, attending schools of taxidermy and shows of taxidermy, working for taxidermy-supply companies, entering taxidermy into taxidermy competitions, forming nonprofit organizations of taxidermists, sitting on boards of directors for taxidermy groups, opening their own taxidermy shops in small towns and haggling over the prices of a mounted squirrel or Dall sheep. Taxidermy lives. And it's changing through technological developments and shifting attitudes toward animals. What's useful about looking at Carl Akeley's life story is the way contemporary issues and questions facing taxidermy can find roots there. How and whether to preserve someone's pet. How to learn the mechanics of mounting animals. The presentation of specimens in museums. Organizing taxidermists around the country and the assessment and judgment of their work. The need to collect animals, the defense of taxidermy as an art form, the ethics of murder and death. Carl had a hand—both hands, really—in all of it.

I've avoided writing Akeley's life as a biography, or at least an exhaustive biography. Akeley has been given the treatment plenty of times, chiefly by his second wife, Mary Jobe Akeley, and by the former archivist Penelope Bodry-Sanders. Instead, my treatment of him is like a pointillist sketch, making up just a part of a larger project. In wanting as multifaceted a look at taxidermy as I could get, I've filled the book with facts, culled both from nerdish research in hard-to-find books and from personal observation around the country. All the same, I've eschewed any attempts at being authoritative. Authority as I understand it is something granted, not claimed. As a kid growing up with two older sisters, I revered my friend Clay as I would a brother. He was two years older and lived right across the street and was considered by me an authority on all things from math to four-square. Once, I must have been six, maybe seven, Clay told me and another neighborhood kid that human eyeballs had a certain kind of weak but potent power. "If you take, like, thousands of people," Clay said, "and get them all to stare at a specific point on a brick wall, if they do it long enough they'll all burn a hole right through it." I remember this conversation perfectly; we were sitting on the sidewalk and curb between our two houses in the late afternoon hours of a slow midsummer's day, just before dinner would be ready, the sun bisected by his house's brown roof. Wasn't it plausible enough? What reason did I have not to trust him that this could, in fact, happen? I carried that trust into my teens, at one point sharing the "fact" with some friends, all of whom subsequently stared at me as though I'd confessed to illiteracy or to enjoying the taste of my own dead skin. When I confronted Clay about it later, he had barely any recollection of that afternoon and was surprised that I did. "I never expected you to believe me," he said.

There are so many lies out there, but what's harder to understand is how many truths can exist simultaneously with one another. Carl Akeley took painting lessons as a boy so that he could create backdrops for the birds he mounted. He considered these to be the first attempts at incorporating painted backgrounds into taxi-dermy displays—Mary Jobe, in her biography, affirms this claim—but Charles Willson Peale had done this decades earlier, to say nothing of similar work done throughout Europe. Likewise, most taxidermy historians write that a rhinoceros dating to the early 1500s is the ear-liest extant piece of taxidermy, but this rhinoceros doesn't actually exist. Are we being lied to? We make myths of the real. We do this every time we write down stories. One of my goals in this pointillist treatment of Carl Akeley is to avoid such mythmaking, but it hasn't been easy. There is so much romanticizing to be done when writing about the dead.

And here, then, is something we can't avoid. Taxidermy is an art form that begins at the moment an animal dies. This is a gentler way of saying that taxidermy needs animals to be dead. It is wrong to say that taxidermy kills animals, but it is not wrong to say that any close study of taxidermy is going to have to get comfortable, or "come to terms," in therapy parlance, with death. Taxidermy is the arrange-ment of an animal's skin over a premade form in an attempt to make that arrangement look alive, and so taxidermy does traffic in acts of resurrection. But to live eternally and to live again a thing must first be dead, and this is what taxidermy is. Death. The dead. Taxidermy is the neat red pinhole popped in the throat of a whitetail deer one morning in November, the high five from father to son that sounds out in the quiet forest dawn. Taxidermy is a mountain lion crossing an interstate too far from home, smacked in the hip by a car's front bumper and now rolling to the road's shoulder like some lost cargo, left to bleed herself empty. Taxidermy is two ring-necked pheasants, one rooster and one hen, unmoving in a corn-stubble field one North Dakota winter, watching and listening for another footfall of the man eyeing them along his sight. Taxidermy is the click of the trig-ger, the crack in the air, the explosion of feathers that go flying up-ward. Best to just admit it. Get it out in the open. Taxidermy is the American, the Englishman, the Frenchman, the Russian, the Western man of means in stately khakis, sturdy leather boots; it is the pack of paid-for Kikuyus, the mother elephant sussed out of the jungle, the war story that gets told for generations, the trophy hung dramatically overhead. Taxidermy is the old brown owl found beak down on the floor of the barn one morning. It's the family dog that lived for seventeen years now gutted, his fat stripped away from the flesh, his brains pulled from the cranium, his eyes replaced by hard plastic. The family dog that lived for seventeen years rotating slowly for a week, two weeks, in a stainless steel freeze-dry drum. Taxidermy is a set of antlers screwed into the skull of a jackrabbit; it's a fish tail sewn to the torso of a monkey; it's a chicken's head stuck right on the body of a stillborn lion cub. Taxidermy is the capture of all these. Taxidermy is their deaths and the deaths of the polar bear, the alligator, the chipmunk, the gorilla, the canary, the moose, the brook trout, the iguana, the joey, the three-toed sloth, the human, the marlin, the dik-dik, the fox, the armadillo, the capercaillie, the ring-tailed lemur. Let's come to terms. Every animal dies. Taxidermy is what comes next.

Very few of us would gladly spend his or her time mucking about with a carcass. This accounts for taxidermy's queasy, kitschy qualities, the way all movie taxidermists are weirdos and fringe characters. Norman Bates is not a man we aspire to be. But very many sane people do choose to spend time with a dead animal, removing the skin, curing and tanning it, draping it over a manikin, and lovingly detailing the end product. Some of these people are hunters, yes, but some are scavengers. Some are scientists. Some are scholarly men and women in charge of museum collections. Some are young boys and girls tinkering around with what they know as "God's creation." If it's true that the number of people willing to put their hands on a dead animal's body is far outranked by the number of those who aren't, then what results is that taxidermists form a small, tight-knit community. A subculture. And as with all subcultures, taxidermists as individuals are impossible to characterize. They are urban and they are rural. They hold graduate degrees and they've never finished high school. They are men and they are women. Young and old. Straight and gay. If there's anything that distinguishes the set of taxidermists from the set of nontaxidermists it's that the people composing the former have something the rest of us do not: an ability to see. Where the rest of us turn away from dead animals, a taxidermist turns toward. We see only the grave. They see possibilities.

This book is an exploration of these possibilities, an attempt to understand what the origins of the taxidermist's vision might be. Put another way, I'm writing this book to answer a small but complicated question: Why do we stuff animals? I want to know where this desire came from, but also how it manifests itself today. We could start anywhere, which is to say "anywhen." We could go all the way back to Lascaux in 15,000 BCE, to the paintings of deer, horses, and bulls on the walls of a cave; the moment, whenever it was, when the first human thought, *I killed this animal but I don't want to forget this animal, not because I want to remember that I killed it, but because I want to remember that it once lived*; the point at which pigment was made from iron ore and clay and applied by careful hands to the wall. The Lascaux Grotto is page 1 in any history of Western art, the first time humans looked at the world around them and put that world to paint. "It seems to be a law of nature that no man ever is loath to sit for his portrait," Max Beerbohm once wrote, and so how refreshing to learn that we weren't even asked to sit for the first portrait ever produced, that our artistic beginning is one of humility. It was nice of us. And telling. Before we ever re-created the self in 2-D, we wanted to depict the other—their swiftness, their size, their strength.

I'm speaking, then, of representations of animals, and thus we have the entirety of human history to sift through. We have the caves at Lascaux. We have the transfigurations of Greco-Roman myth: the Minotaur, the centaur, Medusa. We have the Sphinx and the griffin, the whole of any medieval bestiary. We have the Chinese dragon. We have Ganesha, the elephant-headed Hindu deity. We have the hollowed-out head of the buffalo held on the shoulders of Native American dancers. We have the teddy bear, the Beanie Baby, the Tamagotchi. The whole of human history is riddled with animals, as though our time on this planet were one long, progressive safari, touring curiously through our various countrysides, watching them watch us. We are not them, we've decided, and yet it seems we can't understand ourselves without them.

Depending on whom you talk to, taxidermy is either an homage to nature or a violation of it, man's attempt to lie about the hard truths of life and death. Maybe it's both of these, maybe both at once is possible. The problem, it seems, is one of positioning. No other human activity sits so squarely at the intersection of nature, science, and art. Taxidermy, like nature, like science, like art, has no discernable beginning, but all the same that's where we'll have to start.

ONE

Our taxidermy story begins on a cold night in Clarendon, New York, in the winter of 1876. Everyone in town was asleep. The farmers and shopkeeps. The judges with their offices in Town Hall and Frank Turner, the new town clerk. Chauncey Foster, who owned the Clarendon Hotel. The man who ran the gristmill, a miller whose name just happened to be Miller. The schoolteacher, William Stillwell, who pounded insubordinate students with a notched ruler, and the school-boys trying not to sleep on their bruises. Even the known night owl Dr. Brackett turned in early that evening, the cold being too fierce to get any work done. Irene Glidden, the youngest of ten children—twenty years old and living, still, at home, a brief lifetime of spin-sterhood set out unwittingly before her—had fallen asleep before she could remember to throw another log or two in the stove. In the morning she rose early and shivering to find that her pet canary had frozen to death. She fed fresh, dry logs to the dying embers. She tried to get a fire roaring. If she tried hard enough maybe she could wake her canary up. Maybe it could live again. Maybe miracles hap-pened every day.

Another canary? Another canary was just a day's trip away in Rochester, and yet as any pet owner knows what creates the love between the human and the pet is the notion of custody. *This animal's life is my responsibility.* Every loss of every pet is met with some anxious mix of deprivation and personal shame. Sometimes sobbing alone in one's living room is the only reasonable reaction. Miss Irene Glidden's tears, then, are understandable tears. She had that cold morning in 1876 some complicated feelings of guilt to manage, and she had before her an image no one likes to consider: a bird unmoving, its wings no longer cutting through the air above us.

Enter Carl Akeley. A small boy, thin. His sandy hair slicked flat on his scalp. In certain brands of daylight it looked painted on. A farmer's son, quiet and watchful. Fence-picket shoulders and skin as fair as a lady's handkerchief. She watched Carl enter the house with an empty basket held in his mittened hands. Outside, the wind blew up snowdrifts in slanted curtains of white. Carl said good morning. He left his coat and mittens in place on his tiny body. He was so much like a bird in the frail way he stood beneath Irene that it was too much for her not to keep sobbing right there in her chair.

"Mother sent me for some eggs," Carl said, not moving closer.

She couldn't say it. She only pointed to the birdcage in the corner.

Carl set the basket on the floor and walked over. The cage was a shiny brass thing. Baroque, and glowing in the firelight like a lantern. It hung from a hook in the ceiling, and Carl stretched up on the tips of his toes to see inside. There lay the canary. "Oh Carl," Irene said, standing up from her chair and keeping a distance from the birdcage. "I'm an animal. A monster. What kind of person . . . ?" She drifted off to open the stove and throw another short log in, but by now the fire was blazing. Carl began to sweat. He took off his mittens and stuffed them in his coat pockets, and he pried open the wire door of the cage and reached one hand in.

"I'll fix it," he said. The canary was warm to the touch and felt like breath between his fingers.

He had handled a dead animal before. After the cows on his father's farm had been milked, after Carl had cleaned out the horse stalls in the barn, he liked to walk wordlessly through the woods with another old farmer in town, a man named Os Mitchell, who could train a dog to hunt better than anyone. Mitchell taught the boy how to shoot, and Carl on his best days would clip a bird right out of the air and watch as one of Os's dogs ran off to fetch the animal and present it to the boy. These dead animals led to nothing. They became dead animals and remained dead animals. Before that morning in the Gliddens' home, death was the end of something, and then, suddenly, death was not the end, Carl saw. Death was just an accident, an error in the world he thought he could fix. That morning a canary had died, but before anyone knew it a taxidermist was born.

Julia Akeley was a fire-eyed woman with an acute severity in the brow and a temper none in her household could anticipate. A wronged woman. Her family was wealthy and her husband was poor, having been handed fifty-eight rocky, barren acres on the far eastern outskirts of the property owned by Julia's father, Thomas Glidden.[1] The Gliddens were a large and proud clan, one of Clarendon's founding families, who, according to Carl's older brother Lewis, "ruled the public opinion of the neighborhood." To be a Glidden was to walk through town expecting the faces of its people to reflect envy and admiration. And then there was Julia. Her husband, Webb Akeley, was a man who did not put on airs and had no truck with the airs put on by others. He didn't go to church; he raised livestock. A couple cows, and few pigs, some chickens. He grew oats

---

[1] Back then, in Clarendon, you couldn't swing a dead cat without hitting a Glidden, but no relation seems to have existed between Julia and neighbor Irene. The former Gliddens hailed from New Hampshire and the latter from Canada.

and corn and wheat, but the ground was all clay and rock, and Webb never could have been called a successful man. And Julia saw success all around her. Her sisters all married well and lived in tall brick houses in town with four, five bedrooms. As she walked through town, she heard, she thought, them and the other citizens of Clarendon talking about her family—that run-down farm, that boy and his dead animals. It should have been enough to make her leave. Webb wrote to relative Gliddens out in De Kalb, Illinois (where one of them, Joseph Farwell Glidden, became the inventor of barbed-wire fencing), and received word that out there was wealth and bounty. The Heartland. It had so much promise, but Julia wouldn't leave. Her refusal to break away from the Clarendon Gliddens and their power led, Lewis once wrote, to the Akeleys' doom: "Our father never had a chance for economic independence in the utterly hopeless agricultural situation to which his wife's reluctance condemned him for life."

Julia turned cold and cruel. She snapped at her children and nagged her husband. By age twelve, Carl had learned to remain out of her sights, to stay busy with farmwork, to spend his afternoons far out in the woods of Clarendon. When he got home that cold morning he tried to slip noiselessly upstairs and get right to work, but his mother heard his footfalls from the kitchen. "How many eggs?" she called out, and only then did Carl realize he'd forgotten. He was to have left with at least four eggs, his mother had explained, and eight if the Gliddens could spare them. "And they can," she'd said. Carl had even forgotten the basket. He walked into the kitchen. His mother was sitting at the empty kitchen table, her hands flat on the surface. The canary was safe in his coat pocket, wrapped in a red handkerchief. "I forgot them, I guess," he said. "Shall I go back for them?"

"You forgot the one thing I sent you over there for?" She didn't look his way when she spoke.

"Yes'm," he said. "It was Irene. Her canary—"

"I don't care about canaries. I only care about feeding this family." Her eyes were closed and her face held upward as though in prayer. "But it's clear you don't care as much as I do. Running around without a head on your shoulders. Your father's son, that's what you are."

"I can go back, Ma."

"No," she said. She was looking at him now. "No, you can go up to your room. And stay there. Without those eggs I have too many mouths to feed tonight."

Carl just turned and ran up the steps. "You won't be missed," his mother called after him. It must have been a lie, because by the time dinner was ready she called him down to join them, pleaded almost, though Carl never answered. He wasn't vindictive so much as busy, absorbed in the task of resurrecting Irene's canary. How to get started? Every story ever told about the life of Carl Akeley has begun with this fundamental canary, and part of the mythology holds that he knew what to do because of a book he had borrowed from another boy in town—one that, Akeley is sure to explain in his memoirs, "had originally cost a dollar." It's shorthand for "humble beginnings": act 1 in any Cinderella story. Not that taxidermy in the second half of the nineteenth century was such a strange activity for a young boy. This was a kind of boom era for American boyhood. Twain's *The Adventures of Tom Sawyer* was published the very year Miss Glidden's canary died, and books abounded on how to fish, hunt, and make the world your playground. The children's magazine *Youth's Companion* was in wide enough circulation to have reached even the Akeley household.[2] Add to this knowledge the

---

[2] The recent bestseller *The Dangerous Book for Boys* basically re-creates the kind of outdoorsy how-tos that must have surrounded young Carl Akeley the way manga and video-game cheat books do now. One such how-to, *The American Boy's Handy Book*, was written by Daniel Carter Beard, who would soon play a role in the founding of the Boy Scouts of America. "Before about 1915, boyhood was seen by most grown-ups as a state of

self-sufficiency Carl had cultivated in the face of his mother's temper—she was right: he truly was his father's son—and it's clear that Carl knew what to do with the bird without having to think too much about it.

All the same, he proceeded methodically. First he lay the bird on its back and cut a long incision down the breast, from neck to tail. He used only a small pocketknife, and he took his time. Once he cut away the bulk of the skin he dug into the joints, severing the tibia from the hip, the tailbone from the backbone, the wingbones from the shoulder joints, and the vertebrae from the head. What he then held in his hands was the headless, limbless torso of the canary, shapeless and small like some broken toy. Next he had to remove the eyes and snip out the tongue and scoop the brains from the cranium. Only then was the skin ready for stuffing. He took measurements of the bird before cutting it open and used these numbers to mold from sticky wood shavings called "excelsior" a kind of body. Carl took a sturdy length of wire and fit one end of it into this body and another into the canary's skull and made a neck. He stuck four more wires into the excelsior and attached them to each severed limb and made thighbones and wing bones. Around this poseable doll went the skin, which he sewed up along the seam, keeping the stitches small and neat.

The eye of a canary is a tiny black orb, with a gloss like obsidian. To fill the eye cavities Carl sneaked a hand into his mother's sewing table and found two glass beads. The final stage of any taxidermy project is the mounting of the specimen. For an animal in a museum, what's needed is a re-created habitat built behind a panel of glass. For something a hunter shot, a wooden plaque and some wall

---

natural savagery," wrote Noel Perrin in a forward to a later edition of Beard's book. "A boy of ten or twelve had more in common with wild Indians than he did with his own parents. He probably even had more in common with his dog." Carl was precisely this kind of boy.

space in the den. A pet has its own demands. It was not enough for Carl to make the canary look lifelike. This was an animal gazed upon every day by its owner. It had to look like itself. It had to look as though nothing tragic had ever happened to it.

One Sunday afternoon a short while later, when the weather was still frigid enough to keep herself bundled in a scarf and muffler, Miss Irene Glidden came home from church to find that the cage in the corner of her room was no longer empty, that right there on its swinging perch stood her canary, which she could even push a little, back and forth, back and forth, and she smiled when she saw that the bird didn't falter, smiled knowing that maybe it couldn't swing on its own, that maybe it would never sing again, but that she could touch the animal. She could hold it in her hand and it would never fly away.

The Canary that Carl First Mounted is so central to his mythology that Mary Jobe Akeley, in assembling her 1940 biography, wrote letters to practically anyone still living in Clarendon who may have had information on its whereabouts. She found some success through a man named Glenn Ewell, who tracked the canary's posthumous flight to nearby Holley, New York, where the Glidden family eventually moved, then to a box in their attic, then into the hands of one of Irene's sister's kids. All this thanks to taxidermy, the pet's careful preservation for eternity.

Pets are one of the most obvious ways we make order out of the teeming and daunting animal kingdom. If there were a class system of animals, pets would surely be at the top: The Animals Allowed into Our Homes. In the dark, early days of taxidermy, pets were among the top candidates for preservation. The ancient Egyptians believed in the immortality of cats, and so wealthy citizens would embalm their pet cats after they died, preserving the vessel for that dear soul's return. And one of the oldest mounted specimens still in existence is the African gray parrot that belonged to the Duchess of Richmond, a mistress of Charles II. Before her death, she stipulated that her beloved pet, should it outlast her, must be preserved and displayed alongside her own effigy in Westminster Abbey. The Duchess died in 1702, and, as though in grief, the parrot died weeks later.

By no means are birds the only pets we find preserved throughout history. The Natural History Museum at Tring is a kind of satellite wing of the museum in London—a more intimate museum experience inside what looks like a quaint Tudor mansion. Tring, a town thirty-five miles northwest of London, is also host to the world's most extensive collection of mounted dogs. They've got a spaniel's head, emerging out of a small block of woodwork like a convict from the stocks, but the good people of Tring have chosen to keep this in storage. Which is a total shame. It could be such an instructive image. There is something very unsettling about the fist-sized head of a dog floating on a wall several feet from the floor. It's impossible not to imagine the body that went with it. Why didn't the original taxidermist go to the small trouble of preserving the dog in its entirety? A dog-head mount feels, then, like a bit of a cheat, and suddenly all game heads—moose heads, pronghorn antelope heads, zebra heads—feel like cheats. A deer's head on a wall reminds us that the owner had neither the money nor the space to exhibit the whole of the animal he killed (or had killed). A dog's head on the wall reminds us that game heads of any sort do taxidermized animals a small but noteworthy disservice.

The museum at Tring has plenty of full-size dogs on display—hundreds, actually. There's a pair of Irish wolfhounds, standing proudly erect with chins up as if under official inspection. There's a ratty old poodle dating to 1907 with a haircut that looks far more accidental and scattershot than the one we're familiar with today. A high-eared Welsh corgi standing with its head at a slight, curious tilt. An English pointer, pointing. A Pekingese named Ah Cum, born in 1875 and supposedly the patriarch of the entire breed in England. None of the pets can be petted. All are locked up behind glass panels. Some date back to the Victorian era—a time when gentlemen visionaries had a field day with taxidermy and handled animal skins like the shells of 3-D cartoons they could pose and bend to suit all kinds of gentle whimsy.[3] A Mexican lap dog dates to 1843 and is, thus, one of the oldest mounted dogs in the history of museum taxidermy. Today it resembles something like a guinea pig caught in a wind tunnel.

In a guidebook to the dog collection, Kim Dennis-Bryan and Juliet Clutton-Brock claim the dogs "are unique because they are not just representations of their species, like a stuffed lion or tiger would be; each dog has a personal history that is linked to human social history." It's one reason that a stuffed pet makes most people uneasy: it wasn't just an animal, it was *somebody's* animal. It was some part of a person's family. My vegetarian friends argue effectively against another form of animal classification: edible and inedible. Bessie is large and stands around outside all day eating grass, whereas Fido is loyal and sits by our slipper-clad feet at dinnertime. This doesn't make Fido any less fit for eating than Bessie. But we do this. We create these classes, and this thinking is almost hardwired into our minds: "By 10,000 years ago," write Dennis-Bryan and Clutton-Brock, "the relationship between people and their dogs was already well-established and irrevocable." Pets are honorary humans, in a way. They are animals we give names to and read personalities from like we do meaning from Zen Koans.

One summer afternoon, I learned that my friend Sara's cat was dying. I asked her whether she'd thought about getting him preserved. "It's not too expensive," I said. "Maybe a couple hundred dollars."

---

[3] For example, the full-size polar bear that greets visitors at the entrance to the Tring museum, with a fabricated smile on its face.

We were floating around in her pool, the overhead sun baking our skins slowly. It was so bright I had to squint, and even through the glare off the water I could see her looking back at me as though I'd suggested feasting on the carcass.

"That's so creepy," she said. It was the end of the conversation. When I pressed her to explain why, she said, "It just is."

My sister refused to preserve her cat, Theo, which was fine by me since Theo was a demon of a thing that hissed and spat and bit at my legs whenever I tried to come within three feet of him. "It's not that I'm opposed to that," she told me, carefully, as though preserving animals were some dogma I'd recently adopted. "It's just something I didn't want to do." Likewise, my parents refused to preserve the family dog, Duke, when he died, which was a shame since he had such a thick coat and spent so much time lying still on the floor it wouldn't have been much of a change. "What would we do with it?" my mother asked me, and I made notice of the neutral pronoun.

The veterinarians who euthanized Theo and Duke gave their owners four options. Pet preservation was one of them; both vets had companies they referred grieving pet owners to. Or the pets could be embalmed and returned for burial in either a backyard or what my mother apparently calls "a doggy cemetery." Or they could be cremated and returned in an urn. In the end, my mother and my father and my sister went with the fourth option. Both pets were left in the hands of the veterinarians, who placed the animals in a box and lit them on fire and burned them down to ashes. These ashes they threw away in the garbage. It's one way, I suppose, of honoring the dead.

Pets today are preserved not by conventional skin-and-mount taxidermy but by freeze-drying, like we do with flowers or food for astronauts. There are multiple reasons for this. One is that most conventional taxidermists won't touch pets because too much is at stake. We know these animals too well. A hunter, by contrast, knows his quarry for seconds before he pulls the trigger. Pets have a whole set of characteristic gestures and expressions that no still image can capture in full. Don Franzen, a taxidermist who specializes in freeze-drying, puts it this way: "I've had deer heads mounted in the shop, and customers walk right past them. I guarantee it when people walk into my shop they're not walking past their pet." In other words, pets are recognizable animals; get the hang of the jowls wrong or the shape of the eye, and you've got a tearful customer on your hands—or, worse, one who refuses to pay. (Carl Akeley had so much riding on those black beads he stole from his mother.) Another reason for freeze-drying is that it outperforms taxidermy at re-creating a pet's original form. Pets are fat animals, as a rule. They're well fed and comfortable. It's very difficult to re-create this layer of fatty tissue when you sculpt a bodyform over which to drape the skin. Freeze-drying requires no bodyform. The animal is its own bodyform.

What made Don Franzen a taxidermist was a pheasant he once brought in to some taxidermy shop in his hometown of Wilmington, Illinois. "It came back looking like shit," he says. "And so I said to myself: I can do this just as good." That was maybe thirty years ago.[4] What made Don Franzen a freeze-drying specialist, however, was a great deal he got on a freeze-dry machine. That and the Web. Google "pet preservation" and you'll find more than five hundred hits with dozens of companies and independent taxidermists who will take your dead pet, pose it to your liking, and put it in a machine that sucks out all its moisture. What results is a pet that will last forever. And the industry is growing. Franzen now receives in the mail at least one pet a week.

---

[4] It's a story I've heard again and again while talking with taxidermists— *I can do better myself*—as though the whole field were one ongoing mission of one-upmanship.

Freeze-drying sounds like a cleaner and more humane alternative to skinning an animal, but it's not. Franzen makes a small incision to start, choosing a spot on the body that'll be hidden on its final pose. "The wife is fantastic at stitching," he says. "I can't even find the seams when she's done." Through this incision he removes all the internal organs: the heart and liver and lungs and stomach and intestines. All of it. These can survive the freeze-drying process, but they shrink and lead to warpage in the pet's hide.[5] Next he wires the pet from forepaw to rear paw in a kind of crisscross fashion, turning it into some furry action figure. Eyeballs are all water, so Franzen has to cut them right out. Then he runs a drill up into the skull cavity and scatters the brains. "They're more of a grease product than anything else," he says, and one wants to argue. Brains are the little electric worlds in which our pets remember us. They hold our nicknames and baby talk, the smells of our sofas and of that one time we brought them to the beach to kick up sand and chase crabs. Brains hum and throb with every honest emotion. But a taxidermist is not a man who fetishizes biology. Organs aren't the seats of emotions. They're by-products, waste. Only the skin matters. The coat. The shape of the frame of the body. These are what the customer will look at, and so they're given the utmost care. Once the pet is sewn back up it goes into a wash of Dawn soap and warm water. Then another bath of fabric softener. Then the coat is blown dry and brushed, and in the end it's just sparkling, like a kennel-club best of show. The pretty carcass is then posed in accordance with customer demands and put into the freeze-dry machine, where it's frozen well below zero degrees Fahrenheit. A vacuum pump converts all crys-

---

[5] Shrinkage—the effect of dried-out parts of an animal's body pulling unnaturally at the hide—and drumming, which is a separation, due to an oversight in gluing, that creates a little pocket of air between the hide and the bodyform, are the two main dangers of all taxidermy jobs, freeze-dry or otherwise.

tallized water into gas vapor, which is sucked out of the chamber. The process takes about a week. What results is the same pet you lost—dead, still, but impervious to bacteria and decay. A pet that looks like it's only sleeping. A pet that's going to outlast you.

Freeze-drying can preserve an animal in any pose imaginable. You can make a dog perpetually chase his own tail, for instance, or have a cat do the moonwalk. Franzen sets the levity of this decision squarely on the shoulders of his grieving customers. "I let them tell me what kind of pose they're looking for," he says, "but I recommend they put the animal in a sleeping mode because it's a lot less creepy." It's his word, *creepy*. Sara's, too. When our loved ones die, we bury them or we burn them. Those are the preferred options. No matter how quickly the industry might be growing the fact remains that freeze-dried pets give people the full-on creeps. Even Franzen, a man who preserves pets for a living, admits to some general discomfort. "God, could I freeze-dry her myself?" he says, referring to his aging Brittany. "I don't know. I want to remember my animal in the field hunting birds the way she does." In other words, he doesn't want to remember her as a statuette gathering dust in his house. "I don't even have pictures of my parents around," he adds, cryptically. "But that's just me."

Another taxidermist agrees that she couldn't mount her own pets, but for her the problem was the condition of the carcass. Her ferret, when it died, had suffered from internal bleeding. "I couldn't have made myself look at her insides in that condition," she says, and here we have another key difference between pets and nonpets. Whether we be museum collectors or everyday sportsmen, we hunt animals at the peak of their physical conditions. We want the proathletes of the wild kingdom, the supermodels. We want, however, to grow old with the animals we choose as pets. This creates problems for the pet taxidermist. I mean, no amount of expertise can turn Betty White into Bettie Page.

Who, then, are these people who can happily keep dead pets

around? What is it they have that the rest of us don't? Franzen told me a story about a woman named Sheila, who called him once, asking about preserving her pug, Roxy. Roxy spent eleven years traveling with Sheila and her husband from Massachusetts to Florida and back again, and Sheila wasn't about to let something as paltry as death stop Roxy from joining them on future trips. She had concerns about climate. She had concerns about the threat of decay. Franzen assured her that Roxy would look the same as she always did. "Good," Sheila said, "because I'm going to want to put her in a casket." Franzen said he didn't recommend freeze-drying for a burial. It is a very costly procedure, he said, and time-consuming. "Oh no. You don't understand," Sheila said, patiently. "When my husband or I die, Roxy will be buried with one of us."

"She shocked the hell out of me," Franzen said. "But some people are just so emotionally attached to their pets they can't live without them." Nor, it seems, can they die without them.

We understand grief as an automatic extension of death. For grief to begin, run its course, and conclude, the cause of the grief—the absence of the loved one—must be rendered material by the absence of the body. Present for a time, yes, but then buried and gone forever. To stuff a pet is to keep the beloved around, right there in the corner of the room, long past the grieving stage should be over. The owner of a stuffed pet must still be grieving, we imagine, or must never have fully gone through grief. The owner of a stuffed pet must not have been able to come to terms with the death of the pet and thus might send its corpse off to a man like Franzen or a boy like Carl, who stopped the decay and made it look (kind of) alive. The owner of a stuffed pet is an outsider. She is Faulkner's Emily, without the stench emanating from her house.

Or is she? One of the Web sites I have bookmarked is the discussion board at Taxidermy.net. There, taxidermists come together to give one another tips on how to run a taxidermy business out of the home or how best to care for a bearskin after the hunt. They also bicker like coots over politics (leftists: tread lightly) or issues related to the industry as a whole. It's this forum, "The Taxidermy Industry," I troll most often, and it was here that I found Joshua Knuth, a taxidermist from Oshkosh, Wisconsin, who gave me maybe the strangest pet-taxidermy story I ever heard.

"It was about ten years ago," he said. "I was in school in Wisconsin and doing taxidermy on the side, and this magician found me on the Internet. We agreed on a price, and I mailed over a contract for him to sign; and then he sent me his snake, a fourteen-foot boa constrictor. He'd had this snake for a long time, and its name was Beth." Beth, Knuth explained, died of cancer, and the magician wanted her mounted in a specific position so he could continue to use her in the show. The snake was more than a companion; she was an asset. She was maybe even a celebrity. To deal with the high shipping costs, Knuth agreed to drive the mount to New York City, where the magician and Knuth's brother lived.

"I drove a small Saturn at the time, so the snake was woven through my car, through the trunk. Its tail stuck out a bit and the head came out in front of me and out the driver's side window. Imagine the look on the tollbooth attendant's face when I pull up to pay on the turnpike! So a long and uncomfortable ride out ends without incident, other than the woman manning the George Washington Bridge toll booth who was *terrified* of snakes. She started crying and couldn't stop. I was having trouble holding it together."

On the day he was to pick up the snake, the magician arrived with his assistant, "a busty blond woman wearing a glittery-gold, low-cut showgirl outfit," Knuth said. The magician had a handlebar mustache and wore a black cape. "We are here for Beth!" he cried and handed over the check, and before Knuth knew what to say they'd loaded the snake in their car and left.

"The guy was a nut job," Knuth said, "but at least I got paid."

So maybe those who get their pets preserved aren't necessarily connected to an animal on an emotional level beyond what most of us find rational. Maybe they're just eccentric. A freeze-dried pet can make a good conversation piece, a good joke. Witness Rowdy, the mounted Labrador kept by the roommates J. D. and Turk on the sitcom *Scrubs*. In several episodes, they'd leave the dog in front of a neighbor's apartment door and then chastise Rowdy on his being returned. "We don't know why he always goes to your door," J. D. says in one episode. "Do you have a stuffed cat?"

In 1798, the English poet Elizabeth Moody published her first collection, called *Poetic Trifles*. One such trifle was "An Address by a Gentleman to His Dead Dog; Which Was Stuffed, and Placed in a Corner of His Library":

Yes, still, my Prince, thy form I view,
Art can again thy shape renew:
But vain I seek the vital flame
That animated once thy frame.
Extinct the vivifying spark,
That tongue is mute—those eyes are dark.
In vain that face I now explore;
It wooes me with its love,—no more.
No more thy scent my steps shall trace
With wagging tail and quicken'd pace.
Nor e'er again thy joyful cry,
Proclaim thy darling master nigh.

    Alas! thy shade alone remains,
Yet Memory all thou wast retains;
Still on thy living image dwells

And all thy winning fondness tells.
She courts the muse to spread thy name
Beyond life's little span of fame.
Well pleas'd could verse stern death defy,
And bid that *Prince* may never die.

We imagine plastic-eye technology wasn't so hot in 1798, not like it is today. And today it's quite good. For dogs, a taxidermist can usually substitute wolf eyes, of which they make dozens and dozens of kinds. What size do you need? What color? Some brands even have reflective backs such that when you shine a light on the eye it gleams back at you like a tiny headbeam. And yet Don Franzen suggests a sleeping pose. A lot less creepy. What he means by this is that the eyes are the windows to the soul, proverbially, and here, it's a window looking in on an empty room. This is what the gentleman is mourning in the first part of the poem, and this is why pet taxidermy has not made many converts. And why it may never. A stuffed pet is a dead thing. It's not a monument to something that once lived and then died. It's a dead thing.

But the second half of the poem argues the opposite. "Still," it says, and "Yet." The stuffed dog is more than a portrait, does more than a portrait can do. The stuffed dog is like statuary, except more authentic because the materials used to re-create the body are the materials that used to *be* the body. In the end, the stuffed dog is a tool of memory, personified in the poem as some light deity, able to resurrect all the good times the gentleman shared with the dog. So the dog lives on eternally. The pet, in fact, outlives the master. Moody's poem is more than two hundred years old, which means that stuffed pets are even older. The technology may have changed from the eighteenth century to the twenty-first, but the desire to keep a deceased pet around in one form or another has remained, unchanging, unfaltering in its hope that Prince the dog may never die. Or Beth the python. Or Roxy the pug.

Or the famous frozen canary of Clarendon, New York. The canary's name has been lost from public record, but the bird itself is still intact. That niece of Miss Irene Glidden held onto the bird long enough to donate it to the American Museum of Natural History. And there it sits, today, shut up in a box on the floor of some dark room. The canary is more than 135 years old, but it hasn't aged a day.

TWO

Some animals seem to laugh at us. Hyenas, of course, and certain primates. But even everyday animals like birds and squirrels. We could be walking happily to some second date and trip over a break in the sidewalk. From above our heads, a chattering in the trees, a bushy-tailed thing bent over in convulsions. More alarming is the animal that smiles. The sloth. The orangutan. The viper. Because we can't know what they're thinking as their gaze falls on us, we can't know what these smiles might mean. Indeed, the most disturbed and untrustable creature of all that Alice comes across in her adventures in Wonderland is the Cheshire Cat, and whenever he leaves, he's sure to let that big grin linger. "It's the most curious thing I ever saw in my life!" she says. Curious, yes, and sinister, too. It doesn't help that most grinning animals are reptiles—what with their long, pliable jaws—and we've known since Eden that reptiles aren't to be trusted.

The grin of an alligator is made even more sinister by the teeth that punctuate it at each end—the very things we know that can rip us to shreds. Like a spokesmodel's smile, an alligator's smile is a natural expression, even when it's sleeping, even when it's laying eggs, even when it's coming in for the kill. Even, it seems, when it's being hacked to bits. One Wednesday evening in the summer of 2007, about fifty taxidermists and I watch Tom Voyer, a reptiles and amphibians expert from New Hampshire, remove the skin from an alligator about the length of his arm. It's not going so well. For some animals, the membrane that holds the hide to the flesh is thin and delicate—like sausage casings maybe. Easy to slice through. An alligator's hide—or maybe just *this* alligator's hide—is bonded tightly to the flesh. Voyer, a stocky, swarthy man with a heavy New England accent, has to take it slowly, making hundreds of small repeated cuts around the belly of the animal with nothing more than a razor blade, the kind used in box cutters or to mete out lines of coke. "I'm no good with scalpels," he says with a grin of his own. It's all a big, fun, jolly time, the skinning. After a few cuts with the razor, he'll set it down and grab the part of the hide he's already removed and just tug and tug at it, trying to rip away more from the body. It looks a lot like pulling up a well-tacked piece of carpet, and when he does get it separated, the hide makes a sound like Velcro ripping. Voyer works barehanded.

It's an extremely gory process, and though I'm maybe forty feet away from the guy, I can tell because between us is a cameraman who's careful to get in close, and to the left of Voyer on the stage is a screen on which his now slimy hands are being projected, about ten times their actual size. We're all in the back corner of the Grande Exposition Hall at the Silver Legacy Resort Casino in Reno, host this year of the biennial World Taxidermy Championships. Voyer's seminar on skinning and prepping a gator is one of thirty being offered over the WTC's four nights, and it's actually a last-minute addition to the schedule.[1]

-----

[1] The taxidermist originally scheduled to lead a seminar on constructing an artificial tree got in a car accident on his way to Reno. Voyer happened to have flown in with an intact alligator carcass. He packed it on ice in a cooler. This, the airline had no problem with; dead animals get classified as food.

"I'm losing the battle with these front legs!" he says, and in order to get a better angle on the job, he tosses a garbage bag over the split-open back half of the gator's body and brings his left knee up on the table, clamping the gator in place and freeing up a hand. Everyone chuckles at this—*whatever it takes* seems to be the esprit de corps here. Soon it's clear that not even an extra hand will help him. Some animals just don't want to be skinned. Voyer decides to save time by splitting the legs' hide down the length of them, making a cut like the seam running down the back of a pair of nylons. This will mean more sewing later, the most tedious, finger-aching part of any taxidermy job.

Soon he starts fleshing the hide, once he's got it all the way removed. It's a lot like cleaning a fish. He lays the skin on the table, scales down, and scrapes the flesh off with a small metal tool shaped like the eye of Nefertiti on a short wooden pole. Here the gore is undeniable. With every few strokes, Voyer has to flick the accumulated gunk off his fleshing tool. Spread all along the table (which was covered in thick tarp well before he made a single cut) are piles and piles of alligator meat—it looks like the errant debris from a watermelon fight. If we were alligators, we'd be nauseated or maybe just mad, maybe ravenous and vengeful. But we're humans, and most of the folks here are taxidermists, and so instead of recoiling we watch the big screen closely, passively, as though what we're being shown is nothing more alarming than the evening weather report. A few people take notes. Three seats down from me, a sturdy blonde in her forties is crocheting a border onto a baby blanket, biding her time while her husband learns some new job skills. We are a room desensitized. At one point the cameraman zooms right in on the front of the gator to catch Voyer scissoring through the left shoulder joint. Up in the corner of the screen, the alligator's grin spreads in a way that isn't so much sinister anymore as it is tragic. Or maybe noble. Again, I can't tell what it means, and soon the camera cuts away, and the grin is gone.

Animal-rights activists would be up in arms about all this. What goes on in many seminars at annual conventions across the country is the systematic butchering of an animal that once lived and ran or swam or flew or sometimes did all three. Of course this is no different from what happens every day in slaughterhouses, suburban kitchens, or the more severe parts of the wild. Except it *is* different. Here are four dozen taxidermists serving as an audience, and they're not here as voyeurs, like some slasher-film audience. They're here to learn. Conference seminars are like grad school for taxidermists, most of whom get their education through experience, trial and error, maybe a book or video they bought from the same catalog that supplies their headforms and hide paste. Conferences at the state, national, and international levels give taxidermists the opportunity to study a very specific and often advanced technique in workshops such as Painting a Brown Trout, Mounting a Walking Turkey, Altering Life-size Manikins, Mounting a Ptarmigan, and Skinning and Prepping an Alligator—all taught by working taxidermists known to be the best in their fields. Taking a course at one of these conferences is like taking Villainizing the Law Firm with John Grisham or a special master class in Boomer sanctimony with Don DeLillo. Except all it costs is $145 plus airfare, and everyone's invited.

Taxidermy is a lonely trade. Maybe the larger outfits—Jonas Brothers in Colorado or Nature's Design in Wyoming—have three or more taxidermists working alongside one another. Maybe some husbands and wives pair up. But for the most part, you've got a man in the basement with his tools. You've got a man in the garage with a freezer full of animal pelts. It's a lot like Buffalo Bill from *Silence of the Lambs,* another basement dweller who did noteworthy work with skins, except that a taxidermist comes upstairs to have dinner with his family. A taxidermist drives her kids to their dentist appointments. But then it's back downstairs, working solo often past midnight, learning only from past missteps. The taxidermy seminar, then, is as social as it is instructional; taxidermists get that singular comfort we all feel when we at last find ourselves among people who share our obsessions. There's even a kind of uniform, as if in celebration: denim jeans worn cowboy tight if one is from certain Western states but loose and bag-assed otherwise; polo or button-down shirt with either a hunting-related joke[2] or the logo of one's own taxidermy company embroidered over the left breast; a ball cap. And then that kind of camo I can only call sportsman's camo, in which the greens, browns, and blacks of camouflage are clustered into tighter, thinner blades than the round, leafy splotches you used to find in the army, back when the army fought in forests and jungles. Most important, though, is everything that gets shared among taxidermists at seminars—or maybe *swapped* is the right word for it. In many ways, a taxidermy seminar feels like an hour-and-a-half-long "Hints from Heloise" column. I sat one afternoon in North Platte, Nebraska, and listened to Joe Kaiser—a round guy with a young face who looks kind of like the way rock singer Meat Loaf used to—explain the process of mounting a crappie.

"I'm going to spread some of that Purell stuff over this now," he said, coating the fish skin with the gooey hand sanitizer, clearing off all the grease and making it more pliable. The men in the room clucked and chuckled like a brood of roosters. "What?" Kaiser said. "Give it a try. Seriously. I ran out of denatured alcohol once and I started looking around the house and found this in the bathroom and it's just alcohol. It's pretty much just straight alcohol. But it sticks better to the scales. I love it now."

From the handful of seminars I've sat in over the years—always with a little notebook, usually the only one taking notes, often the

---

[2] "If a man is alone in the woods and no woman can hear him, is he *still* wrong?"

youngest guy in the room, never wearing quite the right outfit—
I've learned that Windex is a great thing to spray on artificial eyes to
make them shine. I've learned that deer hides feel great when washed
with Tide but that bird skins are more delicate and should be
washed with a little bit of Dawn dish soap. I've learned to spread
peanut oil around the eyes, nose, and lips of a game head to prevent
the skin from cracking. I've seen incredible things done with a dentist's sickle probe and have heard that "a guy can spend a lot of time
on the inside of a nose." It's a lot of trial and error, as I've said.
One solitary taxidermist tries something new—like Kaiser and his
Purell—and the result is so stunning that he can't help sharing it.
And it's not just the experts leading seminars but the part-time taxidermists sitting next to one another at the final awards banquet; any
time's a good time to share tips. Any place is a good place to learn to
stuff a deer.

Carl Akeley found his place in Rochester, New York. He moved
there in 1883, happily leaving Clarendon at age nineteen. Throughout his adolescence, he used what he learned from that borrowed
book to stuff the animals caught and trapped by his fellow towns-
people, and they treated Carl like some kind of misfit. A boy—a
Glidden boy!—spending his days in the company of dead animals.
In response Carl ignored their sidelong glances as he went about
town and threw himself further into the profession he found to be
"the most satisfying and stimulating to a man's soul," as he wrote in
his memoirs. He mounted any dead animal he could get his hands
on, building little cases for his work and painting nature scenes on
the backgrounds. In Rochester he hoped to get a job as a taxidermist
at Ward's Natural Science Establishment, a company that outfitted
natural history museums around the world with the stuff of exhibits:
mammals, birds, fish, yes, but also fossils, shells, gems, and meteors.
The demand for such stuff was great in the decades after Darwin's

theory went public, and Henry A. Ward, a scientist and explorer, capitalized off such a demand. Carl arrived at the front gate one cold morning and saw hanging from a set of whale jaws a wide sign warning off visitors: "This is not a museum but a working establishment, where all are very busy." All the same Carl knocked on the front door and was ushered into Ward's office. There he found a thick-set man with a full white beard who glanced up at him distractedly. "What do you want?" he barked. It was well after ten o'clock, but Ward was only now tucking into a plate of ham and eggs. Carl felt this gave the man some vague sort of advantage.

He didn't know what to say, hadn't prepared any grand speech. He took from his coat pocket a business card that he'd had printed back in Clarendon:

CARL AKELEY
ARTISTIC TAXIDERMY IN ALL ITS BRANCHES

—

HINDS ROAD, CLARENDON, N.Y.

Ward held the card at a distance from his face and took the time to chew and swallow. "Artistic, eh?" he said. "How about just taxidermy. Can you do that?"

Carl smiled and nodded and assured him that he could.

He made less money a week than it cost him to live, so he shacked up with a cousin and worked long hours: 7 A.M. to 6 P.M. Ward was the kind of man happy only when the people he employed looked busy. He wanted a roomful of noisy, determined men manipulating tools and putting out product. There was no time for planning or design, and it was depressing, monotonous work. Factory work, really. The process taxidermists at Ward's used to mount each specimen was fast and cheap and crude. They mounted skins for museums that subscribed fully to the specimen-in-glass-case model of scientific exhibition, and thus every animal, no matter the size, was given the same rigid treatment. Rudimentary skeletons would be constructed from an animal's leg bones, and a wood beam for the spine. Over this they'd hang the tanned skin and stuff it with straw until no more could fit. Mounts looked bloated as a result, their four legs all splayed and akimbo like Macy's Day balloons.[3]

Carl set himself to change his profession. For him, the central question was this: Couldn't taxidermy do more than just preserve an animal? Ward's had already established a reputation around the world for life-size mounts that captured the attitudes of an animal. They could pose it, in other words. At the entrance to the establishment was a gorilla with his arms up in the air, his jaws open and teeth bared menacingly. Still, it was to a live gorilla what a sock monkey is to a real monkey. If it had muscles, they'd been abandoned. If his body had proportions commensurate with nature, those proportions were disregarded for whatever the taxidermist who stuffed the animal felt like doing. The hardest work Carl did while at Ward's was looking, thinking. He wanted to see an animal more closely than anyone had seen it before. So he spent a lot of time at the Rochester Zoo. He stared and stared at photographs of animals running over the African plains. And Ward hated him for it. Here was the youngest man in his employ, and he was nothing but a loafer. He lollygagged and took his sweet time.

He came to Ward with unusual requests. One day an intact zebra carcass arrived at the establishment, and Carl saw an opportunity. If he could take measurements of the animal, maybe even cast it in plaster, he could replicate the body as a manikin the skin would fit to perfectly. That afternoon, he went into his employer's office, a bright room flanked with windows, the sunlight falling on the

---

[3] To be fair, it was at Ward's, far before Carl ever arrived, that the beginnings of sculpted manikins can be found, thanks mostly to the work of William T. Hornaday. But such posed, lifelike specimens were rare and cost Ward's clients more than they were usually able to afford.

many trophies Ward picked up in his travels around the world. An echinoderm fossil in a little glass case. The head of an asp set up on a high shelf. The pillow on which he rested his head in Africa while recovering from smallpox. Ward himself was hidden behind that morning's newspaper, and Carl stepped right up and cleared his throat. "Sir?"

Ward lowered the paper, and in the light that came in through the room's back windows he spoke to Carl in silhouette. "What is it?"

Carl explained his interest in the zebra carcass. "I'd like to make a cast of her," he said. "I think the finished piece would be a lot better."

"That zebra needs to be in Pittsburgh by the end of next week," Ward said. "Go skin it and get back to work."

"Sir, please," Carl said.

And here was this boy begging for more favors. Hadn't he given Carl enough? Hadn't he hired the kid with no recommendations, no references? Hadn't he looked the other way all those times Carl seemed to just be sitting around, staring at an animal like it was something in a museum?

"I'll be done tomorrow morning," Carl promised.

Ward picked up his newspaper and made a promise of his own. "If you ruin that hide, I'll ruin yours."

The preparation room at Ward's was about thirty feet square with three windows along the back wall. Four tables were spread around the room, a few platforms on the floor for larger specimens. In this room, skins were stretched and fleshed and cured on one table, manikins were built on another. Over in the corner was a big crate of straw, over which mounts could be hung from a pulley and stuffed. By 6:30 P.M. the room was empty, and Carl cleared a kiwi mount from one of the tables and lit a couple of lanterns. He was a short man, slight in all dimensions. The zebra was larger than he was the way a mother is larger than her preteen, and he struggled to heave it up on the table. To cast the full body of an animal in plaster takes three steps. You coat one side of the animal and the outside of the legs and wait for the plaster to dry. Then you flip the thing over and do it again. Finally, you coat the underbelly and the insides of the legs, and in the end you have three puzzle pieces that come together like the animal's phantom shell. It took Carl the whole night. The whole point of this was to give himself a reference. If he wanted a finished mount to look real, he'd need to match the brisket muscles to those on the carcass. He'd need to count the ribs and measure the space between them. He'd need to get creative with sewing and stuffing. He'd need to look very closely. When he was a boy, he went with his father and Lewis into Rochester for a free exhibit at the Powers Building downtown. Inside were fifty-some cases of mounted birds and small mammals. It was the first time Carl had ever seen a piece of taxidermy, and he stayed far longer than his father wanted to. But to be so close to a falcon or a beaver! They weren't alive, but this was the next best thing.

To kill an animal and then keep it around like this had some gruesome implications. When you grow up on a farm you grow up with a respect for animals threaded through your body like a nerve or the need to breathe. They are your clothes; they are your food; they are your livelihood. Carl, at a very early age, saw that taxidermy was a way to honor an animal but that shoddy taxidermy, lazy stuffing, imprecision in general was a mean form of disrespect. It was like taking someone's picture while they clambered out of the bathtub.

He finished the casts around six in the morning, in time to clean up before the arrival of his coworkers at seven. Carl leaned the casts in a corner of the room and went home to sleep for a couple hours. By nine he was back at work. He took a shortcut past the trash bins and saw a small white heap of crumbled plaster. He went straight to Ward's office.

"They were in the way," Ward said, and that conversation was over.

—————

Such is the story of Carl's experience at Ward's. Here was a young kid whose crackpot notions on what taxidermy could become just got in everyone's way. The kid who, though no one knew it, would go on to become maybe the most famous taxidermist of all time. Or, at least, such is the way the story of young Carl Akeley has been told by those before me. I'm trying my best to resist deification. Carl wasn't a saint, maybe not even a hero. He was just a man with a talent. A man who worked as hard as he wanted to and spent most of his free time studying or reading on his own, sometimes going out to lectures and plays with his friend Bill Wheeler, another Ward's associate. A man who developed quite early an infallible sense of self-reliance that led him to ignore whatever or whomever he saw standing in his way. He found Henry Ward more of a nuisance than a mentor, and as the myth of Carl Akeley goes, just months after he began working at the establishment he was fired for being such an individual. A visionary. For refusing to toe the company line. Mary Jobe Akeley writes in her biography that Carl "became so dissatisfied at the limitations imposed upon him that friction with Professor Ward ensued and the young taxidermist was suddenly dismissed." Carl reportedly was "stunned by this sudden turn of events." The truth of the matter is that in growing up in the same house as his mother Carl had developed a quiet disregard for authority, and whatever dictates Ward would have given him Carl likely ignored in favor of his own methods. That he even asked Ward to make those casts of the zebra, as he reports in his memoirs, instead of just doing so on his own seems doubtful. Months into Carl's employ, the shop foreman noticed the new kid was missing for a few hours every afternoon. No one knew where he'd run off to or when he was due back. Eventually the foreman found our hero way up in the building's attic, dozing on a bed of animal skins to be mounted.

"Wake up, Ake," he said, giving him a little kick in the shoulder. "We don't pay you to sleep."

"Last I checked, you don't pay me much of anything," Carl said. "So I don't know what business it is of yours what I do up here."

Carl was fired on the spot and spent the winter of 1884 stuffing small animals in novelty scenes—squirrels tending bar, moles sitting in armchairs reading the paper—at a dirty shop in Brooklyn. He made even less money than he did at Ward's and produced many more mounts each day, all of them embarrassments. He was miserable—"a more dreary six months I never had spent anywhere."[4] None of this novelty work exists, or at least none of it has arisen, which is a shame. Finding this work would be like finding a tourist's caricature Pablo Picasso sketched while working one lonely summer at a forgotten beach resort.

What ended Carl's exile was the awareness, on Ward's part, that Carl's mounts were realistic enough to fetch prices far higher than his colleagues' did. He hired Carl back, with a raise, just in time for the death of Jumbo, the world's biggest African elephant, owned and widely exhibited by P. T. Barnum.

On the morning of 15 September 1885, Jumbo was hit by a train in St. Thomas, Ontario. Barnum had hired Ward's to preserve the elephant, and Carl Akeley and his colleague William Critchley arrived on the scene days later. By that point the sun had been beating down on the carcass for days, and as Carl circled the animal, assessing the damage, the stench stuck right in the back of his throat.

As a taxidermist, he'd become used to the smell of dead animals. It's the sort of thing that goes along with the job, like the sight of

_____

[4] Carl's weird brushes with fame began in Brooklyn; he shared a room with Isaac Kauffman Funk, the future publisher, and with Adam Willis Wagnalls, of a whole mess of reference books.

blood for surgeons or the permanent stains under a mechanic's fin-gernails. But Carl had never been this close to an elephant before, and here was an animal that weighed six tons when alive. Elephant skin is about one inch thick (yours is about four millimeters), but the flesh can run as thick as a foot. Here, Carl found, was a lot of rotting flesh. We humans have a terrible grasp on our sense of smell. Nearly every animal is our superior in this regard. As a result, our vocabulary for describing smells is poor—practically nonexistent. Think of all the names we have for colors and try to come up with a comparable list for smells. All we can do to describe a scent is to get at it by way of analogy. It smells like ammonia. It has a fishy smell. We cannot possibly know what the butchering of Jumbo's carcass in the late-summer sun must have smelled *like,* but without question it smelled awful. Akeley once wrote that the stench was enough to "gag a maggot."

The butchering took days, but eventually the hide was removed, salted, and shipped back to Rochester. Barnum, as we'll see, was a man who knew well the draw that taxidermy held on the public of the time, specifically "creative" taxidermy. With the mounting of Jumbo he saw the opportunity to capitalize on it and requested that Ward's add some height to the final mount. In 1885 there was very little precedent for mounting animals of Jumbo's size, and Carl knew that to use Ward's standard procedure for quadrupeds wouldn't work on such a scale. There was no way they could hang the ele-phant skin and wooden framework upside down for stuffing. From the techniques perfected during his private experiments, he and Critchley built a manikin to scale, but Carl added an extra step: lay-ering strips of wood that had been treated so as to curve and provide a texture to the body that would replicate the elephant's muscula-ture. To make Jumbo's hide fit on a manikin *larger* than the original body, they had to cut the hide into many pieces and stretch them across the form, securing them in hundreds of places with counter-sunk nails. The result was monstrous, not in its size but in the seams that ran all over the body, like a patchwork elephant. Carl made a gray putty that he sculpted over the entire surface, building up parts of the musculature that he couldn't capture in the manikin itself. It was the first time he felt like an artist, not just a man stuffing things.

Jumbo's skeleton went to the American Museum of Natural History, where Akeley would eventually end up as head taxidermist. The museum still has it, locked away in some storage facility in Brooklyn. When Barnum had got everything he was going to get out of the mounted elephant, he donated it to Tufts University, where he was a trustee. The mount was destroyed in a fire in 1972.

But in 1886, in February, Barnum unveiled the finished mount to the public. Everyone was amazed at how alive the animal looked. How real and ready to charge. This was in the Powers Building in downtown Rochester, the same place Carl had seen his very first taxidermy exhibition. When his name was called he walked up on stage and shook Barnum's hand. He waved to the crowd below. Here was Carl, getting an audience of his own. He was twenty-two years old.

By the turn of the century, museums in America were hiring their own staff taxidermists and funding their own collecting expeditions, and demand waned for the goods Ward's could produce. But the legacy of Ward's is that it was a training ground not just for Carl Akeley but for all the major taxidermists of the late-nineteenth-century museum boom in the United States. Ward's may have been the first time in the history of the world, definitely in the history of this country, that so many working taxidermists were working together so closely and that taxidermy was such a collaborative process. One man skinned the animal, a second built the manikin, a third stuffed the skin, and a fourth sewed up the whole thing. Yes, this led to a lot of rushed and shoddy work, but it also led to a lot of shared ideas. Anything that would make the work easier, anything that would fetch a higher price from the customer, would be shared and tried and soon became standard practice. Sort of like natural selection. Akeley and his colleagues developed at Ward's the spirit that all innovation is collective, all practices are shared. The point of taxidermy is never (or should never be) the glory of the taxidermist; the point is the glory of the animal.

In 1935, a *New York Times* article commemorating Akeley African Hall[5] claimed that Carl kept his techniques a secret until the day he died, and it was enough of a slander for Mary Jobe Akeley to write Carl's brother Lewis, insisting he get the paper to print a retraction. For Carl wasn't secretive in his work. It's true that he never published his methods in print—unlike William T. Hornaday, who wrote an entire book that practically every taxidermist of the era scoured cover to cover—but this doesn't mean he was all hush-hush. By all accounts the door to his studio was always open, and Carl was happy if not eager to walk visitors through his techniques step by step. He had several protégés, notably James L. Clark and Louis Jonas, who learned closely from him and went on to share this knowledge with other taxidermists. And they in turn shared with other taxidermists. And so on. Not only was the Akeley method of taxidermy preparation in national if not universal use well before Carl died, it's clear from all accounts that he never made a penny off it.

Back then, the museum side of taxidermy was an open book. But once commercial taxidermy started to grow as an industry in the early twentieth century, providing a much-needed service for the growing trophy-hunting craze, things were very different. Commercial taxidermy was always a tight-lipped industry. To learn anything, one became an apprentice—just as one did in medieval

---

[5] The hall is now named Akeley Hall of African Mammals, but in 1935 it had this designation. Carl referred to it simply as African Hall in his plans and writings, so this is how I refer to the hall throughout.

guilds. Otherwise few options existed for learning taxidermy, until the state and national organizations started forming in the late 1960s and early 1970s. It was a way to attract customers: get taxidermists together to share what they knew and set up a system of fair business practices. Then the members of a state organization would suddenly be a lot more attractive than their competitors. Before that, things were sort of like Ribfest. If you've ever been to a competitive barbecue festival, you know that anyone competing guards his recipe with his life. Ingredients, cooking times, grilling techniques—all of these are a kind of currency to be hoarded. Professional taxidermy isn't like this, not anymore. If the big winners of competitive barbecuing taught workshops on smoking and grilling and published a full list of ingredients in their rubs and sauces, they'd be a lot like taxidermists. Except their festival wouldn't scare off the little ones.

If there were several taxidermy correspondence courses available in the United States during the twentieth century, all have been forgotten, displaced by the behemoth that was J. W. Elwood's Northwestern School of Taxidermy. Talk to ten taxidermists older than forty, and if one was self-taught and another learned in an apprenticeship, you're still going to have ten former Elwood correspondents on your hands. It was that popular. Elwood was for budding young taxidermists what Charles Atlas was for ninety-eight-pound weaklings, and both men advertised their solutions to a happier life in the backs of magazines, Elwood favoring those read by hunters: *Outdoor Life*, *Sports Afield*, *Field and Stream*. "Be a Taxidermist!" one such ad from 1939 exhorted:

> **SAVE Your Valuable TROPHIES**
> **MOUNT WILD-GAME AND PETS . . .**
> Mount **BIRDS**

AND ANIMALS, HEADS, FISH;
tan furs and leather.
A wonderful, profitable hobby . . .
Investigate at once.
SEND COUPON FOR FREE BOOK

Wild game
is growing **scarcer**. Trophies now more
valuable than ever! Shoot **FEWER** and
MOUNT them true to life. **IT'S PROF-
ITABLE!** many earn $12 to $15 per
week spare time mounting specimens
for hunters. Why not **YOU?** Learn to
make **USEFUL** articles from mounted
specimens. (See squirrel lighter to left.)

The ads were effective. If the school's materials are to be believed, by the 1960s, more than 400,000 students had investigated what Elwood had to offer, all of them enchanted by the promises of trophies and "useful" articles and, of course, profit. In all of its materials, the profit incentive is what Elwood stressed the most, and rightly so. It remains true even today that taxidermy is a profitable endeavor.[6] The overhead is incredibly low. Many people work out of their own basements or garages. The materials you need—pastes, epoxies, clays—are cheap and last through multiple mounting projects. Most skins are tanned by a third-party commercial tannery, the cost of which is forwarded on to the customer.

A taxidermy education, then, for Elwood, was an education in business as much as in a technique. Indeed, it may even be that, for Elwood, taxidermy education was really only a business—the man

---

[6] Note that Elwood never says taxidermy will make one rich, just that it'll make one a profit.

was never a taxidermist himself. Around the end of the nineteenth century, Elwood was living in a small rural town in Iowa, working as the principal for the local high school. According to an official Northwest School of Taxidermy history, Elwood at some point "conceived the idea of teaching taxidermy by mail" and opened the school in Omaha[7] in 1903. What happened between conception and birth is kept a secret, but one thing I know is that Elwood got his hands on two key books: Hornaday's *Taxidermy and Zoological Collecting* and Oliver Davie's *Methods in the Art of Taxidermy,* both published at the end of the nineteenth century. The first illustration in Elwood's book 1—an etching labeling all the parts of a bird's body—is taken from Hornaday, who himself took it from Joel Dorman Steele's *Popular Zoology,* though Elwood fails to give this proper credit. Subsequent illustrations throughout the other books are taken from Davie, though no credit whatsoever is given for these. Also, when it comes time in book 4 to learn how to make papier-mâché, Elwood writes, "We can do no better than to quote that excellent authority Wm. T. Hornaday," and proceeds to do so, word for word.

This is all the Northwest School of Taxidermy course is: a full-size how-to manual on taxidermy delivered incrementally to the customer's—I mean student's—home, peppered throughout with encouragements that "the school is taking **great interest** in your progress" (that is, encouragements that the student continue to be enrolled in the school and thus continue to send scheduled payments).

One weekend while visiting my parents I came across a stack of mail from the Northwest School of Taxidermy at an antique store, sent back in 1949 to a Mr. Epps in Prince George, Virginia. It's a set of six faded, crinkling manila envelopes that contain a booklet about the size and shape of a church program and a letter from Professor J. W. Elwood, BS, himself. The course begins—as Carl Akeley did, and

---

[7] About as "northwestern" as Evanston, Illinois.

as so many taxidermists do—with birds. Specifically, a pigeon. One didn't actually receive a pigeon carcass in the mail, thankfully. One needed to obtain a pigeon on one's own. Most lessons open with a discussion on how to go about acquiring a specimen:

> If you secure a specimen alive, or when shooting you only "wing" the bird, you should kill it in such a way that the blood will not flow out and spoil the plumage. Grasp the bird with the hand tightly just beneath the wings and squeeze very hard for a few minutes. This will prevent breathing, and in a very short time the specimen will be dead. The most humane way of killing a specimen, however, is to make a paper cone, in the bottom of which you deposit a small roll of cotton, after which pour chloroform liberally over the cotton and insert the bird's head in the cone for a few minutes.

After the bird comes small-mammal taxidermy (recommended specimen: squirrel), large-mammal taxidermy ("if you cannot secure a whole animal as large as a deer or bear, then . . . perhaps you can secure a calf, fox, or dog"), game heads, fish and reptiles, skin tanning, open-mouth specimens, and finally the preservation of insects, eggs, and nests. Also contained in the full set of lessons are a few pages on novelty taxidermy. This we'll be returning to in chapter 6, but it's worth briefly mentioning here for the way it enabled Elwood to reach a customer base that didn't "ever go for the hunting of wild animals."

If you've ever seen a jackalope, you've seen novelty taxidermy before. It's what Carl Akeley spent the winter of 1884 doing for little pay. Incorporating the fanciful and sometimes the absurd, novelty taxidermy might best be defined by Elwood in book 3: "it has to do with mounting specimens in 'human' situations." The quotation marks are, I think, appropriate. Elwood provides some sample images, just to get the budding novelty taxidermist's brain percolating with ideas. There's *The Billiard Players,* which fashions two rabbits around a billiards table, one lining up his shot with a miniature cue stick. There's *The Frog Orchestra*—a five-piece outfit, comprising cello, trumpet, violin, clarinet, and snare drum. There is also a conductor. My favorite is *The Barber Shop,* in which a standing barber-rabbit "shaves" the "beard" of another rabbit who is reclining in a chair and whose "fingernails" are getting a "manicure" from a third rabbit, this one sitting on a little stool and wearing a little apron. "You can sell groups like this easily to barbers everywhere," Elwood argues, without ever giving the curious taxidermist any idea on where to pick up, for instance, a four-inch-tall barber's chair.

Taxidermists today see Elwood's lessons as doing more harm to a potential taxidermist than good, and if we consider that they're over a hundred years old this isn't an unfair assessment. Studying these lessons today would be like getting Henry Ford to teach you how to drive. Too much has changed in the last hundred years. These days, there are whole bodyforms to order out of any number of catalogs, so why bother learning how to construct a wooden manikin? These days, there are far better chemical preservatives out there. These days, you can send skins out to be tanned and get them back in a week. But while Elwood's step-by-step techniques may be old-fashioned, his lessons do make for a self-sufficient taxidermist. Sculpting a manikin yourself is time-consuming, yes, but it's far more precise with respect to the final mount than would be any premade body-form, which you'd inevitably have to resize anyway either by building it up with clay or shaving it down with a rasp. In other words, the Northwestern School of Taxidermy and all the old how-to manuals taught the student how to become a taxidermist. These days, taxidermy instruction teaches the student how to become a customer in the taxidermy industry.

———

Dan Rinehart is the host of his own taxidermy television show on The Sportsman's Channel, one of those hyperspecific networks in the high-numbered tiers of your digital cable package. It's called *Taxidermy for the Sportsman* and it airs at hours convenient only for the DVR-owning viewer or for a certain kind of taxidermy enthusiast and writer who stays most days in his robe past noon. It's ostensibly a how-to series, showing the complete process of preserving an animal—skinning the carcass, tanning the skin, preparing the manikin, mounting the skin, and finishing the whole piece. But most projects are split up over two or three half-hour episodes, and because The Sportsman's Channel airs each episode several times throughout the week, it would be as difficult for a viewer to, say, tune in and work alongside Rinehart as it is to tune in and paint alongside Bob Ross. The pleasures of the show are spectatorial—if, that is, you can stomach a ten-minute segment on skinning a fox, with camera close-ups on the fleshing of the inside of the face. It's exactly like what I saw Tom Voyer do in Reno with an alligator, except Rinehart's doing it right in my living room.

Rinehart welcomed me to come see firsthand the sixty-thousand-square-foot warehouse where he films his television show. Here he also runs Taxidermy Arts Supply Company (TASCO) and teaches a taxidermy school accredited by the State of Wisconsin Educational Approval Board.[8] I agreed and planned a trip during his school's whitetail deer course. ("This is the BIG one!" its promotional materials promised.) Dan Rinehart Taxidermy School is located in Edgerton, Wisconsin, a town with a population of 4,900 set near I-90 about an hour south of Madison. It's rural, rolling-hill country, and on the October afternoon I arrive in town the trees have

---

[8] Rinehart's school is at the time of writing one of only two taxidermy schools in Wisconsin than can claim such accreditation. The other, Wegner's School of Taxidermy, is more expensive than Dan Rinehart's, but it does offer its own separate turkey week.

turned every honest color we expect from autumn and the cornstalks stand high and hollow in the long-threshed fields. Edgerton has a Piggly Wiggly, a firehouse, and a tightly clustered business district of two-story brick buildings. At the far southern end of Main Street I find the warehouse, where after I walk through the heavy steel door I see a college-age woman clicking a mouse at a desk, who gets up and takes me into the main room of the school. To the right, lined up almost like voting booths along the south wall, are twenty worktables where people in jeans pull tools out of various drawers. I set my coat and backpack down by a bookcase full of paintbrushes and power drills and paints and chemicals in small plastic tubs. There's a stereo here, a copy of *The Best of Jackson Brown* resting on top of it. I don't know it yet, but where I'm standing as Dan Rinehart comes out from the supply-company side of the warehouse to shake my hand is almost exactly where he stands when shooting his television show. "Here's the worktable I use," Rinehart says, pointing out a freestanding booth in the center of the room—picture Lucy Van Pelt's psychiatry office if she were standing, except this booth has a mirror hanging above the table at an angle of forty-five degrees. You can see the entire work surface just by glancing upward. "When we do the show," Rinehart explains, "we've got a camera aimed right at me, and one down near the floor, angled up at this mirror." This is how they get the overhead shots that fill much of each episode. I've always assumed they had a camera hanging above Rinehart and angled directly downward. *Taxidermy for the Sportsman,* it's clear, is a low-budget production, and already I'm shamed at how taken I am by its easy and obvious teletheatrics.

Rinehart's classes have a watch-and-do structure. Students gather around the workbench and watch him do one step; then they return to their own workbench to try it themselves, grabbing Rinehart from his room pacing when they have a question. I'm here on a Thursday, and students have spent the previous three days preparing their capes for mounting.[9] Today's the exciting day they get to actually put these skins onto the forms, but first those forms need to be prepared to receive the skins. If you've never seen a taxidermy manikin before, rest assured you're not in the minority. A manikin resembles the real animal almost contradictorily the way a socked foot resembles a bare one. The shape is right, but the color is all wrong—the pale, fresh-butter color of spray foam. It has veins and musculature, but no eyes or ears. Just flat spots where those parts should be. And manikins these days are mass-produced. No matter the animal a taxidermist may receive in the studio, he can pick up a catalog and order the manikin based on a few measurements. Rinehart's TASCO catalog requests only two measurements: the tip of the nose to the tearduct of the eye, and the circumference of the neck at "the atlas"—which is the point where the topmost vertebra meets the skull. (Taxidermists as a rule know far more anatomy than you or I do.)

Step 1 for Rinehart's students is to prep the manikins with spray cans of Garry Bowen's Mannikin-Prep (TASCO item number 4072, $9.95) and then to coat them with sawdust ($29.95 for a forty-pound bag). Everything the students use is sold by TASCO. The manikins they work on. The pressurized tanner their skins just came out of. Even the needles and thread with which'll they sew up the skins. This connection between all the parts of his business is something Rinehart's done by design. The plan "from the get-go" has been to build a school—which makes a little money—that's supported by a supply company—which can make a lot. And as the supply company develops new products, Rinehart incorporates those products into his curriculum. "That way," he says, "someone just learning taxidermy

---

[9] A *cape* is the term given for all the skin that'll end up on a game-head mount—namely, the skin of the face, head, neck, and shoulders. Flayed out before mounting, it looks a lot like a cape though couldn't actually be used for one.

is up-to-date." He explains all this to me while the students work at their individual stations, and throughout the day, when the "watch" part of the instruction is done and the "do" part begins, Rinehart moseys over to my somewhat fixed post on a stool by his own workstation, chatting all about the various aspects of his business. He's a friendly man. Watching his show, one of the first things I noticed about him was that he was always smiling. I am a person who finds smiling rather easy and smiling genuinely a little less so, but smiling while talking seems impossible. Rinehart's a pro at it, however, smiling with his eyes so that when he says something like, "We need to take careful measurements to make the fish look a lot more dimensionally natural," it comes across as a compliment would. I'm almost blushing by episode's end.

Which isn't to say that Rinehart's beloved throughout the industry. Some people criticize him for the very business model he's developed: isn't incorporating products into the curriculum more about teaching students how to be good customers than to be taxidermists? One old-school taxidermist I spoke with says that Rinehart and others like him teach people only how to select and work with the right manikin. He doesn't teach how to build your own bodyform. As a result, taxidermists of this latest generation are limited in the kinds of animals they can mount, and thus they are limited to the kinds of customers they can attract. If a museum were to come to them with a warbler or a monkey, there'd be no manikin they could order. "People are becoming excellent technicians," said one taxidermist, "not artists. This isn't to say they're not creative, but there's a difference between a technically creative piece and an artistically creative piece." Some folks take umbrage at those TASCO manikins that come with preset eyes (which Rinehart has selected for this week's course, thus depriving his students any instruction on sculpting a proper brow with clay) or preformed nostrils. "I think it's cheating," one taxidermist told me. This is a taxidermist who never sculpts his own manikins, who instead mounts every job on premade bodyforms he orders from a catalog, but the point here is that the technology of the foam manikin has taken over the industry to such an extent that it's not even considered a technology. It's as much an inherent part of the process as the skin itself is. What this means is that all the work Carl Akeley and his forebears strove so hard to accomplish—musculature, attitude, anatomy—has been done for the taxidermist before he even begins. What's left, then, for taxidermists to distinguish their work? As we'll see in chapter 4, it's the finishing details. The eye and nostril, but also the lips and inner ears. The finicky stuff that most laypeople barely notice when beholding a beast on a wall.

To Rinehart's credit, there are so many products involved in taxidermy that it helps to be given some suggestions, and it's not like TASCO's products are shoddy. At one point, while students are pouring sawdust over their manikins, Rinehart directs everyone's attention to a deer head mounted on the wall near his workstation. "See that deer there?" he asks. "If I told most taxidermists that that deer has all that musculature you see down in the brisket area, that I got all that without pinning [the hide to the form as it dried], they'd never believe me. But you can do it, if you fully prep your manikin before skinning." The key to champion taxidermy is a perfectly rendered eye, but the key to even passable taxidermy is good musculature. This is what Carl Akeley knew in the 1880s. You can sculpt the most realistic bodyform in the history of the world, but if you can't get the hide properly skinned and fleshed and cured and tanned and stuck onto the form, all that musculature will be lost.

All the students seem to take this to heart. I count nine of them in the room, two are women, both of whom are younger than forty. Two men are older than forty. Five of the students wear ball caps, four of which are camo ball caps. They've come to Edgerton from as far away as Phoenix and as near as Janesville, ten miles down the road. Most of them are hunters, many of whom are looking to start a new career. Brian, the man from Phoenix, got laid off when the factory he worked in for years was shut down. He grew up in southwestern Wisconsin and heard the Rinehart name enough that he thought to come back and give it a try. Jim is a twenty-eight-year-old mechanic from Flint, Michigan. He's here for the week with his dad. "I was kinda hating my job and looking for a change," Jim tells me. "Being from Michigan, our economy's in the garbage. I seen what they charge for mounting an animal, and I thought, *If they can do it, I can do it.*"

Which is true in theory. But because ours is not a country with a taxidermy track, so to speak, not a country where fresh-faced taxidermists send out résumés and put up profiles on Monster.com and buy sensible suits for interviews at taxidermy firms, the fact of the matter is that while anyone can be a taxidermist, not everyone can do taxidermy for a living. Know-how is maybe half of it. The scary steps that follow—quitting your day job, starting your own business, and working every day with every responsibility resting on your pajama'd shoulders—aren't for everyone. "I have nothing but respect for the students who come here looking to make a change," Rinehart says. "Because I know what it's like to step outside your comfort zone, and it's a risk. It's a big risk."

Rinehart's path to taxidermy was somewhat laid for him: he's a legacy. His father, John Rinehart, started one of the first full-time taxidermy schools in the country way back in the mid-1970s and had his own shop since before Dan was born. "My daycare was basically a professional taxidermy studio," Dan says, and by the time he was thirteen he was helping his father teach in his school and traveling to state-association conventions to give seminars for taxidermists three, four times his age. What happens when you are born into a profession the way Dan was (his father, brother, and uncle are all well-known taxidermists) is that there's never a way to divide your life into before and after. Dan's always known how to mount a deer. He's always known how to preserve a fish. "It's almost like osmosis. When I actually decided to go into taxidermy profession-ally, even though I'd never done it before, I knew how to."

Rinehart takes me on a tour of the taxidermy arts empire he's try-ing to build. The building used to hold Edgerton's largest tobacco-curing warehouse, back when Edgerton was the tobacco capital of the world. All told the TASCO operation doesn't even use a quarter of the total space. In a room behind the classroom I see piles of card-board boxes TASCO products get shipped in and some proprietary manikin-construction machinery I'm asked not to take notes on or photographs of. I see a pinup on the far wall of "Miss TASCO 2008," depicting a blonde in a black bikini who's bent over on all fours in a classic position, except here it's more like all threes, with one hand draped over the shoulders of a 100-series deer form. The manikin's head is turned almost indignantly away from the model, who happens to be a taxidermist and who happens also to be a for-mer student of the Dan Rinehart Taxidermy School. (TASCO was unable to find a model for its 2009 catalog.) I see the loft upstairs where the ceilings are thirty feet high and the floorspace is virtually empty, ready for a major expansion. I see one of the soon-to-be-released CAD series of headforms. CAD as in "computer aided de-sign," which Dan and designer Steve Rotramel have used to sculpt a perfectly symmetric form. Even more exciting, though, are the nostrils they were able to design, which are so detailed that no lon-ger will taxidermists need to sculpt a realistic nostril with putty or clay. "The finishing process as we know it is virtually nonexistent with this new product," Rinehart tells me, to the chagrin of taxi-dermists everywhere. He's got a prototype for me to look at, and I peer into its nostril and decide that, yes, it's very lifelike, even though I don't think I've ever looked into a live deer's nostril before.

Back in the school, every manikin is coated in sawdust and it's time to set the antlers. Everyone is working with antlers. Some have been brought from home, and some have been furnished by the school. Most of them are ten-point, but some are eight-point.[10] One is four-point, and Rinehart makes a little joke about how small these are. When their owner protests, Rinehart says, "Hey, a trophy is in the eye of the beholder. I would rather mount someone's first kill than some world record." Jim is mounting the antlers of a deer killed by his great-grandfather. "To me that's awesome," Dan says at one point. "See, you're not just mounting a deer; you're preserving memories."

Antlers have to be drilled right into the top of the form's head, and for them to fit properly, students need to trim off the bottom of the skull. This is done with a bandsaw, behind which everyone lines up to wait their turn, like in a Soviet breadline. All the students wear goggles, prudently, and at the saw they hold the antlers such that the thin dome of its skull bone is perpendicular to the ground. As the saw blade eats through the bone the room fills with the kind of shrieking we know from construction sites, except here the context is different. What's being sawn isn't a series of two-by-fours but rather the skull of a dead whitetail deer, and appropriately the sound is higher, something more nasal than the growl of saw teeth gnashing through wood. "Don't force the blade on a bandsaw," Dan warns. "Let it do its job." I've never seen a sawn skull before, so I get closer to take a peek. I see a blurry metal blade slicing off a ring of skull bone, neat and crisp like a pat of butter. There's this white dust that fills the air and coats everything in a couple feet's vicinity of the saw, and from this dust comes a smell that's hot and pungent and not good. It's a lot like the smell of burnt hair—or no: *drilled teeth*. A sawn skull smells precisely like drilled teeth, and doesn't this make a lot of sense?

The students quickly screw their antlers to the tops of their head-

---

[10] I used to think this designated some arbitrary score given to a rack's inherent majesty, but it's actually just the number of tips one can count on the antlers.

forms, and now suddenly whitetail deer are starting to appear. Because their manikins have preset eyes, all that's missing from the rows of headforms is the skin itself. Well, ears, too, but it's easy to overlook an absence of ears when you've got antlers sitting tall and pretty like little bonsai trees. Rather than begin the actual mounting of the skin, Rinehart sends everyone to lunch, and in seconds all nine students file out the door.

I'm not quite sure where they're going to. Edgerton has a Subway, a McDonald's, and a Denny's-esque restaurant by the Town Edge Motel where I spent the previous night. They could be going "home"—which is to say to the house in the center of town owned by the taxidermy school, which rents it out by the week. Dan's whitetail course lasts from Monday to Saturday, but Dan offers a whole meal of taxidermy instruction: there's a fish course, a bird course, and a full-size mammal course. Most of the students I've met today are here only for whitetail, but there are a couple that have been here since the end of September, when the full four-week semester began. Housing for these students is only thirty dollars a night. Not bad for a full kitchen and laundry facilities.

I head over to the Subway, and there I run into Mary Beth Parks, one of the two female students this week, and she kindly invites me to sit with her. Parks is a thirty-seven-year-old mother of three who owns with her husband an archery-based sporting goods store in Brookfield, Missouri. Parks Outdoors is the name, and I can't tell if any wordplay is involved. She and her husband are "big hunters." They've got good deer out there, and bobcats, and she's traveled around the country to hunt bear and moose. All of these Parks has had mounted by a taxidermist in her area, but he was self-taught. The work was suitable, but nothing spectacular. "None of the taxidermists in maybe a sixty-mile area have gone to school for it," she says. This is why she's here this week. Already they have a solid customer base in their sporting goods store, and for Parks—who recently sold her commercial sign business—it seems a logical thing to add taxidermy services to everything else they're already doing. "Plus, I needed something to channel my creativity."

Before this week she'd never done a single bit of taxidermy, and when she arrived Monday morning, she was completely overwhelmed. "I thought I'd made the biggest mistake of my life," she says. Though in the three hours I watched they'd only prepped the form and attached the antlers, these steps have plenty of substeps and Rinehart's instruction as such is brisk. I saw maybe one student ever take notes. Parks worried at first that she wouldn't be able to keep up. "But now I'm very happy with it so far. It's almost amazing where we've come since Monday."

And suddenly I can't help myself. I start to say a lot of dumb words. I'm pretty sure I use "gender" in a past-tense verb form. I have trouble discerning between "female" and "woman." I lead the witness, so to speak. What I want from Parks, I know as I ask the question, is some feminist nugget of postgender wisdom. Because what a boon for whatever it is I'm trying to write about: a female taxidermist! It's like a doctor who smokes, or a Log Cabin Republican. Right? I point out to Parks what she already knows, that she's one of two women in the classroom, and I ask her if she feels there's anything about her being a female that makes her situation special. I want her to respond this way: "I know that my presence here subverts the dominant paradigm, and I've noticed that I and the other woman in the classroom are surpassing some of the men with respect to things like detail and patience, but while I could talk to you this afternoon about the need for gender equality in a field as commonly chauvinistic as the taxidermy industry, I really just want to stuff animals."

Instead, Parks responds this way: "I guess there aren't a lot of women who get into something like this. People have always said I'm strange, like 'Oh, she's one of the guys!'"

Of course there are women taxidermists. That I was ever surprised by this, that it's even a topic of comment or worthy of note, is a factor not of some novelty within the field but of some pervading sexism we may not want to admit. There are taxidermists who are women just as there are doctors who are women. Police officers, too. Ask a female firefighter what it's like being a female firefighter and rightfully she'll stare at you without an answer. Because what are you asking her? Are you asking her what it's like to do her job or what it's like to be her sex, the sex she's been her entire life? Our biological sex is not some hobby we take up. My assumption that taxidermy would ever be a domain exclusive to men betrays a fundamental misunderstanding about the effect animals can have on us all.

We finish up our sandwiches and head back down Main Street in our separate cars. Back in the studio, people are pulling deer capes out from a refrigerator I hadn't yet noticed, where they've been stored in plastic bags since coming out of the tanner, lest they dry up and become unusable. Shrinkage, though, is unavoidable, so for upward of five minutes, everyone grips onto the edges of the hide and pulls outward. The skin's surprisingly resilient, almost like taffy. The next step for the mounting process is to smear all over the manikin a thick coat of hide paste—a tacky hummuslike goo with a musty, moldy smell one normally finds in old closets. Deer capes are slit down the back of the neck, not only because this is the part of the final mount that faces the wall but also because most quadrupeds have a thick tuft of hair, like a mane, that runs along the backbone and hides stitches easily. Everyone maneuvers his or her headform down and around so that it looks even more dead, staring blankly up at the sky, and finally they're ready to receive the skin. Earlier in the day, when students had just begun prepping their manikins, Rinehart said that they hadn't done any taxidermy yet. "Taxidermy," he insisted, "is the art of moving the skin around." Now, with students fitting the muzzle of the form into the empty socket of face skin, spreading the rest of the hide evenly around the neck, trying not to create too many wrinkles, Rinehart announces to the room: "Congratulations, everybody, you just started doing taxidermy. Four days into class and you just started doing taxidermy."

I could argue with him. Does the baking of cookies begin only once the dough is in the oven? Is setting up an easel and smearing colors on a palette not painting? That is, aren't the steps preparatory to the process really just a part of the process? I could argue with him, but why ruin the moment? Everyone's grinning at one another because it's this exact moment they all signed up for: the flat, flayed skin now made three-dimensional and familiar. "They're starting to look like real deer now," Rinehart tells me, and he's dead right.

That's when this strange remorse hits me. Shouldn't I be standing there, near a workstation of my own, arranging my own deer skin over the manikin I prepped myself? Shouldn't I be attacking this whole stuffing-animals thing through full immersion in the practice—like George Plimpton on the football field? If I'm here today to get an idea of how taxidermy education works, wouldn't it have been the smart thing to do to enroll myself in the course? Not just to talk to people who have come here with no taxidermy experience, but to come here with my own lack of experience and see firsthand—and *feel* and know in my bones—how this wacky, impossible act of preservation comes together? This is what people keep asking me when I tell them about this confusing book I'm working on: *Are you going to do some taxidermy yourself?* And so, why am I not? And these people are my friends and my family and the taxidermists I call on the phone or approach at conventions. I'm not a taxidermist. I'm not a hunter. The whole truth as I understand it today is that at some point in my life what was a mild interest in habitat dioramas became a confusing obsession with taxidermy, an obsession that has led me around the country to try to talk with people who *are* taxidermists, people who *are* hunters, people who can take my shallow ideas about the nonhuman organisms that live on this planet and maybe deepen them a little. People like Jim and Brian here, who for so long have been working jobs that no longer work for them, honest people for whom hunting has been a part of their lives for as long as television has been a part of mine. And this, I realize, is why I didn't sign up to take a course myself, why I shouldn't have ever signed up and enrolled. These nine students are looking to change the trajectories of their lives. What, I wonder, would it be like for me to sit next to them, looking only to talk "big ideas"?

I leave the students to their work, their futures, and thank Rinehart for his hospitality. I think what I've always liked about schools are their transformative qualities. Anyone can walk into that building— some land-grant university, some small warehouse, some fifteen-building complex in Rochester, New York—and, by working hard enough, emerge as a different person. Maybe smarter. Maybe better read. But also maybe meaner, more self-involved. And schools don't work for everyone. They never really worked for Carl Akeley, but they've always worked for me, and they just might work for the nine curious people in the room, all of whom are now wrapping the nose, lips, and eyelids of their deer in wet towels, lest these bits dry out overnight. Dan Rinehart Taxidermy School's shop towels are a deep aqua blue, and as I leave I take a look at all the almost-finished deer. Their ears are generally in place, and the skins are sewn up along backbones. And their faces are covered in blue cloth. As a group, they look like a contemporary art piece—*Without Laughter* or some such triteness—but come the end of the week, they'll just look real.

THREE

The history of the natural history museum isn't necessarily bestseller material. It's not baseball or jazz or the Civil War. It's not salt or mauve or the *Oxford English Dictionary*. And yet the natural history museum is something with which we're all familiar. When on vacations, or when bussed cityward on grade-school field trips, we've all strode briskly past the geodes and interactive bug displays to gape drop-jawed at the dinosaur bones in the back hall. Maybe we've even seen the taxidermized animals posed behind the glass panels of habitat dioramas or the cabinets of birds all frozen in time. We read in the newspaper about a new exhibit opening in our natural history museums. We get in the mail another carefully worded letter entreating us to become members of our natural history museums. What is the history of all this? The museum: hasn't it sort of always been around?

Taxidermy is an act of preservation. It is to animals, or more properly their skins, what Mylar bags are to comic books. The whole point is to keep something fragile and precious and susceptible to decay around as long as possible, if not for eternity, and so it comes as little surprise to know that the first taxidermists were collectors. Sometime toward the end of the Renaissance it became important to a certain class of people to have animals both familiar and exotic on display as a kind of curiosity. Taxidermy was the way to show these collections off, without having to worry about the feeding and care of an animal that, given the chance, would crush you, tear your limbs from your body, or otherwise make misery of your courtly life. Where, though, did this need to collect animals come from? For that answer, we need to go way back, for it seems that as long as human beings have been living with animals, we've been trying to understand them, and our understanding begins with classification.

One of the first written attempts to classify and characterize the animals occurs in a genre known as the medieval bestiary. These works were hand copied in manuscripts and listed what was then all of the animals in what was then the known world. They sought to describe not only their behaviors and physical characteristics but also the relation of the animals to Christian doctrine. The bestiaries were the second-most-read type of text in medieval Europe after the Bible. And they were fully illustrated (for a less-than-literate public), each animal drawn in thick, flat outlines with little to no shading and posed in wooden but elaborate postures. There's the same expressive eye throughout: womanish and coming to a kind of Arabian point.

The bestiary is to zoology what astrology is to astronomy, which is to say the men who wrote them got a lot wrong. Here's T. H. White's translation of a twelfth-century Latin bestiary:

> Scientists say that Leo has three principal characteristics.
>
> His first feature is that he loves to saunter on the tops of mountains. Then, if he should happen to be pursued by hunting men, the smell of the hunters reaches up to him, and he disguises his spoor behind him with his tail. Thus the sportsman cannot track him.
>
> It was this way that our Savior (i.e. the Spiritual Lion of the Tribe of Judah, the Rod of Jesse, the Lord of Lords, the

Son of God) once hid the spoor of his love in the high places, until, being sent by the Father, he came down into the womb of the Virgin Mary and saved the human race which had perished. . . .

The lion's second feature is, that when he sleeps, he seems to keep his eyes open.

Note the careful, assertive tone. The bestiary includes the unicorn ("which is also called Rhinoceros by the Greeks") and griffins, and it lets us know that "there is an animal called an Elephant, which has no desire to copulate." It's particularly illuminating about "Castor, the Beaver, none more gentle," whose "testicles make a capital medicine. For this reason, so Physiologus says, when he notices that he is being pursued by the hunter, he removes his own testicles with a bite, and casts them before the sportsman, and thus escapes by flight."

A beaver's testicles, we know now, are internal, and couldn't be bitten off if the animal were even so inclined as to try. Whence these little myths about animals we live among today is the basis for much contemporary study of medieval bestiaries, all of which stem from "the Physiologus"—a sort of ur-bestiary produced by an unknown Greek writer around 150 CE. The word means "naturalist" in Latin, and in many ways its writer, called Physiologus himself, is Western science's first taxonomist.

A bit of etymology before we move on. *Taxonomy* shares a root word with *taxidermy*: *taxis,* Greek for "arrangement." Combine this with *derma* ("skin"), and we have an easy summary of the taxidermist's art, arranging skins. That-*nomy* suffix comes from the Greek words for *law* and *distribution*—it's essentially a way in English to refer to a branch of knowledge. Hence astronomy, physiognomy, and so forth.[1] While the word itself isn't coined until the nineteenth

---

[1] A beloved verb among taxidermists today is *taxi,* as in: "Now, the glue hasn't dried yet, so you can still taxi the skin around on the manikin."

century, taxonomies—systems of arrangement or classification—
were being developed in the natural sciences as early as the seven-
teenth. These early taxonomies were specific to plants, following an
invigorated interest at the time in studying and documenting their
medicinal uses, and the rare attempts at classifying the animals of the
world were arbitrary and of little use to anyone other than the taxonomist. (And often embarrassingly unscientific; it wasn't until the
1690s that unicorns and other mythical beasts began to be dropped
from animal taxonomies.)

But then again: aren't all methods of classification subjective and
arbitrary? Who can say they have *the* method for sorting a group of
creatures that spawned and grew so unmethodically? Or a group of
anything, for that matter? Give a shopful of Brooklynites a sizeable
record collection and you can easily come away with more taxonomies than you'd hoped for. Do you need a chronological arrangement, forming a kind of historical narrative? Alphabetical by name
of band or artist, making lookup simpler for the nonaficionado?
Generic, clustering sounds and styles together? (Once, I asked such
a Brooklynite where a particular CD by The Feelies was located
among his shelves. "It's in Jangle," he shouted from the other room,
as though this were all the information I needed.) It's the question
that haunts every collector: how do you choose to order the things
you have before you? The answer lies in what you want to get out
of your taxonomy. The problem with most of the pre-Enlightenment
taxonomies is that they each formed a closed system. That is, they
took stock of all the known species of the world and fit them into as

---

Which is to say "to shuttle to and fro," similar to what happens to us
between landing in an airplane and walking out of the gate. But contrary
to appearances, this *taxi* and *taxidermy* don't share any common root
words. The former comes from taxicabs, which get their names from
taximeter, the device that measures how far you've gone and how much it
costs. This word, *taximeter,* is derived from Latin terms for *tax* or *tariff.* So,
to sum up: *taxidermy* is Greek; *taxi* is Latin.

few categories as the taxonomist could come up with. This is fine given a finite number of species on this planet, but as we know scientists are still discovering new species, and given the wrong kind of taxonomy, this would be like buying a Laurie Anderson record and finding "new wave" and "spoken word" at opposite ends of your collection.

The person credited with devising the first open and useful taxonomy (and therefore the same taxonomy we use today) is another landmark Carl: Carolus Linnaeus, a Swede. In 1753, he published *Systema Naturae,* a work of just eleven pages that not only classified the animals, the vegetables, and the minerals but also further subdivided the same into classes, orders, genera, species, and varieties (taxonomists would later add the phylum above class and the family above genus). Linnaeus, then, was the first taxonomist to use the same system for plants that he did for animals. He's known foremost as the progenitor of binomial nomenclature. Previously, any living thing in a taxonomy was assigned a genus, and then species were given a set of descriptors to explain how they differentiated themselves from others in the genus. These resulting names got unwieldy. Linnaeus gave a single word to both the genus and the species of an organism—*Canis lupus, Homo sapiens, Ursus arctos*—which was above all extremely economical. It made him akin to the first person to come up with *frenemy* or *J-Lo.* But more than economy, binomial nomenclature was the first system of naming that had built into it room for the discovery of new species. You just had to look at the body; there were orders and classes of similarly structured creatures waiting for new members. Most new discoveries of the present day happen at the species level, and scientists are getting a sense of humor (or honor, depending on your point of view) in their naming. There's a spider named *Myrmekiaphila neilyoungi*, and one named *Aptostichus stephencolberti.* A new kind of dinosaur was found in the United States recently, and the species was given the name *Dracorex hogwartsia* because of what it inspired in the paleontologist who dug it up. There's even a slime-mold beetle with the name *Agathidium bushi* after a rather slimy former president.[2]

What do all these celebrity species look like? you ask. Sure you can find images online, but as new species keep being discovered and added to our animal taxonomy, wouldn't it be great to have a central location where all these new species could be collected and put on display for a public eager to learn more? Welcome to the situation facing botanists and zoologists of the eighteenth century. Binomial nomenclature begat a refined system of classification. Classification begat collection. Collection begat an issue of storage and a larger one of preservation. The very first animals stuffed were done so literally, with straw for large animals and cotton for smaller ones. To prepare these specimens, the skins were merely left out to dry and rubbed with salt or herbs to get rid of any excess grease or moisture. After about fifteen years the feathers became frayed and swatches of fur were gone from the hides—the mounts experienced the natural decay they would have had the animals inside them been left alone. No matter how clean the skin, no matter how long it was set out to dry, there always remained some organic matter that certain insects find irresistible. These are mostly beetles, and specifically the beetles in the *Dermestidae* family, commonly called carpet beetles or skin beetles because such is what they like to eat.[3]

The problem of decaying mounts was solved at last in the 1740s, when a French chemist and naturalist named Jean-Baptiste Bécoeur invented arsenic soap. It was kind of a godsend. Scientists knew a lot

---

[2] While on an expedition in the Olympic Mountains in Washington, Carl Akeley's colleagues named a new species of mouse after him: *Peromyscus akeleyi.*

[3] We'll come back to carpet beetles later; it turns out the most hated enemy of the taxidermist is also now one of his best resources.

about arsenic as far back as the Middle Ages, when alchemists would toy with and oxidize the element for its medicinal properties. During the Renaissance, arsenic was prescribed to treat such varied ailments as ulcers, tuberculosis, and syphilis. Of course, everyone knows arsenic as a poison, and indeed for a long time it was a much-loved method of the aristocracy for getting inconvenient relatives off the throne. Arsenic in its natural state is a powder that's odorless and tasteless, and so for much of the Middle Ages and Renaissance it was untraceable following, say, one's brother's sudden keeling over after some royal banquet. It was also impossible to get arsenic to adhere to an animal's skin long enough to penetrate and kill off any bacteria. That is, until Bécoeur's conversion of arsenic into arsenic soap. His formula was so valuable he kept it a secret throughout his life, but it was later published around 1800:

  320 g arsenic
  120 g carbonate of potash
  320 g distilled water
  320 g soap
  40 g lime
  10 g camphor

Once prepared, this soap could be rubbed all over the inside of the skin and left to dry. The arsenic, being poisonous, would kill off anything dermestid beetles could feed on.[4] Collectors could then stuff the skin, set it on a shelf, and never worry about it having to die a second, undesirable death.

----

[4] One would expect that Bécoeur's invention would lead to a spate of taxidermist deaths, the way the mercury used in the felting process maddened many old-time hatters, but studies taken of census records by Christopher Frost and others have found in taxidermists no earlier age of death than average.

Ask anyone—any by "anyone" I mean the four or five of us who spend our time investigating the history of taxidermy—about the oldest mounted animal still in existence and you'll get any number of answers. Some will point to the Duchess of Richmond's parrot we saw in chapter 1, which was preserved on account of its being stored in a cold underground crypt, devoid of insects. Others refer to the crocodile held at the Natural History Museum in St. Gallen, Switzerland, that dates from 1623. But most will tell you it's the rhinoceros at the Royal Museum of Vertebrates in Florence that dates way the hell back to the 1500s. Go to any major source: Christopher Frost's *History of British Taxidermy,* Rachel Poliquin's otherwise authoritative taxidermy blog RavishingBeasts, a how-to manual on taxidermy dating to 1944. Even Penelope Bodry-Sanders's biography of Carl Akeley. They all cite the rhinoceros at the Royal Museum of Vertebrates in Florence that dates back to the 1500s. Try, however, to find the Royal Museum of Vertebrates in Florence and you'll come up empty. It's possible that in the days before unification Florence may have had a Royal Museum of Vertebrates, but now the closest thing around is the Museo di Storia Naturale, which is part of the University of Florence. That museum opened in 1775, more than two hundred years after everyone says the rhino was first mounted.

Clearly, there's some confusion. The botanical garden attached to the museum dates to 1545 and has held in its time a menagerie of exotic animals. Perhaps the rhino was exhibited here? But this is a stuffed rhino we're talking about, not a live one, and virtually every piece of taxidermy mounted before 1750 has decayed and no longer exists. What did the Florentines know about preservation that the rest of the world did not, enabling them to keep something as gigantic as a rhinoceros perfectly preserved for two hundred years before everyone else caught up?

Ask at the Museo di Storia Naturale and they'll tell you they don't have a rhinoceros dating back to the 1500s, which is to say it doesn't exist. Or, at least, it *probably* doesn't exist. While no one is able to produce a picture of this rhino, much less the skin, there is a story of the first rhino seen in Europe that may give us some answers. The story, found in papers of such authoritative entities as the Swedish Linnaeus Society and documented quite thoroughly in Silvio Bedini's book *The Pope's Elephant*, goes like this: in the winter of 1514, the governor of Portuguese India sent a live rhinoceros to his king, Manuel I. It arrived in 1515 and was soon a sensation. This was the first rhinoceros that had been seen in Europe since Roman antiquity; most people had thought it mythical, some relic from the bestiary. The animal was immortalized by Albrecht Dürer, the famous artist of the Renaissance, who made a woodcut based on an eyewitness account of the rhino that made its way to Germany. That is, Dürer never actually saw the rhino himself, and we all know from the old saw about the blind people feeling all sides of an elephant what the dangers are of not getting full visual evidence. Dürer's woodcut, as a result, is bulked up and overworked. Its armor, for starters, looks as though it were wrought in a smithy, and Dürer included a superfluous unicorn-like spiral horn right between the animal's shoulder blades. It's close. A good rendering. But it looks more like a child's action toy than a rhinoceros.

After about a year of enjoying his rhino, even going so far as to put it up in a coliseum-style death match with a baby elephant (the rhino won), King Manuel I decided to regift the animal and shipped it to Pope Leo X. On its way to Rome, the ship that carried the rhino sank; chained up in a cage, the animal went down with the ship. Or *did* it? Both Bedini and the Linnaeus Society cite two contemporary accounts that say the rhino washed up on shore and that its skin was shipped off to Rome. It arrived at the Vatican in February 1516. According to Bedini, the saga of the rhinoceros seem[s] to have terminated with its arrival in Rome, and art historians have sought in vain for some trace of its disposition thereafter. The missing rhinoceros continues to intrigue many merely because of its sudden disappearance. . . . It was presumed to have been destroyed in the sacking of Rome in 1527, if not earlier. Still, another possibility offers itself: Pope Leo X, or perhaps his cousin Guilio de' Medici after he was elected Pope Clement VII, may have sent the mounted beast to Florence to become part of the natural history collection maintained by the Medici family. . . . A search of the records and of the present collections of the five natural history collections in Florence failed to bring anything more to light.

And *yet*! Here's the Linnaeus Society: "Although there appears to be no confirmation at all about the continued existence of such a mounted rhinoceros, there is still a chance that the first Lisbon rhinoceros is preserved." So the myth of taxidermy's oldest extant specimen lives on. As far as myths go, it's a small one. It would be a bit of a stretch to say that we "know" the oldest mounted specimen is the rhino in Florence like we "know" Pluto is a planet or like we "know" that Iraq had weapons of mass destruction in 2003. Which is to say, this myth isn't really harming anyone. It doesn't have the capacity to change anyone's life. And yet for some reason it's so important to taxidermists that they're willing to set aside any doubts or questions about the myth's veracity—unwilling to make follow-up phonecalls or go digging around in the literature—in order to keep asserting it as true.

What seems to have happened is that back in the early 1890s, George Brown Goode, a curator at the Smithsonian (then the United States National Museum), got some facts mixed up in conversation with his colleague, Robert W. Shufeldt. "Probably, as Mr. Goode informs me," Shufeldt wrote in the museum's 1892 annual report, "the oldest museum specimen still in existence is a rhinoceros still preseved in the Royal Museum of Vertebrates in Florence. . . . It dates from the sixteenth century." The Smithsonian then published this footnote, and Shufeldt's scholarship was otherwise strong enough that others read and quoted it and the error was passed on as fact. This is inevitable in the slipshod task of reconstructing histories: the apocryphal is too narratively alluring to pass over. Where, for instance, did a twelve-year-old boy get his hands on some arsenic in mounting his neighbor's canary?

When I try to think about what's so alluring about this myth, I can only go back to that Lisbon rhinoceros and the tragic story behind it. To aver that *this* animal was the first preserved is to assign for taxidermy such noble beginnings. Noble in both senses: righteous and aristocratic. Here was an animal given as a gift to both a king and a pope. Here was an animal immortalized as a woodcut. Could anyone argue that such an animal shouldn't have been preserved for future generations? It behooves taxidermists to place their art form's origins here, with a one-of-a-kind collectible and not, say, with a deer that some hunter shot and wanted to show off. Or some maligned and unspectacular animal such as a rat. Being that taxidermy is something we can enjoy only at a great cost—some animal's death and dismemberment—we all want to believe that cost is worth it.

Had the rhino survived, he would have been kept in the menagerie Pope Leo X built in the Vatican's Belvedere Court, where it would have lived among lions and tigers and bears (and monkeys and the famous elephant Hanno). If, though, only the skin survived, it would have been exhibited in the pope's cabinet of curiosities, if he had such a cabinet, and records show that he did not. Somewhat of a fad among the worldly aristocracy of Europe's High Renaissance, the cabinet of curiosities usually wasn't a cabinet at all but an entire room lined floor to ceiling with glass cases containing all manner of objects. A belt buckle from "the Orient" carved from ivory. The bill from a platypus. A portrait of the daughter of the Grand Duchess of Wherever. All were exhibited alongside one another, the only criterion for inclusion being a thing's rarity, the level of curiosity it could rouse in the viewer, and, thus, the level of prestige it could bring the owner. These cabinets of curiosities were the very beginnings of museums, and it's a private, elitist beginning. The grandest of cabinets were owned by royalty, the men who received the gifts sent by foreign dignitaries or ambassadors and who could afford to buy the paintings and sculptures made by artists both foreign and domestic. Those cabinets not owned by royalty were owned by the wealthy citizens allowed into their court. One such citizen, Ole Worm of Denmark, was the personal physician to King Christian IV. For much of his adult life, Worm (pronounced with a *v*) assembled so thorough a cabinet it was among the first to be designated with the word *museum,* meaning "seat of the muses." The Museum Wormianum, as seen in an etching made in 1655, shows every available surface filled with things Worm wanted to show off. A primitive canoe hangs upside down from the rafters alongside a stuffed duck and several breeds of fanged fish looking ferociously down at the floor. High on the right wall are two large tortoise shells, like family crests, one mounted right above the other and flanked on one side by a flayed-open snakeskin and on the other by an iguana and an armadillo preserved and hung from strings affixed to their backs, like grotesque Christmas ornaments. Opposite these are an array of antlers as large as and wrought as tree branches and some horns made to carry gunpowder. Running along the lower half of the far end of the room are shelves filled with trays labeled CONCHILIATA, HERBAE, METALIA, LAPIDES, ANIMALIUM PARTES. Ole Worm himself taught Latin and Greek and medicine in Copenhagen. He studied the branch of alchemy called iatrochemistry, which sought an elixir that would heal all ailments and cure all diseases. He was the first to show the link between the horn on the mythical unicorn and the tusk on the very real narwhal. So, a bit of a polymath. Couple all this with his tendency when the Plague hit Denmark not to flee to less toxic climes but rather to stick around and treat those who suffered and you've got in Ole Worm a pretty stand-up guy.

Shame he died of a bladder infection in 1654. Fortune, though, smiled down on the Museum Wormianum in the form of Christian IV's son and heir, Frederick III, who purchased the full collection to add to his own: the *Kunstkammer*. *Kammer* translates to "chamber," but this doesn't do the job of describing Frederick's collection. Here was no chamber or cabinet but rather a whole museum, laid out in nine different rooms on three floors of Copenhagen Castle. Weapons of armor from far-off lands were exhibited in the Arms Apartment. Scientific instruments and clocks could be found in the Mathematical Chamber. Specimens from nature were right in the First Apartment; here were the wonders (read: freaks) that brought Frederick all the renown he wanted. Deer antlers that had somehow grown through the bark of a tree limb. Also: a crocodile skull. The most endearing aspect of the *Kunstkammer* was the misguided way its objects were labeled with the same certainty we recall from the bestiary. "The Shinbone, which is believed to be from a giant" is the way Frederick labeled the left thighbone of an Indian elephant. "A piece of Indian Wood grown like a large Arm and Hand" is a branch from a pitchapple tree that, indeed, looks a bit like a loose fist. "The Head of a Walrus" is actually the skull of a hippopotamus. All of these objects have been unearthed from errant collections and relocated to the Zoological Museum at the University of Copenhagen. There are a number of preserved animal skins, too, though time hasn't been kind to them. The chameleon skin is a frightening, nauseating relic, its whole body swollen and ash black, as though left in an oven for far too long.

The only people who ever got a look at the *Kunstkammer* were personal guests of the king. Thus is the way these early museums were kept as pleasures for the wealthy for more than a century. It wasn't until this passion for collecting made its way to the post-Revolutionary United States that cabinets of curiosities were created with a mind for public education. There were a few notable cabinets scattered here and there along the eastern seaboard in the 1780s, but inarguably the most thorough belonged to Charles Willson Peale—an artist, collector, naturalist, and taxidermist called by one historian "the leading pioneer of taxidermy in the U.S.A." Most folks remember Peale as one of America's first major portrait artists. He painted several portraits of George Washington—a lifelong pal—and some of the best known are those of George in soldier drag, the younger, earlier portraits when his cheeks were still rosy and round. In 1782, Peale built an addition to his Philadelphia studio with many broad skylights and flat, open expanses of walls. He made this a gallery for showing off recent paintings to friends. It wasn't until he was commissioned to make a few drawings of some mammoth bones that had been discovered in Kentucky that Peale realized the potential for expanding the kinds of objects he exhibited there. Those bones were kept in a corner of the gallery, and every time Peale would bring people around for a look at his wall art, they'd continually drift over to the bones. After all, they'd *seen* Washington. They'd seen General William Smallwood. Maybe they'd even seen John Beale Bordley, Peale's patron, and the sea captain Mordecai Gist. Maybe not in person, but a two-dimensional likeness could only be looked at from a distance. Mammoth bones were right there in three dimensions on a table, as touchable and real as that morning's breakfast.

Peale hobnobbed with Washington and Thomas Jefferson and Benjamin Franklin. He was the most famous painter of his time, commissioned by statesmen and the wealthy class of the Revolutionary era. He named his sons Raphaelle, Rembrandt, Rubens, and Titian. Maybe he wasn't an aristocrat by definition, but he certainly couldn't be called an average Joe—not by a long shot. And yet from the beginning, as Peale began to collect more and more specimens of natural history, the goal for his gallery was to become a museum for the people. A collection, argued Peale, shouldn't be valued just for its encyclopedic properties—the thoroughness or rarity of its holdings—but for pedagogic ones. Museums had appeared in Europe at this time, most notably the British Museum in 1759, but these institutions made clear divisions between their research and exhibition components—always favoring the former over the latter. The European museum was a place where serious scholars came together for serious study. Peale wanted his museum to be a place, as he wrote in an early advertisement, where "individuals . . . may gain from it information, which, with pleasing and elevated ruminations, will bring them nearer to the Great-First-Cause."

This shift from private research to public exhibition has a lot of implications regarding our grander subject here. Karen Wonders, in her exhaustive study on habitat dioramas, argues that preserving an animal for up-close scientific and taxonomic study leads to a dull, bare-bones (forgive the pun) mount. It's called a study skin, and it's still created today in museum collections. When a specimen comes into the museum—and some institutions such as Chicago's Field Museum continue to get specimens donated almost daily[5]—a preparator skins it and sets the carcass inside a terrarium filled with carpet beetles. Yes, those same carpet beetles that taxidermists spent centuries trying to outwit. Turns out they like to eat more than an animal's hide, and nothing will clean a carcass as thoroughly as a

---

[5] Remarkably, there exist two competing groups in Chicago—Flint Creek Wildlife Rehabilitation and Chicago Bird Collision Monitors—that wander downtown and collect the bodies of birds who've collided into skyscraper windows. Those that don't make it get dropped off at the Field Museum's doors. Some 1,700 birds are donated each season, according to Dave Willard, the collection manager for birds.

swarm of beetles. Whenever I visit a museum's collections I always ask to see its dermestid colony, usually as a form of self-torture. Always, the beetles are kept behind a sealed door, sometimes two, and as a result the air inside the room is thick and stale. The smell of several skinned corpses slowly being devoured hits one very quickly. It's a sharp, thin stink that tends to pinch in the nostrils. I have recurring nightmares involving insects and their crawling on and near my body. The simple locomotion of six wire-thin legs—even the thought of this, even the typing of this sentence—is enough to send me screaming from a room. And yet every time, I go in for a close look, peering down into the tank from above and seeing the larvae of these beetles eating the flesh off a skeleton, crackling in group mastication like some giant rotten bowl of Rice Krispies. It ranks among the most gruesome sights of my life, and yet one of the most honest. Here it is, every time: the circle of life.

While the colony chews on the specimen's bones, the preparator cleans and cures the skin and stuffs it with wads of cotton. Some wires get driven along the limbs to keep the body in place, and the whole thing gets sewn up and placed in a drawer somewhere alongside many others just like it. Once, on a tour through the collections of the University of Nebraska State Museum, I asked Dr. Trish Freeman, caretaker of the collection, why she needed so many skins of the same species. An entire drawer, two feet by three, filled with twenty-some-odd yellow warblers. She looked at me like I was some kind of idiot.

"Are you the ideal human specimen?" she asked.

Touché. It ranks among the best dressings-down I've received. Her point of course is that variation among species is minute but widespread and that only with multiple specimens can a zoologist see exactly how they vary and what these variations might signify. And the best way to study these variations is to muck around as little as possible with the carcass. It's almost like what we do to humans before a funeral, except that we expect with study skins to open the coffin repeatedly—and for decades.

But if you want to get a sense not just of what a yellow warbler looks like but of where and how it lives, a study skin will have little to tell you. You'll need something more lifelike, something mounted in a way to suggest its habitat and behavior. Peale, in filling his gallery space, learned taxidermy by trial and error, reading books by Louis Dufresne and other European taxidermists, improving their techniques through his own experimentation. One of Peale's first successful mounts was the pair of Chinese pheasants George Washington donated, a gift from General Lafayette. Peale caught the graceful curves of the birds' tails and plumage quite well and manufactured his own glass eyes to give them a realistic finish. When it came time to put them in a case, he painted a little background of some theoretical landscape on which these birds could be innocently standing. It was the first time anyone had done this, and so bully to Peale for being an artist by trade and doing just what came naturally. Says his biographer Charles Coleman Sellers: "Here was the origin of the habitat groups which would be brought to full perfection a century later (and with the éclat of a new discovery) at the American Museum of Natural History in New York." He's partially right. As we'll see, habitat dioramas were made ("to full perfection" I might argue) elsewhere in the meantime, thanks to our friend Carl Akeley.

To fill his museum, Peale asked for donations and "the assistance of all persons who may be possessed of things curious that they can spare; whether they be of America or any other part of the world." The plea was effective, and, by 1790, when he renamed his gallery The American Museum, Peale had amassed more than a thousand objects, most of them donations. Sellers catalogs as many of them as he can stand to: a petrified snake, a root that looked like a human face, a two-headed pig, and a cow with five legs and six feet (*and two tails*) that actually lived with the Peales for a while. In short, the natural was abandoned for the surreal. "People presented," Sellers writes, "what they themselves delighted to see."

This line gives us a new way to think about an older one: *that oughta be in a museum*. Because, when you are building the first museum in a nation's history, one of the first museums in the world, deciding what *that* might designate isn't so simple. Nor is it even today. *What* ought to be in a museum? Most of us would agree that museum-inclusion status is deserved only by one-of-a-kind items. Archie Bunker's chair, for instance, which is on exhibit in Washington, D.C. The jersey worn by Cal Ripken Jr. the day he broke the most-consecutive-games-played record in baseball, on display in Cooperstown, New York. Roy Rogers's famous horse Trigger, originally on taxidermic display in Branson, Missouri (but bought at auction in 2010 by the owner of an Omaha television station). But when it comes to biological specimens—animals, specifically— the question is a lot more difficult to answer. We go to museums to see the things we can't see at home, and so a squirrel or a sparrow or a house cat isn't going to bring strollers and field trippers through the door. Unless it's an albino squirrel or a two-headed sparrow or a hairless house cat. We should be able to see, say, a rhinoceros, but what kind of rhinoceros? White or black? Male or female? What may not matter to the general museumgoer matters dearly to the zoologist.

Peale tried to find a balance between these oddities (which drew the crowds) and scientific specimens (which drew greater prestige), but in the end, it was too difficult a balance to maintain. The fate of Peale's American Museum matches that of any American museum today: admission fees weren't enough to sustain operations. By the 1800s, Peale was perpetually hit with financial trouble and struggled to keep his museum open. After his death in 1827, the museum went to his sons Rembrandt and Rubens, who even through expansion museums in Baltimore and New York had no further success. In 1854, they sold all Peale collections to a man far more adept at drawing the crowds (and their money): Phineas Taylor Barnum

Barnum's life has been exhaustively documented elsewhere, including numerous times by the man himself. Indeed, he may be the only figure in this book to have a Broadway musical written about him. But given the way he spent the earlier part of his career completely changing the position of the museum in American culture and the influence he had in the development of American taxidermy (recall our discussion of Jumbo, mounted by a young Carl Akeley), it's worth spending a little more time with the guy.

In the early 1840s, before the Peale museums went belly-up, Barnum was looking for a way to get back into show business after the public uproar that surrounded the unveiling of his Joice Heth hoax—a woman who he claimed had been a nurse to the infant George Washington and was more than 160 years old. Turns out the Tammany Society in New York City was looking to sell its museum, and Barnum saw his opportunity to move away from the traveling freak-show circuit and settle into a burgeoning new business. Barnum's American Museum opened on New Year's Day, 1842, featuring most of the oddities he'd inherited from the Tammany Society, including taxidermized birds and reptiles, some famous wax effigies, and a dog named Apollo that could play cards. But Barnum set immediately to acquiring new specimens and attractions that would bring more people through the doors. Unlike his museum predecessors, Barnum never asked of a potential acquisition, What can this teach us about the world? Rather, he asked, How can I get people to pay to see this? And thus, for a time, did the museum in America change its purpose from educational to sensational, a shift that would make Barnum's museum the most profitable and best-attended museum this country had ever seen.

One of the first things Barnum got a hold of was the Feejee Mermaid. Originally discovered in 1817 by a Boston sailor, the mermaid was really the head and torso of a monkey sewn onto the lower body of a large fish—probably something from the salmon family. After this sailor's death, his son had no use for the mermaid and sold it to Moses Kimball, a friend of Barnum's and the owner of his own museum in Boston. Kimball wasn't able to see the mermaid's potential as spectacle. Barnum, though, pounced when he got a look at this monstrosity.[6] The face was wrinkled up and gape-mouthed, the gnarly little hands of the creature raised up and outward, as though it were fending off some violent attack. He tried to find a seam where the two corpses were sewn together, but no matter what he could see up close, he knew that if he kept it in a case, the illusion would remain intact.

The Feejee Mermaid was an immediate hit, thanks to the dubious stories about mermaids that Barnum was able to place in various U.S. newspapers in the weeks preceding its unveiling. A month after the public first got a glimpse of the creature, Barnum's door receipts had nearly tripled from the previous month. It got so famous that imitations of the mermaid (which is to say, taxidermic fabrications of a taxidermic fabrication) began popping up in rival museums, including that of the Peales in Philadelphia. To his credit, Barnum never tried to "solve" the mystery of whether the Feejee Mermaid was real; he simply presented the mystery as a mystery, encouraging the public to speculate on its own about the mermaid's authenticity. Take a look at the carefully crafted language Barnum used to advertise the mermaid in his public notices:

> The FEEJEE MERMAID! positively asserted
> by its owner to have been taken alive [in] the
> Feejee Islands, and implicitly believed by many
> scientific persons, while it is pronounced by
> other scientific persons to be an *artificial* produc-
> tion, and its natural existence claimed to be an
> utter impossibility. The manager can only say

---

[6] No one seems to know how much he paid. When Rubens Peale sold the entirety of his family's collection to Barnum, the latter paid $7,000 for it, if that gives us any indication.

> that it [h]as such *appearance of reality* as any fish
> lying [in] the stalls of our fish markets—but
> [who] is to decide when *doctors* disagree.

Notice how worry-headed and untrustworthy "scientific persons" and "doctors" are portrayed in these three sentences. Clearly, it's the audience who needs to see for itself. James W. Cook, in his book on Barnum, puts it this way, "The question Barnum's 1843 patrons are asked to decide, however, is not whether mermaids exist as a species in nature, but whether this particular exhibitory commodity . . . is in fact what the promoter claims it to be."

In this way, with his Feejee Mermaid and other such curiosities, Barnum can be said to have taken Charles Willson Peale's notion of the truly democratic American museum to its most excessive conclusion. This had both a pecuniary cause and a museological effect. Maybe some people, Peale thought, would pay to see natural specimens classified according to scientific data, but many more people, Barnum realized, would pay to decide for themselves what was authentic and what was, in the parlance of the day, "humbug." All this thanks to taxidermy. The Peales couldn't compete with this new mind-set for a public museum, and once they sold their holdings Barnum had become the king of American museums, and the American museum had become indistinguishable from the circus sideshow. Except, of course, the walls were a lot more permanent.

Barnum's American Museum burned down in 1865, taking the Feejee Mermaid and other exhibits with it. He rebuilt immediately thereafter, only to have that one burn down in 1868. By this time, the Civil War was over and here, again, was a United States of America, and the public was ready to move away from the sideshow curiosities that Barnum had built a career on and toward a more encompassing center of knowledge like the museums they were hearing about or seeing firsthand in Europe. And yet here was a museum-going public that had in many ways been reared by Barnum and expected in their museums a modicum of entertainment, and maybe even a little spectacle. In short: the staid hall of carefully labeled glass cabinets wouldn't cut it. Harvard and Yale had opened their collections to the public by the time Barnum was out of the scene, and by 1874 natural history museums had been founded in both New York and San Diego. The National Museum of Natural History settled in a more spacious building in Washington, D.C., in 1881 (to be permanently moved to its present-day location on the National Mall in 1910). By the end of the nineteenth century, every major city in the country would open a natural history museum—all of which needed taxidermized specimens to show. Many of them went straight to Ward's Natural Science Establishment, where the demand was so great, as we saw in chapter 2, that taxidermists were told to produce mounts quickly and to Henry A. Ward's dictates. Here were the most talented taxidermists in the country, and they were also the most overworked—producing far more hack pieces than any artist or professional would prefer to.

After the thrill of mounting Jumbo had faded, Carl Akeley went back to the assembly-line work he was being paid for and soon became bored and anxious. If this was the future laid out for him, maybe he didn't want to be a taxidermist anymore. Maybe he should follow his brother Lewis and become a professor. After his friend Bill Wheeler left Rochester, Carl threw himself into his studies, hoping to enroll in the Sheffield Scientific School—Yale's science and engineering college. For weeks he did nothing but get up in the morning, stuff animals for eleven hours, walk home, and read until he fell asleep. The stress of it was too much for him, and the morning of his entrance exams he broke down and couldn't bring himself even to sit for them. Lewis was disappointed but understood it as a necessary act of self-sabotage. "Carl," he once wrote, "had sense enough to see that college would be [the] death of all his dreams."

It was around this time that Wheeler wrote to Carl, inviting him to come out to Wisconsin, where the new Milwaukee Public Museum was rapidly expanding and looking to acquire a taxidermist. Carl began working on contracted pieces in 1887 and was hired full-time in July of 1889. But before we move on to the next stage of Carl's professional life perhaps it's a good idea to stop and go over some personal matters, because I want to believe that a man is more than his résumé. And when all the people who wrote about Akeley after he died—both of his wives, numerous friends and colleagues, later biographers—get at these more personal matters, he's painted so often as a passionate man. Stormy in the depths of his heart and driven. But is it true? The trouble in writing about historical figures after their deaths is that we can read their lives only teleologically. Hidden inside every small gesture or every grand decision is the seed of what we know will bloom in adulthood. There were no delicious cans of soup eaten in Andy Warhol's boyhood is what I mean. Only portentous ones.

Here's Akeley's chief biographer, Penelope Bodry-Sanders, in a characteristic moment of reverie: "Young Carl Akeley rose before dawn after a sleepless night. He might well have watched Orion in the night sky through his window—Orion, the famous hunter blinded by an angry parent, exposing his empty eye sockets to the rising sun to recover his sight." He might well have indeed. He might well have risen after a cloudy night. He might well have never learned how to locate Orion in the sky or the legend behind the constellation, but given everything we know about Akeley's past trouble with his mother and about Akeley's future as a big-game hunter, isn't it better to think he had? We remember our heroes by making myths of them, and starting from the presumptions I had at the onset of writing this book that taxidermists were a knowable, finite demographic, I've learned quickly to distrust myths. And yet I've been guilty of this in my own painting of young Carl Akeley. How do I know his shoulders were like fence pickets? Where did that egg basket come from, the one he left behind as he fled the Gliddens' house? Here's Roy Chapman Andrews, the former director of the American Museum of Natural History and a man so mythic himself that it's said he was the model for Indiana Jones: "Every day [Akeley's] respect and affection for animals increased, and he seemed able to understand their psychology, to enter into their minds and anticipate their thoughts, as only one who really loves them can do."

In just one sentence, Andrews has turned Akeley into Aquaman, with preternatural powers of telepathy. I'm not trying to argue that these writers are wrong in their beatification, just that such remembrances—of anybody—make it nearly impossible to get beyond this mythic remove. Every reconstruction, even a taxidermic one (perhaps *especially* a taxidermic one), is an abridgement and thus an idealization. We're given with Carl what feel like important details. We know he liked to go to the theater those years he lived in Rochester but hear nothing about it after he left. He once read *Alice in Wonderland* in a single sitting. We know he had a pet dog, a stray he found one day back in Clarendon, a pointer that was stolen from him one afternoon by a passing hunter. Carl never owned another pet again. What might this signify? How can this clue us in to the kind of person he became? We know that he avoided his mother and had a special bond with his father. But Carl himself never fathered anybody. Is this why?

Here's something else we know. In Milwaukee, Carl met the woman who would be his first wife. Her name was Delia. She was maybe fifteen when they met, maybe fourteen. She came from a flat little prairie town so far from the big brick buildings that hold our records and educate our young that neither she nor her parents could ever accurately say when little Delia Denning first fell down on the world. December 5, 1875, is the best guess out there. But by 1889 Delia was in Milwaukee, a just-pubesced runaway who had earlier that year married a dentist, Arthur Reiss. Her husband was a man settled and Carl, Arthur's hunting buddy, was a man on the move, a recent transplant, a plank-thin boy of twenty-five who spent his time skinning dead animals and putting them back together. This boy from New York. Carl was an exotic creature, and in him Delia saw another way out, a way farther from whatever fate had been sealed for her in her girlhood.

Delia, it must be said, grew up a brat. She hid behind bushes and waited for the boys in town to walk past on their ways home from the community well. At the right last moment, she'd spring herself on them with a tiny sticky fistful of dirt, tossed like a donation into their pails. The boys would have to head all the way back for fresh water, and Delia would laugh at all their slumped shoulders. In the mythology of Delia Akeley, these boys were the boys who teased her, but this story and others like it have been told only by Delia, and so who knows whence her motivations came? Who knows why she stole one of her father's shoes one night and stepped with it on every single still-wet brick made at the yard near her family farm, ruining a whole day's work? Did the men in the brickyard incite such careful revenge? Did they not understand where this demon of a girl got her nickname, Mickie? Her biographer, Elizabeth Fagg Olds, says it's "doubtless inspired by her combative headstrong Irishness," as though simple heredity were to blame. Or not *blame* so much as to be *given due credit,* because in all accounts it's Mickie's Mickieness that defined her character, her Mickieness that gave her the wild, misguided gall one day, after having failed to bring water to the farmhands as her father had asked her to, to yell directly into this man's face and never look back. Years later, when asked about this, Delia would mention what little choice she had, given that "washing dishes and making beds for a family that did not hesitate to criticize my efforts was to my mind a waste of precious time."

By the time Carl Akeley was named staff taxidermist, the Milwaukee Public Museum was only five years old. Carl's friend, Bill Wheeler, was at only twenty-three years old the "custodian" of the MPM. (Today he'd be called a director.) Two other employees, an assistant to the custodian and a janitor, rounded out the full-time staff. The MPM didn't even have its own building at this time but instead rented space on the first floor of the city's Exposition Building, which also held an art gallery, a concert hall, and, of all things, a fish hatchery. For lack of space the four men in charge lined each wall with deep glass-fronted cabinets as high as most men, and they filled the center of the room with shorter display cases, setting what didn't fit inside cases on top of them. They named the room Lapham Hall after Increase A. Lapham, a Milwaukee naturalist whose private collection became the basis for the museum's public one. In this way, the MPM's origins are much like those of Frederick III's *Kunstkammer*, and indeed early photographs of Lapham Hall look a lot like the Museum Wormianum. Enormous tortoise shells cover the top of one cabinet, and articulated skeletons of whales hang high over museum-goers' heads. One tall cabinet contains more than a dozen mammals, including a brown bear, kangaroo, llama, and giraffe—all staring in different directions as though they'd never seen one another before.

Akeley's day-to-day routine at the MPM was to skin and preserve the specimens he and others donated almost continually. Owing to the lack of space, few of these specimens got the full pose-and-mount treatment, and thus Akeley became for a while a preparator, putting together study skins that would be left to fill drawers. It's not as though he didn't try for greater. The awful thing about a study skin and about the single mount inside a glass case is what a lie they tell about the animals fated for such treatment—that is, the lie of solitude. So many of the creatures Carl watched during his boyhood in Clarendon and during the weekends he'd been hunting with Arthur and Delia Reiss moved across the earth in groups. Sometimes as few as a pair, and sometimes whole great flocks that covered the sky above in some instinctive system of interdependability he'd never know. Why, then, this persistence of the lone animal? Carl went several times to the MPM's Board of Trustees with this problem. He had the full support of Wheeler, whose time at Ward's let him see both the educational and monetary benefit of group displays. But these men on the board weren't taxidermists. They were neither scientists nor artists. These were city councilmen and school superintendents— men bred, it seemed, to keep both eyes on a budget's bottom line. "It was the old, old story of starting a thing and having to give it up because of lack of support." This is how Akeley put it in his memoirs. And so rather than remain a simple study-skin preparator he buckled down and gave the aldermen of the board what they and future audiences wanted. He built a little model of a proposed diorama: a group of muskrats in and around their den at the edge of a pond. He brought it before the board one afternoon and the men all gathered around. Every brow furrowed as they got a closer look. Carl knew these men had perspectives over the long term, and he made sure to speak carefully. "This diorama won't be the end of it, gentlemen, but the beginning." Carl saw an entire series of dioramas depicting the fur-bearing mammals of Wisconsin, which would not only bring a more sensory experience to exhibits but also set the MPM apart from other museums around the country. Here, for once, was a local focus, which was sure to draw the locals.

There were reluctant nods, skeptical nods, and Carl got to work right away. Here in Milwaukee he had his own studio, filled with no one but himself and the animals he was preserving. And Delia, who as Carl got more and more busy found that their hunting trips became more and more rare, and who thus began to hang around and watch this exotic creature do his dirty work. Here was Carl's first awareness of the joys of keeping his studio open, working for an audience. Delia asked questions about anatomy and habitat, while Carl tried to perfect the techniques that would make him famous: casting every animal in plaster and making manikins out of papier-mâché that were just as sturdy but much, much lighter than clay manikins. It must have been like trying to do your homework while your little sister sits at the same table as you, asking what photosynthesis is. He couldn't get annoyed because she was so earnest, so endearing. And Delia, for one, never asked why he was taking so many measurements of each muskrat's body. Delia never wondered what was taking him so long to skin the animals. Delia never shouted for him to sew faster, to *get it done* and to move on. Henry A. Ward's influence runs throughout the origins of the MPM—in that Ward in 1883 sold the trustees more than fifteen hundred specimens to fill up Lapham Hall at the price of $12,000—but the one influence that never gets acknowledged is the steady torment he fed Carl Akeley in Carl's four years in Rochester. For what else could get this man to produce such innovative work his first time out? Surely, Akeley's muskrat diorama has any number of antecedents, but if the American museum of the nineteenth century was a stuffy old building full of glass cases, the twentieth century museum was made up of dioramas, of theater, and Carl Akeley's muskrat group is that century's quiet beginning.

Who were you when you first saw *Citizen Kane*? I was a recent high-school graduate heading to college where long-since-abandoned dreams of directing movies would get me to major in film studies, and knowing everything I did about the status of Orson Welles's films in American cinema, I rented the tape one night and watched it. I was underwhelmed. The acting was superb and there was that nice sudden reveal at the end (the mystery behind which was spoiled by a boyhood spent in front of the television set). But the greatest film of all time? Not hardly. Such was my diagnosis until I entered film school and listened to my professor lecture on the movie before screening it. Then I saw it again, and then I knew. *The greatest American film of all time*. I simply had to be told what to look for. I had to be shown Gregg Toland's deep-focus cinematography. I had to be shown all the photographed ceilings on the set, all the monumental low angles. A person fed on Hollywood movies made after *Citizen Kane* can't in any other context appreciate all the innovations Welles came up with that changed the grammar of cinema so wholly as to be virtually unrecognizable today.

This is why Akeley's muskrat diorama is so seminal. Not because it's the first, because it's not the first. Birds were mounted on artificial branches before, and as we saw with Charles Willson Peale they'd been shown with painted backdrops before, too. Akeley's diorama looks at first like any other you've seen in a museum, until you look closer. Until you see it alongside the other dioramas his colleagues were producing at the time. To get a sense of muskrats' natural habitat, Carl went out on the Wisconsin landscape and got a good look. He got some artificial reeds and piled them up in the front left corner of his diorama to make the den. Or part of the den. To show that this pile of reeds was more on the inside than it seemed, he let the front panel of glass cut the den in half, like one of those Damien Hirst cross-sections, and what was revealed was the hollowed-out burrow where one of the five muskrats sleeps, adorably. Akeley stood another muskrat on its hind legs at the top of the den, "outside" if you will, with its tongue sticking out as if concentrating on a task. Two other muskrats he set on a log in the mud— all of this painstakingly constructed by hand—and the fifth muskrat, the magical one, he knew he wanted to show swimming. But how to feature a muskrat swimming when including water in a diorama was an impossibility? Akeley took another sheet of glass and installed it about eight inches up from the floor of the diorama, building the landscape under and around it until it looked like the surface of a pond. And to create the illusion that the muskrat was half-emerged in the water, doing a little doggy paddle, Carl sculpted the manikin and then sliced it laterally in half, along the backbone. He then did the same to the skin and mounted each half separately. One got glued to the underside of the glass and the other just above it. Magic.

The muskrat diorama was installed in the MPM in 1890. In the museum's annual report for that year, Wheeler writes:

> The great difficulties in accurately imitating the boggy earth, the half dead vegetation and the stagnant water have been very successfully overcome by Mr. Akeley. The mounting of the animals themselves is most admirable. The case containing the group was planned by Mr. Akeley and presents great advantages over the cases commonly used for such purposes.

It would be the last case of the fur-bearing animals of Wisconsin. Wheeler resigned the following year to begin a fellowship at Clark University in Massachusetts, and in 1892 Akeley left for Chicago.

There's lots more to tell about the muskrat diorama—the V of geese painted on the curved backdrop,[7] the shells and bits of bone lying around—but any description of the diorama will do as poor a job of getting at its effects as do all the extant photographs (all black-and-white, for some reason, and all making Akeley's work look like garbage). Much the way I'm sure Akeley's diorama of a group of taxidermized muskrats must do a poor job of conveying what an actual group of live muskrats must look like, would I ever get the chance to come upon one—which I won't. Not like this. And so rather than rely on some old tired photographs of an old diorama to give me a sense of Akeley's masterpiece, I went to Wisconsin myself. If this—the adoration of habitat dioramas, the iconography of the mount—is your religion, there are any number of pilgrimages you can make. You can go to the Akeley Hall of African Mammals at the AMNH to see some of the most astoundingly seamless displays ever. You can go to the Carnegie Museum in Pittsburgh to see its

---

[7] John Jeske, a local artist, did the backdrop for the muskrat diorama. Despite those art lessons back in Clarendon, Akeley was never much of a painter.

Arab Courier Attacked by Lions diorama (1867), probably the oldest group mount still on display. Or you can go to where it all began.

On my pilgrimage to the MPM, I have one goal, one object of contemplation, and I walk straight to it when I arrive, past the basement café, up the staircase to the main floor, past the mount of the beloved local gorilla Samson, and behind *A Sense of Wonder,* a display that re-creates an eighteenth-century-style cabinet of curiosities—its artifacts packed on top of one another. There, be-tween opposite walls of elevators, stands Akeley's diorama, in a case that raises the scene up to eye level. I get up close to the glass, and it may be the museum's regulated internal temperatures, or the cold from the Milwaukee morning that's still stuck in my clothes some-where, but I find myself getting a chill when I look at the muskrats. It's silly, I know, but something happens to us when we see in three dimensions an image we've spent a long time looking at in two. I didn't get the chills when I met Dan Rinehart, but the whole morning I hung out in his school was a little unsettling, particularly when I looked over at him and caught him at a rare moment when he wasn't smiling. It was like some kind of adulteration of his per-fected image.

Here, though, nothing is adulterated. The muskrat diorama is just stunning. I can only keep staring at it after I've already stared so much at it. Key to the success of any diorama is that sheet of glass, which not only demarcates all that's held inside as some kind of closed entity—operating similar to the covers of a book or the frame around a portrait—but also invites the viewer to step close and pretend to be a part of what's contained. What makes Akeley's muskrats so great, then, is the self-conscious way he constructs the scene around panes of glass. The primary pane, the one facing us like a window, also gives us a kind of omniscience, opening up for us the den-burrow that normally would be hidden from any live bystander. The sec-ondary pane, creating the water's surface, is extended right to the front of the case, and I can't help crouching down to see what he's hidden under there. Mud. Reeds. What looks like half an oyster shell. And feet! The little curled-up feet of the muskrat ruddering him to shore.

It's 2008 when I'm standing in front of the muskrats, which means they were mounted almost 120 years ago. I step back to take some pictures and a group of girls gets dislodged from one of the many packs of field-tripping schoolkids and runs over to the display. "Look how cute!" one says, pointing to the swimming muskrat. "It's like a big hamster!" another girl squeals before her more studious friend points to the display label and corrects her. There are robotic dinosaurs right at the other end of the hall. How is this dinosaur of an exhibit still attracting kids?

Wendy Christensen-Senk is the staff taxidermist at the MPM, which is one of only two institutions in this country to have a full-time taxidermist still on the payroll. She meets me by the muskrat diorama and tells me of its restoration back in the mid-1990s. This sounds about right. Over the past twenty years, many museums have had to restore their taxidermy, which has, in some cases, faded under harsh fluorescents or come apart at the seams because of hide shrinkage. In some cases even arsenic has leaked out. Christensen-Senk spearheaded the restoration of the muskrat diorama, resetting the curved background painting that had warped over time and fixing some of the broken plants and shells. When I ask her if she repainted the muskrats themselves, she shook her head. "I felt it was not right for me to do that to Akeley's work," she says. "I considered it, but then I thought: *I'm just going to leave it alone.*"

Christensen-Senk, who invites me to call her Wendy, is a strong-shouldered blond woman in her mid-forties with the open, inviting face of a teenager. Eyes bright and wide whenever she talks. She takes me on a tour of the MPM's many habitat dioramas, and though Milwaukee is one of this country's lesser cities its museum is enormous and its dioramas are maybe the best I've seen. The quality of lighting is such that you can not only tell the intended season in the scene but also practically feel it. So many dioramas in so many museums are cramped into a tight little box full of branches, but here the habitat floors are generously deep, running far back from the front panel of glass, and the back walls are wide and curved, adding to the illusion that what you're looking at extends for miles. A good number of the dioramas are open, meaning there's no glass panel at all between you and the taxidermy. Like the savannah bush. Or the bamboo forest, where I could throw my notebook hard enough and hit Timba, the elephant,[8] and somehow this spoils the illusion that I've come across him in the wild. But this disillusionment is easily outweighed by the sheer vastness of these open dioramas, these expansive panoramas that curve almost fifty or sixty feet around a hall and incorporate two dozen mounts of several different species.

How did Milwaukee, of all museums, develop such astounding displays? The Field Museum, just a couple hours south in Chicago, is no kind of competitor in this regard. Very few of its mounts have painted backdrops or artificial habitat. It's almost spectacular how unspectacular they are, and the Field Museum had Marshall Field's fortune and the successes of the 1893 World's Columbian Exposition at its origins. Milwaukee had a long-since-forgotten naturalist and some scraped-together public funds. Moreover, how does the MPM still staff a full-time taxidermist? One answer, Wendy says, is commitment. Most larger and better-funded museums don't have half the commitment to taxidermy that the MPM does. "This institution has always been at the forefront of the taxidermy style you see in museums," she tells me. Of course: Akeley's muskrats. After that diorama, the MPM has never been content to copy what can be

---

[8] Wendy tells me that Akeley may have collected Timba for the MPM, but nothing I can find on record says so for sure.

found elsewhere. It developed the world's first open dioramas and the world's first interactive dioramas. This kind of full-sensory museum experience even has a name: the Milwaukee style. It dictates that too much required reading in exhibit labels, too set a perspective on what the exhibit holds, will deny viewers the chance to come to their own conclusions. Echoes of Barnum, to be sure, but it's a style that began in full with Akeley's muskrats and that continues to dominate museum design today.

Over the past twenty, thirty years museums have found fewer and fewer needs to keep taxidermists on hand full-time. The MPM is an exception, sure, but when Wendy came on in 1982 she was one of three full-time taxidermists. Now she's the only one, in an exhibits department that has dwindled to seven employees total. "I feel I may be the last person hired here as a taxidermist," she sighs. The trend today is for museums to contract their work out to commercial taxidermists—the exact sort of thing the MPM was doing before it hired Carl Akeley on full-time. The problem with outsourcing, of course, is there's little to no quality control in place. "These commercial taxidermists don't have the commitment to the institution that a full-time taxidermist on staff would have," Wendy says. "With me, I'll do whatever it takes to make the mount perfect."

But what if what's needed isn't a single mount or a single restoration job, but rather the complete overhaul of the entire collection of mounts, an entire hall of dioramas? This was the situation at the Smithsonian's National Museum of Natural History back in 1997, when it received a donation of $20 million to renovate, among other things, its Hall of Mammals. The Smithsonian was (and remains) fortunate to be the other institution in the country with a full-time taxidermist on staff, Paul Rhymer, who never would have been able to fill an entire hall with new and restored mounts himself. Simply sewing up the skin of the brown bear, for instance, took two men an entire workday to complete. So Rhymer enlisted the help of the Canadian taxidermist Ken Walker and the nearby Maryland taxidermist John Matthews—both of whom are internationally renowned and regularly compete in and judge taxidermy competitions. The work took more than five years. When the new hall opened in 2003, there were 274 specimens on display, more than 200 of which were new to the museum—all of them donations. About thirty specimens were given, along with the $20 million, by Kenneth E. Behring, a big-game hunter who made his fortune developing real estate starting in the 1960s, and who made even more money selling the Seattle Seahawks to Microsoft bigwig Paul Allen. Behring's gift to the museum (which was combined with $80 million for the National Museum of American History, making the total of $100 million the largest gift to a museum by a single donor in the history of the country) didn't come without controversy. Right around the time he sold the Seahawks, in 1997, Behring was traveling through the central Asian republics of the former Soviet Union on the hunt for argali, a family of bighorn sheep. He took four on that trip—including a Kara Tau argali, of which fewer than an estimated hundred exist—and all of the animals were endangered enough that their remains could not be imported to the United States, and so shortly after Behring donated his first $20 million, the Smithsonian, as an official institution, petitioned the U.S. Interior Department to waive the ban so the sheep could be part of the renovated Kenneth E. Behring Hall of Mammals.

The argali aren't in attendance in the completed hall, but the other specimens Behring hunted are on display, including a giraffe and the brown bear. These specimens, Rhymer tells me, were all collected well before Behring made his donation. "We made sure of that," he says. "We didn't want people to think we gave Behring a shopping trip." Instead, the museum sent out a "wish list" of mammal specimens to zoos and research institutions, looking for donations of any animals that died of natural causes. And soon the specimens came pouring in from all over the country. The two Grévy's zebras came from North Carolina, donated by one of those depressing drive-thru safaris. The orangutan came from the National Zoo, also part of the Smithsonian Institute. The opossum came from the highway, just north of the city, found when Rhymer himself was driving to work one morning. "I knew we needed one," he says, "and I saw what looked like a good specimen. Of course, I was going fifty miles an hour at the time, but I stopped and got out to see if it was okay, and it was. I put it in the back of the truck and froze it when I got home."

Rhymer wasn't always a taxidermist. He started at the NMNH in 1984 as an exhibits illustrator, which was his original passion. But his father was a taxidermist and worked at the NMNH in the early 1960s, and so when a position as staff taxidermist opened up, Rhymer applied for the job. Now that the Hall of Mammals is completed he does little taxidermy for the museum. The day I met him for a tour through the hall, he was working on some fiberglass salmon for the *Ocean Life* exhibit that was set to open in three months' time. He also does very little taxidermy on his own. Maybe a bird or two, for a friend. "I'm a birder," he says, proudly. He recently took an extended vacation to Swaziland, where every morning he was up at 5:30, 6:00 A.M., looking for birds he'd never seen before.

Rhymer's a very tall man. I'm just over six feet tall, and I have to lift my chin to look him in the eye. As he leads me around the Hall of Mammals, I don't see a single recognizable diorama from field trips in my youth. Back before Behring's money came to the NMNH, the Hall of Mammals had a traditional habitat-diorama setup wherein visitors were led down clear, empty corridors to stop every seven steps in front of a re-created scene from nature, with mounted animals posed naturally in the environment from which they were taken. It was the Milwaukee style. Now, however, in what could be called the Smithsonian Style, the number of mounted animals easily outnumbers that of artificial leaves. There's no fake water anywhere, as far as I can tell. Stepping into the hall from the huge open rotunda,[9] one is hit by a visual onslaught of fur and four-legged bodies. Mammals are mounted in the middle of the floor, sometimes scaling up the walls right to the ceiling, all of them behind high panels of Plexiglas as though caught in some hockey-rink penalty box.

The hall is laid out continentally, and one first walks through Africa, where the noise is constant and overwhelming. There's the sound of stampeding antelope running across the plains and of rain thundering through a forest canopy, and every few seconds a monkey's shriek sounds out through an ongoing cacophony of animal noises. It's very intense. To be understood, I have to speak up. I'm standing shoulder to shoulder with Rhymer—well, shoulder to biceps—and I project my voice to him as though he were sitting in the back row of an empty theater. What happened to all the dioramas, I ask, and Rhymer explains that the NMNH made a deliberate choice not to just restore the habitats they had but to construct a completely new museum experience. "We wanted the story to be about the mammals themselves," he says. "Not their habitats." And sure enough, whatever habitats exist in the Hall of Mammals are merely suggested, much the way a single Monet poster on a college kid's dorm-room wall suggests a whole world of sophistication. The floor of the *Sahara Desert* exhibit is made of a rolled linoleum with a black-brown-tan flecked pattern. It's meant to resemble clay or sand

---

[9] The rotunda was also recently renovated thanks to Behring, and it has an elephant at its center that is claimed in a text panel to be "the largest mounted specimen of the world's largest living land animal," which might be true now that Jumbo's been destroyed.

and looks exactly like the floor in my high school's gym lobby. When the NMNH needs to suggest water, this linoleum's background shade changes from off-white to light blue. The cluster of trees in which a giraffe might feed has been reduced, Zen-like, to a single branch emerging out of a wall.

"In my opinion," Rhymer says, "this setup works best for the MTV generation of kids who are used to getting images and moving on and getting another. In the old days, or at the American Museum [of Natural History], you'd be given dioramas with every little twig and feather, and you can get a story out of that, but you've got to be patient. Here you can come in and get one story clearly and then move on and get another. It's better suited for kids today."

So while the Milwaukee style worked to keep visitors planted in front of exhibits for longer, the NMNH has worked toward the opposite, even going so far as to encourage errant wanderings all over the hall. And it seems the overall effect is working. I'm there on a Monday afternoon in the middle of the summer, and so despite the lack of field trips it's alarming how many school-aged kids I see, whipping around the room in some kind of frenzy, with dismayed parents toddling after.

I'm an immediate skeptic. One of the reasons I'm so continually drawn to habitat dioramas is the narrative inherent in each one. Here is a landscape. Here are some animals. What are they doing, right now? Sleeping? Foraging? Migrating? Dying in the jaws of a predator? What is their relationship to one another? Is this a family? Is this a turf war? These are questions I can usually find answers to just by looking hard enough, and though the narratives have a tendency to repeat themselves inside a single museum, and surely from one museum to another, they never get old. The surety of the telling keeps me coming back.

Which is not to say that no narratives exist at the NMNH. Rhymer leads me over to a group mount of two lionesses attacking an African buffalo. One lioness has a claw buried into the buffalo's back and looks about ready to take a bite. The other seems to be trying to avoid getting trampled. Mud splats speckle the buffalo's hide and hooves like barnacles, which Rhymer tells me is often a handy way taxidermists can cover up flaws in an animal's skin (this group was one of the restored projects from long ago). But it's a stellar display, full of movement and despair and incredible attention to detail. From the back, the buffalo's scrotum swings jauntily to the side, as though the animal were barreling through the grassland, and as his tail is raised the anus is clearly visible, as crisp and articulated as the straw insert on a thirty-two-ounce Big Gulp lid.

"Here's a different kind of narrative," Rhymer says, moving to the *Sahara Desert* exhibit, where an oryx calf is mounted suckling milk. "And it's a good one because one thing that makes us all mammals is that we get milk from our mothers." Also in this exhibit is a pair of fennecs (which may be the cutest animals on the planet; picture a Chihuahua with the big, alert ears of a corgi), which in themselves are a narrative of adaptation. Those big crazy ears help the foxes find rodents in the vast, quiet desert.

Maybe the strangest animal on display is the pink fairy armadillo, a mammal native to Argentina that looks like a cross between a regular Texas armadillo and an insect pupa. You could hold the thing in the palm of your hand. "It's a funky, bizarre, weird little animal," Rhymer says when he shows it to me. "I think it's my favorite one we have on display." The little armadillo is exhibited as part of a two-story-tall matrix of animals mounted on plain wooden platforms. It's surrounded by mammals as diverse as a lemur, a walrus, a gorilla, and a bat. Some of the animals I've never heard of before, and I've scoured taxidermy catalogs and many large mammal exhibits in the country—not to brag or anything. Not that I'm any kind of expert, but if before today you were to present me with a flashcard that had the words AFRICAN CIVET or JAGUARUNDI or PA-

CARENA written recto in clear letters I would've had a hell of a time trying to describe the outline of the animal verso. The point here is biodiversity. The NMNH wants ten-year-olds and their families to know that whatever it is that constitutes a mammal doesn't necessarily look like what two different people might find foremost in their imaginations. Across the hall from this is a similar display with a moose in the lower left forefront. Right at its nose, on a small platform hanging in midspace, is a pika, a kind of cold-weather rodent about one-fiftieth the size of the moose. This, Rhymer says, is "really cool." In other words, a mammal can be big and a mammal can be very small. It can swim in the ocean and look like an elephant, as one father described a seal to his son, or it can fly through the air and look, as Nabokov once wrote about a bat, like a cripple walking with an umbrella.

These pieces of taxidermy came from every continent and they're removed from any kind of habitat context. They're arranged in no logical order other than the fact that they're all mammals. And why not? What, after a century and a half of their existence, is the purpose of museums, anyway? You can be shown a hall of mammals and be led down a single corridor, but what will this tell you about mammals? About how mammals differ from birds, also grouped in dioramas across the way? That this planet's fauna constitutes a finite group is a belief that goes back to the bestiary, if not earlier—a belief that it's the zoological burden of every subsequent era to shatter. For its entire history, taxidermy has been the medium for our constant mythmaking of nature, the idea being that if we can arrange the physical form of an animal in a way that will last, we can arrange its narrative. We can fix its fate in the world. It's not that this work hasn't been undertaken at the Kenneth E. Behring Hall of Mammals—skins are still arranged in positions and gestures and narratives suiting the needs of (human) museum makers—it's that this work has happened so free from any apparent plan. Here, in

Washington, we see baby steps toward a kind of democracy. Animals are still unequal, still put on display for us, but at last we can see at the Smithsonian a glimpse of the rough, wild bigness of the world, full of animals that outnumber us in quantities we'll never really know.

FOUR

In the fall of 2005, residents of the city of Omaha started seeing mountain lions in their backyards. One was up in a tree, supposedly. One was sitting on a woodpile. *Mountain lions.* Three reports came in during one week in October, and in November somebody saw not one but three mountain lions running in a field. No tracks or traces remained on the scene by the time animal control officials arrived. Was it a mania? Omaha sits right at the eastern edge of Nebraska, right across the Missouri River from Iowa, far from any mountains in which *Puma concolor* likes to make its home. Yes, they had been seen in Omaha before; in 2003, the director of the Henry Doorly Zoo shot one with a tranquilizer dart and installed the animal in a cage for the public to come look at. It's still there, in the Cat Complex. But everyone thought a mountain lion in Omaha was an anomaly, like a May blizzard or Democratic congressman.

Confirmation that the residents of Omaha weren't crazy came on 6 November 2005, when the carcass of a mountain lion was reported to be lying on the side of Interstate 80 in Gretna, a town just outside city limits. It was a Sunday morning, and the then deputy Brian Fjelstad figured what he'd find as he drove to the site was just another deer. "We'd had a lot of false reports," he says, but when he rolled up to the carcass he saw the small head, the round paws, the long tail lying on the pavement like an empty hose. The mountain lion stretched to about six and a half feet, lying there still and unbreathing with no visible exterior damage. "It might have had blood coming out of its mouth," Fjelstad says. "I don't remember specifically."[1]

The only thing to do was get the animal off the road, so Fjelstad and another deputy wrapped the cougar in a blanket and stuck it in the trunk of his cruiser. But then what? A mountain lion is not a skunk or an opossum. It was hit by a car, but to call it roadkill would have been to miss a vital opportunity. Opossum skins can be had for a pittance, but the skin of a mountain lion? That's worth something. The Sarpy County sheriff is reported to have hoped the skin would end up a few miles north, mounted in the new Cabela's being constructed just off the interstate. Cabela's, a massive, Nebraska-based outdoors supplier, is known around these parts for its three-story-tall taxidermy displays that give shoppers (who've maybe traveled four hours or more to be there) a few fun snapshots. To a sheriff, very likely a hunter himself, such is the pinnacle of achievement for a mountain lion's carcass: a perch in a big-box megastore, right across the aisle from the very tools that could be used to kill it. Unfortunately for Sheriff Davis, guidelines under the Nebraska Game and Parks Commission state that any mountain lion carcass found must be offered first to the University of Nebraska State Museum in Lincoln. When the museum director, Priscilla Grew, heard about this, she fired off an email claiming dibs.

The University of Nebraska State Museum is located in Morrill Hall on the campus in Lincoln, and in the basement are a dozen or so habitat dioramas featuring wildlife native to Nebraska. Sandhill cranes. Beavers. Some bison. It is a small wing of a small museum, but Grew and her staff have worked hard for maximal effect; a few

---

[1] One article in the Omaha *World-Herald* made special mention of the blood that stained Fjelstad's boot hours later.

of the dioramas have been "brought out" onto the floor, the rocky ground of the Platte River display extending past the front pane so you can step on it and feel even more a part of the scene depicted. They've even had to apply decals of birds in flight to the glass because kids (and, yes, some adults) kept walking into it. The staff of the Nebraska State Museum has thus become quite familiar—too familiar, perhaps—with the sudden *boom* of a human face colliding with heavy glass. "If you hear some tears, you're okay," says Grew, whose office is just beyond the hall. "But if it's quiet afterward, you wonder if you've got a dead kid out there."

In the far back corner of the room is a scene from the Niobrara River valley, a region in north-central Nebraska, and it's here that Grew decided the mountain lion would go. It was, after all, the most likely home for the very cougar killed in Gretna. Nebraska Game and Parks has tracked a couple and found that big-cat overcrowding in the Black Hills of South Dakota had begun to force pumas to follow the Niobrara and Missouri rivers southwest, which got them as far as Omaha and even parts of Iowa. This placement of the Gretna mountain lion in the Niobrara scene was contingent on two things: money (as always) and whether the hide was in good enough condition to show in a museum. The animal was hit by a car, after all. It wouldn't do to have wads of fur missing. Torn limbs or ears. The former required the kind of fund-raising effort museum officials make their careers on. The latter required something a little more peculiar: the work of a good taxidermist.

The story of the Gretna mountain lion fascinates me because of its improbable narrative arc: a car hits an animal on the interstate and soon a taxidermist gets a phone call. But which taxidermist? Open up the phonebook and you'll find any number of them, right between taxicabs and tea houses. Lincoln's phone book lists eight. Of course, it's a gamble selecting any one. How can you find a good one? How can you tell which will do the best job?

One option is to stay abreast of trade periodicals. As soon as

Thomas Labedz, the collection manager for the state museum, was given the task of finding a taxidermist to mount the puma, he recalled an article from 2002 in *Nebraskaland* magazine—a *Field and Stream*–type glossy put out by the Game and Parks Commission—about Todd Kranau, a taxidermist out in Blue Hill, Nebraska, who in 2001 took a mounted boar's head with a rattlesnake in its mouth to the World Taxidermy Championships and walked away with the Best in World medal. The writer of the article spent some time in Kranau's shop, fawning over the realism of the bobcats and whitetail heads he found there, and came to this curious conclusion: "Examine the awards he's won at dozens of taxidermy competitions . . . and you know for sure: This guy is really good." The layperson, it seems, can never know whether a taxidermist is any good until he or she sees the awards. Taxidermy, then, is just like any other art form—it has its aficionados, and it has its dilettantes. *I don't know taxidermy,* many of us might say, *but I know what I like.* But what is it about taxidermy that the average person likes (if the average person likes taxidermy at all)? When we talk about "good taxidermy," what do we mean, exactly? Honorable? Awesome? Technically proficient? All of these at once? At Charles Willson Peale's museum in Philadelphia, as we've seen, people donated whatever oddities they wanted to see. Show folks a stuffed panda fighting a snow leopard and they might think you're a pretty good taxidermist. But, the argument goes, it won't be *true* until the awards come in.

The end of the *Nebraskaland* article makes mention of Dick Cabela, the man behind Nebraska's own megastore, who, after hearing of this world-show win, hired Kranau to design and mount an entire trophy room in his Sidney, Nebraska, home. "Kranau hopes," the article reads, "the Cabela project leads to similar jobs for museums." Three years later, Thomas Labedz picked up the phone.

Kranau was one of the first taxidermists I met. It was the summer of 2005 at the Nebraska State Taxidermists Association's annual convention in North Platte, where he took Best in Show with dual shoulder mounts of a chamois and a tahr.[2] He also won Most Artistic Mount, an award sponsored by the taxidermy supply company WASCO. It's easy, then, to extend the awards for the work to the man himself, right? In 2005, Kranau was the best and most artistic taxidermist in Nebraska.

Whether or not the accolades for the work apply to the taxidermist, it's all relatively small potatoes compared with Kranau's 2001 Best in World win. *The best piece of taxidermy in the world.* It's worth taking some time to think about. Who among us can claim to be the best in the world at, say, keeping our garages tidy or maintaining a recipe blog—whatever it is we think we do well? The weird thing about accolades is we're never fully satisfied having given them. The gold medal winner at any Summer Olympics knows, in four years, barring World War 3, a medal equal to his in size, shape, and significance will get draped around the neck of another athlete. Miss Universe only gets a year before she has to give up her crown. And yet we continue to stage year after year these global contests, weeding through all six billion of us to find the one we can isolate, the one we can name The Best. Kranau was the best in 2001, but today that's claimed by some other taxidermist. It seems so fleeting, this accomplishment, but look at what it led to. Kranau's work is now enshrined behind museum glass—we'd be hard pressed to come up with a more permanent kind of victory.

Randy Holler is not the best taxidermist in the world, but he hopes to be. Even though he's only been doing it for ten years. Even though he's never competed at the world-championship level before. Most of his time is filled managing an auto-parts store in Hettinger,

---

[2] These are animals I'd never heard of either; the former looks like an oversize jackalope, its ears as high as its prongy antlers, and the latter like a shaggy-haired ram.

North Dakota, and raising two teen daughters with his wife, Wendy. He's got a little shop on his property where he does part-time work, mostly on upland game birds. Grouse, quail, partridges. It's not all he's good at. The first time he went to nationals he won blue ribbons for a turkey and an antelope. The second time he got the Pheasants Forever Award for a ring-necked pheasant.[3] It's not Best in Show, but it's an achievement, and what else could be next but the 2007 World Taxidermy Championships? "I know the quality of work there is really high," Holler says. "But I want to experience it for myself. I want to compete and just see: Where do I stand? How much more do I have to learn to be able to compete with the best of them?"

It tells us something about the nature of competition. Get enough guys together—or maybe just people, maybe it's not as gendered as I think it is—who all do the same thing, and it's only a matter of time before some will feel the need to sort and rank one another. This is stuff we learn very, very early, going back to recess: *race you to the end of the blacktop.* It tells us only that one kid is better at sprinting than another, but that superlative adjective is so important. *Better.* A is better than B, and we know this because they competed head-to-head. But this is only half of it. A desire to sort and rank leads to the forming of competitions, but these competitions' existence itself fuels the desire to compete. Holler may have been satisfied with eventually winning Best in Show at the national level, but there was a greater, more prestigious competition lying above it. He wasn't driven exactly to put his work up against taxidermists from Europe, but he saw that the World Taxidermy Championships were there,

---

[3] Sponsored by the conservation society that bears the award's name. Many awards at taxidermy competitions have sponsors behind them. The Safari Club International sponsors one at nationals for "the mount that most displays the importance of habitat conservation." There's even a Research Mannikins–Delia Akeley Award that goes each year to a female taxidermist.

open to anyone with enough ambition and entrance-fee money, and it wasn't long before he thought, *what if?*

Prince William of Wales is older than the World Taxidermy Championships. So's the Nintendo Entertainment System. Which is to say they haven't been around very long. Unlike the Nationals, which are put together by the National Taxidermists Association, the WTC is a fully commercial affair, organized and funded by *Breakthrough* magazine, one of the few taxidermy trade publications out there. When I first heard of the WTC, I'd pictured such pageantry, all the nations of the world sending their best taxidermists to . . . oh, Lillehammer maybe. I pictured opening ceremonies with flags and anthems, a solemn parade of all the many beasts that were in the course of a week to be slaughtered, skinned, and brought back to life for the purposes of a bunch of medals. I pictured international scandal. In-fighting among the judges. Tainted taxidermist urine.

As soon as I could, I booked my ticket.

Turns out I was way off. The WTC is held every other year in some wayward corner of the United States: Springfield, Illinois; Lawrence, Kansas; Macon, Georgia. Little cities, in other words, where a hotel full of taxidermists and their dead things won't draw too much attention. How fitting, then, that in 2007, the year Holler decides to hit the big time, the year I fly out with grand delusions and a bag full of notebooks, the show is held in the biggest little city in the world: Reno, Nevada.

I arrive Wednesday morning at the Reno Events Center, an arena downtown that seats just seven thousand, the kind of place best suited for niche markets—a gay rodeo, say, or floor-hockey tournaments. Around me, taxidermists are ambling through the wheelchair-accessible doors, mounts in hand, or pushing massive wooden crates they got off the loading dock. One excessively primped woman walks by carrying what looks like her pet Siberian husky in her arms, but on second thought is actually just a shoulder mount of a wolf. It's early enough in the week that any animals I see I assume to be alive. (By the end of the week, this will not be the case.) Around me, everyone's face broadcasts unease. Some people even shout at one another. The buzz in the lobby is the damage plane travel has inflicted. Past WTCs were all held in the Midwest, and most folks drove their mounts to the show, but this year's choice of Reno means more perilous travel arrangements for anyone east of the Mississippi. Any mount larger than one's luggage has had to fly in the cargo hold, and as boxes are opened people are finding that what looked like a winner back in the studio now looks like the victim of a tragic accident. Tail feathers have been snapped in two. Whole body parts have fallen right off. As soon as a taxidermist hands an entry in at the registration tables, it gets whisked onto the competition floor not to be seen (or touched) until all the judging is complete, and so the WTC staff have lined the lobby with half a dozen banquet tables where taxidermists clamber for space to clean up their mounts. Everyone's taking his time to fussily primp feathers and furs. It's like backstage at a burlesque house.

Holler's driven down from North Dakota with his wife and daughters, so he's able to hand over his ring-necked pheasant—an alert-looking male mounted on artificial snow—in pristine condition, as though it were a gift for the judges. Others aren't so lucky. In the corner of the lobby I watch Raymond Kowalski, a tall, kind-eyed man from New Kensington, Pennsylvania, delicately rub a wad of cotton through the feathers of his mount. He works as careful as a nurse, except that what he's nursing isn't a sick patient. "It's a griffin," he says. "G-r-i-f-f-i-n." Kowalski's griffin is made from a lion cub's body ("stillborn," he assures me; "I didn't go hunting baby lions"), a ptarmigan's wings, and a white chicken's head, which has been embellished with an artificial beak and skull of a bald eagle to get that classic griffin look. The effect is magical and cute, a griffin you could cuddle up with at bedtime.

"I took it out of the box when I got here and the head was just hanging off," Kowalski says. "That's what I'm trying to do now is smooth it out."

He's got time, but not much, and he's desperately trying to keep a smile on his face. If he can get it on the floor, his griffin will turn heads. Of the 389 entries at the 2007 WTC, Kowalski's is the only one that's never existed in this world.[4] In fact, the fantastical and the whimsical have little place in the world of competitive taxidermy. Instead, you have realism that's almost Balzacian in its approach— re-create the animal precisely the way it lived. And so by the end of the afternoon the floor of the Reno Events Center has become a mostly boring tableau of animals not doing anything. Turkeys stand around, their tails fanned proudly like halos over their asses. A few leopards show off their big teeth. Two owls stand on a box and look out to the center of the room. A desert sheep, an ocelot, a greater kudu, a water buffalo—they all just stand there, posing for some interminable portrait.

I've never really been an animal lover. I've had pets, sure, but the process of fitting animals into the tangled mess of my understanding has always involved strict compartmentalization. They go over there, with the other nice but unknowable curiosities. Then again, I'm not even sure what I mean by "animal lover." I don't mean anything, you know . . . *pervy*. I don't mean something as specific as someone

---

[4] Despite its long history, the jackalope makes no appearance, not even in jest. At least one of the mounts on the floor *used* to exist in this world: a saber-toothed tiger, made from a female lion and what look like small walrus tusks. Any mounts made from the parts of more than one animal are categorized at the WTC as "re-creations." Perhaps taxidermy's most famous re-creation of late was the panda Ken Walker brought to the WTC in 2003, made from two black bear hides, one of them bleached. It didn't just turn heads, it blew them away, and Walker took Best in World.

who works in a pet store or is a veterinarian. I think I mean at the least someone who can name and appreciate variation among species. I, for example, often get golden retrievers and Labrador retrievers mixed up, to say nothing about the whole confusing mess of the terrier group. Animal lovers, on the other hand, can hear "springer spaniel" and form in their heads a picture that would never form in mine, not without the aid of a reference. Animal lovers can look at a bird and say what species of bird it is, not because animal lovers have some kind of pathological need to be precise, but because a barn swallow, say, has characteristics that make it deserving of recognition. Deserving of being named. A person who looks at his family or his friends or any grouping of others like him and sees only "humans" drawing in the same hot air with the same two lungs, using the same larynxes to make the same loud noises, carrying the same wet genitals between their same two legs—this person can't really be said to love people, can he? Therein lacks a certain form of respect that seems requisite when we talk about love.

The judges at the World Taxidermy Championships are all previous world champions themselves, which means they've been taxidermists for a very long time, which then means they're animal lovers all. Because to judge a piece of competitive taxidermy, you need to get up close and poke and prod a mount. You need to look and look and look at the animal, and in seeing the animal you need to disregard whatever flashy predation drama might be attracting the lazy eyes of the dilettante. This isn't to say that taxidermy isn't full of drama. It's to say that *no one* has spent more time gazing into the soft, liquid eye of a deer than a taxidermist has.

Around six thirty that first evening in Reno I head up to the judges' meeting on the second floor over the events center, inside a skybox-type room with a whiteboard and conference tables. If the world of competitive taxidermy has an A list, the people in this room would compose at least half of it. And at the head of them all is Larry Blomquist, who, as editor and publisher of *Breakthrough* and chairman of the WTC, is pretty much a taxidermy mogul. He stands at the head of the room like a schoolteacher,[5] quieting everyone down, going through the guidelines and schedule for judging over the next three days. It's an arcane system, involving three divisions, each with sixteen categories (e.g., Large Gameheads; Cold Water Fish; Reptiles, Amphibian, Other) and more than fifty subcategories. Every mount on the floor will be assessed individually by three judges, who will each score the mount on a scale of 1 to 100. These three scores are averaged together for the competitor's final score, making the earning of 100 average points nigh on impossible. In the history of the World Taxidermy Championships, no one's ever done it.

Once Blomquist releases the judges to their work, it takes only fifteen minutes or so for them to form packs and travel together from mount to mount. According to the rules of the competition, they're each supposed to work individually, but instead they're shuffling around the room chatting about what they see. "That guy's got a nice little attitude on him," judge Frank Newmyer says about a Bahama pintail duck. "He's cute. He's a cutie." All names of the taxidermists who mounted each piece have been removed from the mounts, but I recognize Holler's pheasant and am happy to overhear one British judge call it "a very impressive piece." Another judge rubs the neck of a curlew, a long-beaked coconut-size bird with speckled brown feathers, and pronounces this neck too thick. The others nod in agreement. I'm alarmed by all this rampant manhandling. On every table in the room sit computer printouts that shout "DON'T TOUCH!" in high letters, warning the bystander that no matter how lifelike a mount is—how strange or inviting or smooth textured or just how irresistibly *touchable* it may be—he's to keep his soiled hands to himself, thank you very much.

---

[5] Blomquist taught high school biology before turning full-time to taxidermy back in the 1970s.

Jack Fishwick, one of the bird judges, tells me what they're looking for first off is an overall impression of the mount. "We ask ourselves, Does it look like a live bird? If the head is in this position, should the feet be to the left or right?" In short, they're looking for the animal that most accurately re-creates its live version. That's the mount that will earn the title Best in World. Here, in Reno, sixteen people are going to earn it—in theory. Though there are sixteen categories of competition, the rules stipulate that, "If no mount scores at least 90 in a subcategory of a World Title category, there will be no Best in World in that category." This is a decision completely at the discretion of the judges. And tonight it seems that at least two categories may come up empty at Friday night's awards banquet. The large life-size mammal judges are unhappy with what they're seeing. "There's still TP on his scrotum," Marcus Detring says after having squatted down to check with a flashlight the undercarriage of a spotted elk, toilet paper being residue from the hide-drying process. He shakes his head and looks at the floor. "It's like, you hate to mark it down for stupid stuff like that, but you know you gotta do it."

Detring's a third-time judge at the WTC and tonight he's at a loss. Not only does the elk have toilet paper on its gonads, but the desert sheep's lip liner is way too long and the hyena holding its child by the scruff of the neck is no good either. From a few steps back, each of these mounts is impressive. Stunning, even. But up close, they're a complete disappointment. "It's just not *convincing*," Detring says, inches away from the hyena's face. That mediocrity could be so present at a world championship is shocking. If this were a figure-skating competition, it's as though every skater tried the triple axel and fell flat on his face. Detring says he has to have a talk with the competition coordinators. "To me, Best in World titles are a pretty big frickin' deal. You don't just give them out to keep people happy."[6]

---

[6] Detring's referring indirectly to the practice of handing out ribbons in the professional and novice levels. At these levels of competition *any*

All around the room, particularly with the birds and small mammals, judges are flipping madly through three-ring binders full of wildlife photographs. These are called "references," and they are inarguably the most valuable tool in a taxidermist's arsenal. *Check your reference. Go back to your reference.* These are things I hear countless times in seminars and judging critiques, and it seems a taxidermist can't have too many photographs lying around. (References are what Carl Akeley always got in trouble for staring at back at Ward's.) On the competition floor, one judge will stand before a goose and hold up a reference that captures a similar pose, and everyone will compare the angle of the head, the fanning of the secondary flight feathers. Fish judges will make sure the taxidermist properly replicated a trout's coloration. I can't help wondering what would happen if the tables were turned, if this room were full of animals that had stuffed a bunch of human beings for competition. Who would be their reference? What photographs would they use year in and year out? How would any of our skins look when mounted to resemble, say, Steve Guttenberg? or Tawny Kitaen?

This isn't how it works, one of the bird judges explains to me. "These birds are selected by Mother Nature as not freaks, but machines. They are walking, moving machines that all work in the same way. Their variation is not as pronounced as it is on humans." It's an argument only a taxidermy judge could make. If you've seen one bobcat, you've seen them all. Time and again I've heard taxidermists decry the practice of "beefing up" mounts. Customers come in with a slender mule deer and ask their taxidermist to thicken the

mount scoring a 90 or above wins a first-place ribbon. Second place ribbons go to mounts scoring 80 through 89, third place for 70 through 79. So you could have a dozen first-place winners, even more. At the master level, though, it's different. Here, only three ribbons are given out per category. Even if you're able to score a 92, if three other mounts score higher you'll walk home with nothing but score sheets.

neck and shoulders a bit on the headform. Make it look like a tough kill. Some taxidermists are happy to comply, but others think little of the practice. Isn't taxidermy about honoring the very animal that died? About capturing that animal's spirit? In competitive taxidermy, the answer is no. Maybe, then, competitive taxidermy follows not so much Balzac as Praxiteles. It's in the constant pursuit of some ideal, an ur-partridge that everyone agrees is what one should think when one even hears the word *partridge*. What'll take Best in World is not the best representation of an animal, but the best representation of the best representation of an animal.

Like the Venice Biennale, the World Taxidermy Championships happens only every other year, and thus what's called for is not just a simple floor competition, but rather a multivenue moveable feast of the taxidermic arts. From Tuesday night to Saturday night, I'm able to experience many, many new things. There are twenty-three different seminars going on; in one I watch a man use silicone to make "flexibilized" tree bark, and in another I listen as the instructor plays a Brooks and Dunn song urging me to believe in myself. I watch the live sculpting competition, where five men in the lobby of the Reno Events Center spend twenty-five hours over the course of three days sculpting, from scratch, life-size animals that could, in theory, be used to make manikins. One of the contestants looks precisely like Stephen King, and would it be such a surprise? Across the street from all this are hundreds of middle-aged white men competing against one another in the National Bowling Stadium at the United States Bowling Congress's Open Championships (and after only one day in Reno I learn that the surefire way in the lobby of a hotel to distinguish a bowler from a taxidermist is to check for camo). And because both championships are housed by the Silver Legacy Resort Casino I'm able to sit for the first time in my life at a blackjack table and swiftly lose ten dollars. There's so much to do that I miss out on a lot of it. I skip out on the WTC-sponsored tours of Lake Tahoe, Carson City, and the "All that Glitters" tour of Reno itself, but these were all available to me. There's even an entire auxiliary fish-carving[7] competition—with its own set of judges and its own schedule of seminars—that I sort of just ignore out of my own confusion about its presence here.

Though Blomquist & Co. try to pack as much activity as they can in four days, there's still a lot of downtime, and the best way to pass that time is, well, probably by losing money in the casinos. If you don't have a lot of money to lose at casinos—or if you're a faithful Christian who won't sanction games of chance, of whom there are more than a few at the WTC—there's always the trade show to wander through for a while. Laid out in four wide avenues at the northern end of the events center, the trade show does what every convention's trade show hopes to do: sell products. Some of these products are mere novelties, like the multicolor T-shirts on sale at the Jonas Supply booth that read

\ veg • e • tar • i • an \ *n.*
Another name for a bad hunter

and

People **E**ating **T**asty **A**nimals

which sell for $9.95 and come in three colors: brick, navy, and—naturally—hunter green. I pick up a fox face for $3. No one's selling rabbits' feet, I notice. Most of the stuff for sale is practical, innovative, designed to make the taxidermist's day-to-day life easier. There are tables for Bug to the Bone Skull Cleaning Service and Artistic Antlers (a major advertiser on Reinhart's *Taxidermy for the Sportsman*

---

[7] That is, the carving up of woodblocks to make replicas of certain species of fish and not, thankfully, the carving up of certain species of fish to make lord knows what.

show). A few wildlife artists sell pastels and watercolors. There are companies that build the wooden plaques you can hang game heads from, and one company that builds coffee or end tables out of glass, big enough to fit—tomblike—your full-size fish or small mammal mount.

Overall, fifty-three companies fill 151 booths, and I kill a whole afternoon walking past every one of them. I talk to Jason and Ben Emrich, brothers who run Montana Rocky Mountain Fur Dressers, Inc., about what a "wet tan" is and what a "dry tan" is, and they tell me it's all in the condition of the skin when they receive it. I see the booth for Knoblochs Chemical Company, which makes a product called Odor Out I heard rave reviews of during one of the seminars. The instructor said it could remove any smell from anything, that just yesterday one taxidermist here at the WTC took a bottle up to his nicotine-stained hotel room and sprayed some around like it was air freshener, and by the time he'd come back from lunch the smell of ten thousand cigarettes was completely gone. *I want one,* I decide, so I sidle up and ask the wry-eyed gentleman working the booth for a demonstration. He pulls out a very small bottle of a milky yellow liquid and sprays some on a spare piece of hide, which he then holds under my nose. What hits my nostrils is the pinch of ammonia mellowed somewhat by the funk of mold. I yank my face away from him. "What *is* that?"

"Doe piss," he says, grinning.

I nod my head as though it were just about to come to me. *Of course, doe piss!* After five squirts of the Odor Out, I'm invited to take another whiff, and I do and smell nothing. Not even the lingering hint of some uric undertone. Not even the musty smell of an animal hide. I smell only whatever the insides of my nostrils smell like, and I drop twenty bucks on a bottle.

Probably the stinkiest, messiest part of the taxidermy process is fleshing, which is the removal of excess flesh from the hide before you can tan it. It can be as frustrating as scraping ice from one's windshield, except the ice is actually meat, and it's raw and warm and terrible. Fleshing machines, then, have a strong presence at the trade show. Everybody needs one, from the little wire wheels used to flesh greasy bird skins to the sharp, gleaming disks of the upright fleshers, the ones that look like radial saws aimed dangerously frontward. Then there's the Whizard Trimmer: The Next-Generation Fleshing Machine, which is set up in a booth at a prominent intersection and looks like something right out of your childhood dentistry nightmares. A human-head-size motor hangs from a six-foot post, much like an IV bag, and is connected by wires to a handheld device about the size and shape of a microphone, except in place of the mic's head is a metal hoop about three inches in diameter. This hoop consists of two spinning blades that will cut quickly and fiercely away at anything they touch.

Compared with traditional fleshers, the Whizard Trimmer is actually much less dangerous. "With the wheel fleshers you're holding up hides that can weigh a hundred, hundred fifty pounds when wet," says Scott Gregory, a representative from Bettcher Industries, which produces the Whizard. "It's also really hard to work the skin of the face with one of those things." *Work the skin of the face.* Gregory offers all this up practically unprompted, having introduced himself after watching me stare and scribble in my suspicious notebook for a couple minutes. We pause and watch a demonstration, in which what might be a plain old deer hide is draped over an incline, and another Bettcher Industries employee is slowly and evenly scraping with the Whizard at the skin, stripping away the wet, puce flesh until only thin streaks of white hide are left behind. These meat scraps litter the board he's working on, litter the tarp spread out on the floor, lying there slimily under the harsh lights. I want to ask Gregory more questions, but I'm struck silent and dry-throated by the stench, so I quickly thank him for his time and hightail it out of noseshot.

The trade show is open only certain hours of each day, perhaps to give the people manning the booths a break every now and then, and so in this three-hour window late Thursday afternoon, it's filled with hundreds of aisle wanderers wanting to shop before dinnertime. I see Holler and his wife, Wendy, looking at a table full of artificial bird eyes, and I mention that I saw him at the alligator seminar last night. "Yeah, my curiosity got me," he says. "It's like, How do you mount an alligator? I never seen it done before."

I ask him if he gets a lot of reptile work in North Dakota. "I've done one rattlesnake," he says. "Wasn't crazy about it, probably wouldn't do another one."

Judging for Holler's division happened late Wednesday, but I'm not sure he knows this. If I had to rate his anxiety level on a scale of one to ten, I'd ask for a new scale. He seems completely relaxed, like unflappably so. Full of small, thin-lipped smiles. Glad just to be here, he says. Looking forward to getting a look at the competition tomorrow.

At one corner I see a group of eight people crowded around a wood duck mounted in a simple standing position on a four-foot-high faux-marble pedestal, its plumage a glossy, patchwork display of every handsome shade in a book of car-upholstery samples. I step up and wonder what it is we're looking at exactly. The duck doesn't seem to be part of any booth. A shaggy-haired man with Sam Elliott's mustache stands behind the duck, but together I don't think they're trying to sell anything, and while the taxidermy job here is pretty good, it's nothing to write home about. It's just a duck on a pillar. But then I realize that no one's been allowed on the competition floor yet, so maybe this crowd just wants to take a look at— Jesus Christ did the duck just *move*? Did that head just bob up and down? I think for a second this must be an animatronics display. The future of taxidermy, *today*! But then, the duck moves again, and this time it's a full-body shiver, running from his beak to his tail feathers, and his wings stretch outward as though ready to take flight. And *ha ha ha,* what a krazy idea! Bring a live game bird to a taxidermy competition and stand it on a marble column as though it were a piece of sculpture! Fool *everyone*! Charlie Thurston is the man standing just behind the duck, and he tells me its name is Seven. Seven the wood duck. "He's a good duck," he says. "I keep him as a pet, bring him to taxidermy shows. People seem to get a kick out of him."

It's not so much a kick I'm getting as it is a kind of comfort. Seven is the only living animal in an arena full of dead ones, and we stare as though he were an alien, come to save us. We're all here for the same reason. We're here to see the same exciting stuff. But no matter the mastery of a competition mount it'll always only be life*like*. Here, on a pedestal, is life, and it's hard for any of us to turn away.

The bulk of the trade show's space is taken up by the big-five supply companies. Jonas Brothers (a name that since about 2007 has become a little confusing to taxidermists with tween-age daughters) takes up seven booths. WASCO (not to be confused with Dan Rinehart's TASCO) fills six booths, as does Research Mannikins. Van Dyke's needs nine booths, and McKenzie—sort of the Macy's of the bunch—takes up a whole twelve booths. All this extra space is needed for the manikins each company wants to show off, many of them making their debut at this year's WTC. McKenzie, for example, is showing off a new semisneak,[8] open-mouth elk manikin, displaying it next to a finished mount in a kind of before-and-after

---

[8] For game heads, at least those of the *Cervidae* family, you have four neck positions to choose from when mounting the animal: upright, semiupright, semisneak, and full sneak. Often this choice is made by the customer and depends on how the animal was holding its head at the moment the trigger was pulled. Deer hold their heads upright when they hear something suspicious. Remember this the next time you see one mounted on a wall.

tableau. This is standard operating procedure for the supply companies; it's very likely that whichever mounts at the opposite end of the events center go away this weekend with a Best in World ribbon will show up next year in supply catalogs, depicted right alongside the very manikins used in their construction. The message is clear, but false: use this manikin; win an award. It's one way to go about choosing a product. How taxidermists decide which company to shop from (and there are dozens) and then choose among that company's many lines of head forms is a mystery to me. Most seem to go with McKenzie. Wendy Christensen-Senk at the Milwaukee Public Museum and Paul Rhymer at the Smithsonian both shop there. Even Todd Kranau, when hired by the Cabela family (who bought Van Dyke's in 1995), went with McKenzie to mount his client's trophies. "You don't buy from Cabela's to mount for Cabela," he says.

There've been any number of landmark innovations that have transformed the taxidermy supply industry over the past hundred years, each one skyrocketing a different company into popularity. While J. W. Elwood can be considered the first major supplier in the country—including with his Northwest School of Taxidermy mailings detailed explanations of how artificial eyes, Borax, scalpels, and even frogs can be had on the cheap[9]—it was Jonas Brothers that built the first large-scale taxidermy supply business in the country, starting in Denver in 1908. Jonas Brothers claims to have been the first supplier of compressed paper manikins "when the taxidermy industry was still in its infancy," according to the company's self-published *The Jonas Story*. But every company likes to claim it's the first at something. Van Dyke's—founded by a South Dakota army veteran in 1949—claims it's the first company to make and ship urethane foam manikins. According to Jay Schriever, a product special-

---

[9] While the popularity of Elwood's instruction waned with the rise of taxidermy schools and instructional videos in the 1980s, his supply company, run by his son, kept shipping to customers through the 1990s.

ist at Van Dyke's, the company began producing foam manikins in "about the early Seventies." Jonas Brothers released its Pos-Tex line of foam manikins also in the early 1970s. McKenzie Taxidermy Supply was founded in 1973 and, according to the CFO, Tom Powell, was "one of the first companies to offer molded polyure-thane manikins."

No one has any idea who did it first. What's important isn't who was first to manufacture foam manikins, but rather the fact that the foam manikin was the biggest revolution in the taxidermy industry—on par with the development of the Akeley method, which begat foam manikins the way radio begat TV. It was quicker and cheaper for the companies to produce and lighter and stronger for the taxidermists to work with. It also did a much better job of capturing the nuances of the original sculpture. Before the foam manikin, all taxidermists had to work with was a dead animal and their own faculty. Everything needed to make the animal look life-like, every inch of musculature, every gesture, every bit of "atti-tude" was put in place by the taxidermist's own two hands. In short, the taxidermist was responsible for everything. Naturally, this slowed things down in terms of output. Maybe they could bang out a couple deer heads a week. Then the supply companies came along, and taxidermists today can do one before lunch and another just in time for dinner. Now at the dawn of the twenty-first century a taxi-dermist is responsible for very, very little. What was sculpture has now become assembly, and with everyone using the same McKenzie forms or the same Van Dyke's forms the only place where taxider-mists can stand apart from one another, the only place where their artistry, such as it is, can shine, is in the finishing details. The paint-ing of the nose. The carving of an eye duct. The positioning of the ears. In short: all the things supplies can't do for them—yet.[10] It's no

---

[10] Of course, the argument can (and should) be made that the supply companies have increased quality of commercial mounts overall. With all

wonder that the bulk of the work the judges do involves the up-close inspection of the finishing process.

This isn't the case in Europe, where taxidermists on the whole sculpt all their own bodyforms, from scratch, each time they set about mounting an animal. To do this well, as Carl Akeley knew, you need to know a hell of a lot of anatomy of a hell of a lot of animals. What if a taxidermist is hired by a museum and given, say, a macaque monkey to mount? If he's European, he knows where to begin. If he's American, he's screwed.

Whether this means that Europeans are at an advantage at the WTC (and there are many of them in attendance this year) is up for debate. But Thursday morning before I decide to mosey around the trade show I sat in on the Avian Challenge, where fifteen taxidermists all mounted a Hungarian partridge—a brown-gray bird about the size of a volleyball with an orange face and a bold black bead of an eye—in the same walking pose, and after more than an hour of vocal deliberation the three European judges picked the first-, second-, and third-place winners. All were Europeans. All Scandinavians, actually, two Finns and a Swede. They undoubtedly made their own manikins using techniques older than any of us in the room. The Americans, however, probably went to their catalogs: McKenzie form number UGB7, Hungarian partridge. Costs just $7.60.

A fun thing about the WTC is that the judges are themselves not exempt from judgment. Or, at least, they don't have to be. There's

---

manikins being premade, and with ear liners much easier to work with, taxidermists are now free to focus their energies on these details that can make a mount turn heads. The deer head hanging above me as I write this, for instance, dates to the 1950s and has lips like dirty strips of licorice, and his ears poke out goofily in front of his antlers. No disrespect to the good folks at J. C. Mirguet, Inc., but better deer have since been made by worse taxidermists.

a special division called the Master of Masters, open to all judges and former Best in World winners (of course there's some overlap). This division, while ineligible for the Best in World title, does cast a bit of a shadow on the idea of those being "the best." It's like the award should be renamed Best in World Outside of Those Who've Already Been Named Best in World. Or maybe just Best in World for the First Time. At any rate, by 4 P.M. on Friday, the competition floor is finally open for viewing, and of the five hundred–plus men and women here to scope out the competition, maybe one hundred are clustered along the events center's west wall, where the Master of Masters mounts are lined up. Because here are the WTC's doozies. Stefan Savides's glorious California valley quail, with his little pompadour head plume. Simon Blackshaw's delicate little hairless baby blackbirds, their beaks wide open for some absent mommy. Of special interest to the crowd is the rather absurd multimedia display of Frank Newmyer's capercaillie (a large grouse that looks kind of like a pigeon, kind of like a turkey, and kind of like a crow). He's got velvety backdrops, tricolor lights, and a hidden stereo playing sounds of nature on a loop. The whole thing looks like Sears Portrait Studio's worst available options all thrown together.[11] The Master of Masters division is judged by popular vote from all five hundred WTC competitors, and every time I walk past the ducks I see three or four people standing nearby, listening quietly to the prerecorded birdsong and the "wind" in the "trees," and it's clear that Newmyer's going to take home a first-place ribbon, what with all his devastating bells and whistles.

---

[11] To be clear, Newmyer is a superstar here. He has his own line of eyes that he sells through WASCO, and he's won Best in World nine times. His name alone carries enough weight that a woman I spoke with at the trade show hyped up the accolades of her company's staff taxidermist by letting me know he beat Frank Newmyer at the Pennsylvania Taxidermist Association's 2002 competition. In the world of competitive taxidermy, it's sort of like outracing Lance Armstrong.

What I'm gunning for are the owls over in the corner of the room, nearly hidden behind this bizarre elk-head display with its antlers webbed in bloody, half-scraped velvet. They're mounted on a plain pine box, the owls. One crouches low and the other, to its right, has its back turned to the viewer, with its head swiveled around in that creepy way owls are able to accomplish. They look at you as if they didn't expect you to be there looking at them. What I like about the owls is that they're not captured in flight or set in the midst of some artificial habitat. These owls on the pine box look like owls. They look like they've somehow been mislaid, ending up in a taxidermy show of all places and needing a place to rest while they plan their escape.

Savides, who mounted the owls, is dashing about the competition floor, chatting with old friends about what he thinks will take home the blue ribbon. He's a tall man, with a razor-sharp Adam's apple visible even through the hunter green turtleneck he wears with one of those tweed newsie caps with the bill snapped up front. I ask him about his approach to presentation. "If you were to mount a bird right here," he explains, pointing to the mediating aluminum rails that have been set up on the floor to protect mounts, "your mind would register it as a live bird, not a piece of taxidermy." Savides thinks that the obsessive attention given to presentation detracts from the animal itself. His California valley quail is similarly mounted on a plain gray box. "A presentation," he tells me, "that [complements] the muted tones of the bird."

This is when I start to get it, start to see why judges are so critical and so dead set on the up-close details of a mount. Habitat is nice. It helps make taxidermy more like a story. But habitat itself isn't taxidermy. It's window dressing. It's book design. A mount heavy on habitat serves only the taxidermist's vision. It doesn't serve the animal. The more minimal one's presentation, the greater the focus on the animal that had to die for one's art to exist. If there's a minimalist school in the field of taxidermy, Savides has to be its Donald Judd—passionate about form, and no less outspoken. "Look at his *bases*!" he says to any number of us in earshot, pointing at the neoclassical column made of black marble that supports Newmyer's wood ducks. Savides would have mounted the animals on a simple cylindrical base with no shine to it, though he's aware that his ideas don't always garner him awards. "Some judges can't get past certain things. They want to see habitat. They want to see presentation."

The judges he's talking about in this case are, of course, the competitors themselves. And who, pray, created this desire in them for habitat and presentation? Maybe these things gradually fail to keep a taxidermist's interest, the way the work of some senior comics comes to adhere less and less to the setup-punchline model. Savides has been mounting birds for forty-five years, and he's won enough awards that he's lost count, and maybe after all this the animal itself starts to be enough, because the object of making an animal look as real as a live one is so difficult, nigh on impossible, that it's worth shucking all the excess work and focusing on what matters. The skin. The form. The thing that gives it its *it*-ness—or what I heard one taxidermist call "the jizz" of an animal.[12]

Savides has won Master of Masters before, in 1999, but tonight anyone can tell from the way he stares at everything Newmyer's thrown together that he really wants to win again and has no idea whether it's possible. It's the bitter truth about serious competition: no amount of awards can soothe the desire for more. Maybe this is a good thing. Once a taxidermist gets named Best in World, what else to keep his work from sliding into stagnation than the Master of Masters division? Then again, there are only so many awards to go around, and every other year, more and more first-time competitors come to the WTC hoping, like Randy Holler, to come back with a

---

[12] From the *OED*: "The characteristic impression given by an animal or plant."

ribbon, to go home with the kind of approval from their peers they can't get from customers or friends.

If, proverbially, there's more than one way to skin a cat, then there are more than a thousand ways to mount one. The divide between minimal and maximal, the subdued and the sensational, goes back probably to taxidermy's curious beginnings. You can line all the major players up and watch them spar with one another. Savides v. Newmyer. Peale v. Barnum. Webster v. Hornaday, which was how things played out at the very first taxidermy competition in the United States, held in 1880 by the Society of American Taxidermists. Founded pretty much by the staff at Ward's Natural Science Establishment, the SAT's mission was "to promote intercourse between those who are interested in the art of Taxidermy in various parts of America, to encourage and promote development of that art, and to elevate it to a permanent and acknowledged position among the fine arts." Operative word here is "elevate." Taxidermy at that time in American museums was passable. It lasted longer than fifteen years, for instance. But it couldn't have been called "good." Bird mounts were lined up in large cases, all in the same unnaturally stiff pose. Mammals, too, were placed in cases and mounted completely devoid of "attitude." The SAT was all about attitude. Arguing against the popular wisdom of museum professionals at the time, the wisdom that claimed there was no room for creatively mounted specimens in a place of scientific study, Frederic Lucas, the treasurer of the society, wrote that

> the Humming Bird should hover over a flower, the Woodpecker climb the side of a tree in search of food, the Goatsucker should sit *lengthwise* of a bough suspended with outstretched wings and gaping mouth, as if in chase of insects. . . . In short, let each bird, so far as practicable, be

mounted in an appropriate attitude and teach some fact in
its life history.

We have the members of the SAT to thank, then, for making presentation and habitat vital parts of a taxidermy mount. And it wasn't
all just speeches and acting sanctimonious in the face of their employer. The SAT also staged public exhibitions of top taxidermic
work. To have been at the first competition in Rochester, another
little city, things would have seemed eerily similar to what I've been
witnessing in Reno. All manner of animals were there, all mounted
by the society's members, hoping to impress their peers enough to
take home the silver medal, which in this pre-Olympics era was
designated for first place. There was a lion with its mouth wide open
and snarling and a tiger that spanned ten feet, nose to tail tip. Lots of
ungulates—bison, antelope, mountain sheep. Even a fur seal. Some
wood ducks. It wasn't called such, but they even had a category for
re-creation or novelty taxidermy, or what Mary Anne Andrei, in
her exhaustive study on the SAT, calls "grotesques." One taxidermist
entered a mount of some squirrels playing dominoes. Another did a
set of romantic kittens sitting on a bench. There were lots of frogs.
Some frogs were drinking. Some were smoking. One was sat up in
a chair, leaning over a hummingbird flayed open on a little table.
This was titled *The Taxidermist,* replete with miniature tools lying
around, and it very well may be the world's first piece of metataxi-
dermy. The most noteworthy pieces at the first exhibition were two
now-historic group mounts: Frederic Webster's *The Flamingo at Home,*
which depicted three pink flamingos in a classical triangle composi-
tion standing before a painted backdrop of some tropical swamp;[13]
and William T. Hornaday's *Fight in the Tree-tops,* which put two male
orangutans amid some artificial tree limbs, one in the act of biting

---

[13] Karen Wonders calls this group mount "the first of its kind" and places
it as a key forerunner of the habitat diorama.

off the other's finger. The victim was howling out in pain, and Hornaday was sure to paint some "blood" seeping out from the wound.

You can see where these guys fall in our arbitrary subdued-sensational dichotomy, and at the first annual SAT competition, the sensational won out. Maybe it's the American way, but the judges of the competition decided that Hornaday's group, which lacked a painted background, was thus the more scientific of the two. And the scientific group in 1880 was the superior group, according to the three museum directors—scientists, themselves—who were chosen to judge the competition, all of them coming out of the slowly dying, boring-old-study-skin-as-optimal-research-specimen school. Webster's flamingos were the envy of his peers in the SAT (save, perhaps, Hornaday), and yet they weren't awarded any medal, didn't even score an 85 to merit a "diploma of honor."

Webster's flamingos went to the Milwaukee Public Museum, and Hornaday's orangutans were bought by the National Museum of Natural History. At the second exhibition, held in Boston in 1881, the two once again went head-to-head, splitting the silver medal between them, notably for solo animal mounts without painted backdrops. Having won back-to-back, Hornaday took a job offer from the NMNH and began immediately to consider himself the best taxidermist in America. In a letter to Henry Ward, his former boss, he claimed he would no longer bother himself with competing, "unless I am forced to it by insinuations that somebody else can lay over me on mammals." The idea was that he should now rest on his laurels at his prestigious job and work to produce high-quality taxidermy in Washington. But of course the competitions themselves would continue without him, and someone else would be awarded the silver medal. And what if it was with a higher score? About a week after penning that letter to Ward, Hornaday entered a polar bear, four game heads, and a seal in the third annual exhibition of the SAT.

William T. Hornaday has been hiding out in the shadows of this book for some time now, popping up here and there at key points.

To be fair, there's a lot he deserves credit for. He single-handedly organized the SAT. He wrote *Taxidermy and Zoological Collecting,* which became so authoritative by the end of the nineteenth century that J. W. Elwood stole about half of it in putting together his correspondence course, the one by which hundreds of thousands of U.S. taxidermists learned their trade. Undoubtedly, it was Hornaday's hard work that put Ward's Natural Science Establishment on the map, not Akeley's. Hornaday arrived at Ward's in 1872, when Carl was only eight. And while Akeley likes to take credit for being the first taxidermist to drape a skin over a premade form, this isn't at all true. Hornaday was the first to sculpt manikins, Akeley merely made them lighter and more durable through his plaster-casting technique.[14] Karen Wonders, in her exhaustive study of the habitat diorama, calls *him* the father of modern taxidermy. Not Akeley.

Still and all, Hornaday was kind of a dick. Another piece he brought to the second exhibition was a "baby elephant not more than six or eight months old." Or so it was listed in the show's catalog. Actually, it was an elephant fetus that he'd salvaged from the body of a pregnant female he shot down in India in 1877. He'd been really hoping for "a tusker," as he wrote in another letter to Ward, and seems to have had an itchy trigger finger when he shot a female. On skinning the carcass he found the fetus "quite well developed" and saved its skull and skin for later use. "The skull doesn't amount to a great deal," he wrote, "but I have a hankering after that little skin to stuff for a library ornament. I must have *some* trophy of my elephant shooting." Later in life Hornaday directed the Bronx Zoo, where he put an African man on exhibit in the Monkey House, even after the city's black clergymen protested.

So you can see what I mean when I call him a dick. Or maybe the

---

[14] In fact, Louis Dufresne, the man credited with coining the word *taxidermy,* wrote about fitting animal hides over preformed manikins as early as 1803.

more accurate slander is that Hornaday was self-centered. He was a profligate hunter and a voracious competitor. Even after his prima-donna threat that he'd never compete again he was right back at it, forcing SAT President Frederic Lucas to call, in the organization's third annual report, for the fair and open comparison of taxider-mists' work and the sharing of ideas and techniques. "We must get rid entirely of the idea that but one man is master of the art, and that one man is ourself," he wrote. In the end it wasn't enough to assuage Hornaday's self-interest. With his steady job, and with other SAT men getting museum work, there became little need to work together—or to show off. The group disbanded in 1884.

Carl Akeley wasn't much of a competitor. He was driven to surpass his own exacting standards for his work, but he rarely kept his eyes on the work of his colleagues. He joined the SAT in 1883 probably as a gesture of camaraderie with his coworkers at Ward's, but he didn't enter any work in the Third Annual Exhibition of that year. The only time Carl put his work up in a competitive show was at the 1895 Sportsman's Exhibition in Madison Square Garden, where his deer head, titled *The Challenge,* won first place as judged by the city's police commissioner—who happened, at that time, to be The-odore Roosevelt.

In truth, Carl Akeley was a private man. Maybe shy and modest, maybe aloof or unsociable, but all accounts put him happiest in the studio, working on an animal. By 1892, after Bill Wheeler had left his position as director of the Milwaukee Public Museum, Carl had no friend at the MPM to champion his projects and felt unmoored, and he resigned on September 20. He lingered in Milwaukee for another year or so, doing commission work for the MPM. He was unsure about the next stage of his career and whether it had anything to do with a certain Mrs. Arthur Reiss. Working on the muskrat group had been exhilarating—no doubt thanks to her continuous presence—and Carl couldn't help thinking bigger, grander. A group mount was all well and good, but what about a group of group mounts? It was in these in-between years that he began planning his next great project, something large-scale and baroque, with a baroque-inspired name: *The Four Seasons.*

Many people know that most female members of the *Cervidae* family do not grow antlers (bully for the caribou for being an exception), and some people know that the male members who do grow antlers shed those antlers every winter. I didn't know this when I began looking a lot more closely at racks of antlers hung up on walls and angled naturalistically behind diorama glass, and I knew even less about the velvet that covers the fresh set of antlers growing on stag heads every summer. But sure enough: here is another way to read the cycle of the seasons. Spring, summer, autumn, winter. Pedicle, velvet, calcified, bald. This is to say nothing about what happens to the coat of a deer as the days grow shorter and colder. Carl, of course, knew all this like he knew he'd one day marry Delia, and one can imagine he planned *The Four Seasons* as a way to solve a problem central to any taxidermy job. For years now, Carl would get word from some uppity-up at a museum that an animal was needed. A deer, say, to be featured in the museum's hall of mammals, and Carl would be left with a hefty set of questions to ask the museum man. What species of deer? whitetail? mule? caribou? Adult or youth? What sex? If male, antlers or no antlers? If antlers, velveted or denuded of velvet? And a deer harvested at what time of year? That is, how thick or thin shall the coat be? What the museum man usually wanted was exactly what Carl's commercial clients went after, the deer we all see in our heads when we hear another person say "deer": an adult whitetail buck with calcified antlers and a coat of the medium thickness one finds in the fall. Imagine doing hundreds of these a year. Imagine doing even just a dozen. For Carl it was like knowing himself as a painter and wanting in the spirit of the time to rethink the picture plane in the ways of his European colleagues, and instead having to paint countryside after country-side in the low morning light using the time-honored techniques of classical perspective.

Instead, for *The Four Seasons* Carl would do it all: every kind of whitetail deer imaginable. A whole family of deer—mom, dad, sis, bro—in four different scenes in four different times of the year. Six-teen separate deerskins mounted so as to tell a grand narrative of adaptation and survival.

Delia thought it a wonderful idea, but was now the best time for such an ambitious project? At this point, in 1894, she'd pretty much left Arthur for good (though they wouldn't divorce officially until 1901), and though now she and Carl could spend all their time to-gether, they were unhappy in Milwaukee, just scraping by with Carl's private shop. *The Four Seasons* would take a lot of money and a lot of time, keeping the two of them stuck in the cold, flat country Delia had always been forced to live in. What about Paris? she won-dered. Would Carl not be happier running off to the European capital Delia had known so intimately in her girlhood dreams of distant escape? He could learn sculpture there. He could combine a classical art training with his own self-developed taxidermy know-how and be, maybe, the best in the world. Such were the conversa-tions that drifted between the two in the years after Carl's resignation. Carl, though, didn't care about Europe. He'd tried school back in Rochester and found it tedious. Too abstract. Would art school be any different? He made it clear to Delia that *The Four Seasons* was exactly what he needed to do right now, and Delia relented, and she swore to help him through it.

By 1895, Carl found work in Chicago—again doing commercial trophies as well as contract pieces from the Columbian Museum of Chicago.[15] Delia followed shortly after, twenty years old at this point.

---

[15] So named because many of its displays came from materials exhibited at the 1893 World's Columbian Exposition. The museum's name was

Carl was thirty-one. They worked at a ramshackle studio built on a rented lot in Hyde Park—a shack, really, with no floor and a roof supported only by neighboring buildings. Behind the studio, Carl built a small shed where he kept a live whitetail deer to use as a reference for his new project. The whole space was heated by a small coal stove, and for most of the year the two of them were kept very, very cold. Habitat dioramas demand much from the fingers. Carl had sixteen skins to sew up with stitches small enough that they wouldn't be seen. Delia made upward of seventeen thousand artificial leaves by casting wax in some molds Carl had sculpted. They wore knit gloves with the fingertips cut off and tried to breathe away from the task at hand, lest the steam from their exhales cloud up the freezing air around them.

The Four Seasons took four years to complete. It was not the taxidermy itself that took up so much of Carl and Delia's time and energy; it was the habitat. To set *The Four Seasons* next to everything else Carl did for the Field Museum, it is as though he took the planned habitat materials from two dozen dioramas and stuffed them all in his four deer groups.[16] There were not only all the leaves, but the barks of the trees. The lilypads on the pond in the summer

changed in 1905 to Field Museum of Natural History, after benefactor Marshall Field, which for clarity's sake is the name I'll use throughout.

[16] Carl was hired full-time in 1896, earning two thousand dollars a year, eight hundred more than he made in Milwaukee. Most of this work is still on display today. Whether a factor of the budget of the museum or of Carl's personal priorities, his work for the Field looks shoddy and amateurish when held up against that which he had done for the MPM and what he would mount in the last half of his life for the AMNH. There are no painted backdrops to be seen, and habitat stuff is minimal. The African buffalo stand in lots of straw and mud. The bongo stand amid floor-to-ceiling bamboo stalks. But these are the exceptions to the rule of decay. Granted, Akeley's mounts are 120 years old, but by now the hides are alopecia'd and colorless, with splits and cracks running along many of the seams.

diorama. The pond itself—another tricky pane of glass. There were artificial rocks to sculpt and artificial snow to lay on the winter scene; Delia mixed pounds and pounds of beet sugar with plaster to get a reflective effect. It took Carl months to figure out how to get the velvet to adhere to the buck's antlers (he injected them with paraffin wax, and, since they are porous, the velvet bonded perfectly). All this they did, by hand, step-by-step, in close company. Carl and Delia were living together at this point and, it's clear, sleeping together. But they were still unmarried—Arthur Reiss wasn't exactly eager to sign the papers that would legally allow Delia to tie herself with his (ex) hunting buddy. And so, in the meantime, they threw themselves into *The Four Seasons*—their epic monument to these happy years of wooing each other.

Carl invited the Field Museum curator Daniel Elliot to his studio one day in 1900 to take a look at the finished *Four Seasons*. In Carl's short number of years in Chicago, Elliot had become a mentor. He kept the former supplied with contracts to fill his time and his wallet, and he was the first man to take Carl to Africa. It was a surprise, then, when Elliot said he'd recommend the Field Museum's purchase of one of the four deer displays. "They're a group," Carl said. "I won't see them exhibited alone." Elliot mentioned budget problems, and Carl went right to the president of the museum. "After some discussion," Akeley writes in *In Brightest Africa,* "he asked why it was that the museum couldn't have the four groups. I gave him every assurance that it could." In 1902, the Field Museum bought *The Four Seasons*, paying $5,500 for all four groups. Subtract the cost of materials and Carl and Delia made just about nothing on the piece. But at least they sold it. At this stage in his career Carl still had to wheedle museums into buying his best work—recall the song and dance he performed before the MPM's board of trustees to get his muskrat diorama approved. Later, at the AMNH, he'd get the full support (and budget) of the museum behind him, and it was the success of dioramas like *The Four Seasons* that got him there. The Field

Museum's $5,500, though small, was a major accomplishment. A lasting one. Hornaday's *Fight in the Tree-tops* was deinstalled in the NMNH's recent renovations, and no one at the MPM knows what happened to Webster's flamingo group. *The Four Seasons* may never have earned Carl a medal, but it earned him something far more important: an audience. Money, he knew, can come and go, but museums, we trust, are eternal.

The medals given to Best in World mounts at the WTC bear the face of Carl Akeley. It's from a photograph he had taken back in Milwaukee. Carl looks to be about twelve, dressed up unwillingly for some distant relative's funeral. His jacket, buttoned right up on the breastbone, is one or two sizes too small. His head is caught in three-quarters profile, facing to our left, and the whole open right side of his face is fair and unlined. His hair looks held in place by his mother's loving spit. All of this is made understandable by the legend that runs on the lower curve of the medal—AT THE AGE OF NINETEEN—except that the photograph from which this image of Carl was taken dates to around 1890. He would have been at least twenty-five when he sat for it.[17] At the age of nineteen he must have looked like a toddler.

Friday evening, the Best in World medals are lined up on a table near the stage that's been erected in the Silver Legacy's Grande Exposition Hall. Doors to the hall are set to open at 7:00 to begin seating for the 2007 WTC's awards banquet. It's a complete free-for-all. You grab the best table you can get—unless you're a judge or staff

---

[17] The WTC has Mary Jobe Akeley, Carl's second wife, to blame for the error. Underneath this same photo in her biography is the caption: "Carl Akeley at the age of nineteen, when he mounted 'Jumbo.'" The elephant is depicted on the back of the WTC medal, and it certainly doesn't help matters that Carl was twenty-one when he mounted it.

member, whereby the best table has been reserved for you. For everyone else, it's a bit of a race, and so by 7:10, with doors still inexplicably closed, there's a jittery mood in the lobby and very little elbow room. Taxidermists and their spouses in semiformal attire all stand as close as possible to the dark wooden doors. Bottles of light beer in the hands of the misters, something mixed on ice for the misses. There's a strong Western flavor to the outfits. The men's suits have ornate plackets and bold piping. Here and there: bolo ties. And yet some men have for one reason or another simply not bothered, and stand impatiently with friends in clusters of denim and ball caps. They sip beer slowly, making it last.

Once the doors open, I'm lucky to find a seat next to Randy Holler, who's wearing a black cotton dress shirt and tan khakis. His tie depicts a summertime forest scene in the many greens and browns we're all familiar with this late in the week. At a table for ten, one of about fifty in the room, we all try to talk around the maroon napkins coiled fourteen inches high at the head of our place settings. Holler and another taxidermist, Dennis Nelson, of Montana, talk shop while their wives listen politely. Nelson has a couple fish mounts up for Best in World, and as these two compare techniques there's a clipped nature to their conversation. Whatever calm Holler's achieved throughout the convention is gone now. The medals are right over there. They have to go to someone, right?

Soon a voice comes over the PA system, one very deep and professional like those you hear before the commercials at televised awards shows.

"Ladies and gentlemen, please welcome the Chairman of the World Taxidermy and Fish Carving Championships, Larry Blomquist." Blomquist comes up to the podium amid thunderous applause to welcome everyone briefly and introduce his sister-in-law, Ann Moody, who will sing for us the U.S. national anthem.

It's—do we need reminding?—a *world* championship. There are taxidermists in the audience from Canada, England, the Netherlands, Norway, Estonia, Japan, China, Russia, Sweden, Finland, Iceland, Australia, Denmark, Italy, and the Philippines—among other countries. These taxidermists, all with national anthems of their own, certainly, stand politely while Ann belts out "The Star-Spangled Banner." "Wow, she can really sing," Nelson's wife pronounces, and once Ann finishes, the singing of anthems is over. The banquet, I'm soon to find out, is at least an hour too long as it is, so I suppose there's just no time to sing other anthems. But it's embarrassing. Directly afterward, fish judge Mike Kirkhart invites us all to applaud ourselves, "for loving the Creation so much to make it beautiful in His eyes." We do, and then everyone—well, not *everyone*—begins to chant the Lord's Prayer in spooky unison.

Other than these initial missteps, the nice thing about the WTC's awards banquet is the surety with which it adheres to the traditional model. There's a teleprompter, for instance, situated far enough away from the podium that most folks reading from it have to squint and end up stumbling over their speech. Frank Newmyer skips the teleprompter entirely and goes for impromptu crowd pleasers. Slap a pair of sunglasses on him and you have the WTC's Jack Nicholson. Blomquist, as owner, is our host—Billy Crystal without the song-and-dance hooey. Shortly after he takes the podium to start things off in earnest he's sure to interrupt himself and lean down toward the table at which his wife sits expectantly. "And by the way, Kathy, you look *exceptionally* beautiful tonight." It's unclear whether or not this is teleprompted, but it's a line that will be repeated by nearly every presenter throughout the evening. Every third award or so, someone will interrupt the proceedings to tell Kathy Blomquist she's looking exceptionally beautiful. At first, when judge Tom Powell does it, it *kills*. Smiles throughout the room spread wide open in delight. Is it a dig on Blomquist's cheesy gesture? Is it just a good bad joke to make? But then it keeps happening. By the fifth or sixth time it seems almost obligatory, as if telling Kathy she's looking exceptionally beautiful tonight is a kind of penance one does up at the podium, à la kissing some magisterial ring.

Any awards show worth its salt saves the top awards for last, of course, and the WTC takes its time getting to the Best in World titles. As Blomquist comes to the podium to explain how the Best in World titles are chosen he says they've never had a world show in which all World Titles were given. "This year, only eight were selected." That's eight out of *sixteen,* and this news has left Holler and Nelson—and the hundreds of other taxidermists in the room— nervous and confused. Eight? What happened to the unawarded medals? One imagines a storage facility, some dead-medal office, with Best in World medallions hanging from their red-white-blue ribbons like tasty fruit from a tall tree, its branches just out of reach.

What happened was this. Thursday morning, after the master-division judging was done, the bird judges were all clustered by a couple of mounts they'd already scored the night before. They called Skip Skidmore, the judges' liaison for the WTC, over for assistance. Everyone was trying not to talk at once.

"It's the front portion of the upper eyelid that I have a problem with," Peter Sunesen, the judge from Denmark, said, gesturing with his pinky at the head of one of the pheasants.

"Yeah, it looks staring in a way," said another judge.

"It's flat through here," Stefan Savides said, pointing with a pencil at the curve where the pheasant's neck met its head. "The head is the weak point."

"The body is horizontal," Sunesen said, "but the head is erect here."

Skidmore asked how he could help the judges, because he needed them to move on to the professional division. Sunesen said he overscored the pheasant at a 92 and needed to change his score. "The main problem is the bird's position," he said. "The neck is more suited to a body that's more upright. I thought about this a lot overnight and I don't think this bird should be named Best in World."

"If we give it a blue [ribbon]," said a judge from Texas, "we have a Best in World. We need to come down to an 88."

"When you guys came to me," Skidmore said, "you said that none of these capture *the spirit* of the animal. And if they don't have the *spirit*, as you say—look at those cottonpickin' *owls* in here." He motioned over to Savides's minimalist mount. "Talk about *spirit*. I look at them and I wanna—" and here Skidmore pantomimed an owl attack, ducking a bit and tossing his hands feebly in the air.

"Then you'll back up our decision?" Sunesen asked.

"Absolutely," he said.

"Then we'll have no Best in World in this category," the Texan said.

Sunesen nodded. The thing was done. "Okay, then let's change our scores."

Tomorrow morning I'll find Randy Holler back in the events center, picking up his score sheets and getting a consultation with his judges. It was Holler's pheasant the judges reconsidered. Holler's pheasant they had scored too high. When the sun rose Thursday morning Holler had the best pheasant in the world, but by Saturday it had only scored an 89.

Sunesen justifies the decision by arguing for the integrity of the title, that a Best in World mount must be more than best in division, more than the best-looking bird on the table. "That's why I feel strongly about this," he says. "It's to the benefit of the whole show. It should be an absolute scoring system. There shouldn't be a first place for the sake of it."

One obvious question follows: can't first place be given to the mount that scores the highest? "No," says Blomquist. "In a piece that scores an 89, it's an 89 because it was lacking in some critical area. Neither myself nor Skip have ever gone back and told a judge they gotta give a 90. It infringes on the integrity of the way this contest has been judged for years."

In the months after the WTC, Blomquist published an editorial in *Breakthrough* titled "Giving Away World Titles?" where he wrote, "A World Title at the World Taxidermy Championships® is not something you can win by default; it is an ultimate achievement with the highest degree of respect." At the Olympics, gold medals are just given away. At the WTC, Best in World titles have to be earned.[18]

In the end, it's a night of disappointments. Newmyer's overproduced wood ducks do indeed win out over Savides's owls. Raymond Kowalski's griffin fails to win Best in Show—as do any pieces in the re-creation division. This I take as some kind of betrayal. That a miniature griffin can get no recognition in this room seems a tragedy. A sad lack of wonder in a place that could use some.

When it comes time for the game-bird award, nothing is said. No award is given. The category is skipped, silently, and the ceremony moves on.

"I knew there was a chance of that," Holler tells me later. "But just by walking through the competition area—and again I'm not a judge or anything obviously—but just from walking through there I was really surprised that eight categories didn't have a blue ribbon."

It turns out to be a bad night for America. The Best of Show

---

[18] In 2009, Holler finally earned his. He walked away with a Best in World medal, again with a pheasant, scoring a 91.667. "I think the difference was, you know, the things I didn't do right [in 2007] I made sure they were right in 2009," he told me recently. "My anatomy was off, and I studied anatomy quite a bit in between those two shows. I think I got it better the second time." He added that getting those last 2.667 points to win was tough. "As it should be," he says. "I mean, it shouldn't be easy, right?"

award goes to Norway, first place Avian Challenge goes to Finland, and the Best Professional Entry award goes to Australia. As the audience shuffles toward the doors, the banquet producer cues up "We Are the Champions" by Queen (an English band), and the question arises: Who? Who are the champions—*of the world*? Only eight people are walking out of the Grande Exposition Hall with a medal that validates them as such. But what about everyone else? What about Randy Holler, whose pheasant was only better than every other game bird in his division, and not, as a few people decided, Best in World material? It's a song with meanings loaded well beyond what its title denotes, and this makes it in the end a curious choice to play at a world championship. The whole purpose of the WTC is to bring taxidermy's best and brightest together and separate the best and brightest of the best and brightest, and tonight this has been accomplished to an almost maniacal degree. And yet looking around the swiftly emptied hall, shoulders are slumped, eyes are thinned, and very, very few people are satisfied. This is why there will be another world championship in 2009. And another in 2011. And they mean to go on and on and on and on.

FIVE

As a kid I had any number of ridiculous things on my walls. My collections were few and soon abandoned. I stuck stickers in plastic-paged photo albums the two summers that flanked first grade. Baseball cards for a year or two before puberty. Anything after that was music paraphernalia, probably—cardboard longboxes from the early days of CD sales stapled on one corner of my bedroom's front wall, a column of concert ticket stubs falling nearly to the floor, some of them (vaingloriously) signed. Who knows where these things are now. That they might be festering in a landfill, turning to dirt and earth, is for me no real tragedy. I still have the memories the things themselves were meant to capture and evoke as I transferred them to my walls, and in those memories I think whatever value I might be talking about lies. But I am not an island, and one's possessions have value in the global market, and so while I can rest easy at night knowing the longbox of Camper Van Beethoven's *Key Lime Pie* I once displayed as a kind of bratty, music-nerd challenge to any potential Top 40 visitors is gone forever, somewhere out there is a different kind of Camper Van Beethoven fan who would pay or give any number of surprising things to own such an item. The thing is mine, was mine. I was the buyer and the owner of the object, and yet it seems I'm not the one who gets to decide its value.

As soon as I began thinking more and more about taxidermy, I wanted some. Just a head I could hang on the wall. Maybe even a jackalope, but ideally a whitetail head—taxidermy's C-major chord. The words *buffalo head* in the newspaper's yard-sale listings sent me one Saturday all the way to the other side of town to take a look, but by the time I got there it had long since been sold. The man in whose driveway I stood, forlorn, said he got $400 for it (I'd been prepared to go up to $80), that his uncle shot it years ago, and that it had been mounted by Jonas Brothers. Four hundred dollars was probably a steal, but what did I know? Another weekend at another yard sale I came upon a pheasant and a deer head hanging up in the back of one man's garage. These he had taken himself, and for the deer head, which had a hole inexplicably drilled through one antler and was cracking all over the dried-out hide, he wanted $150. This was outrageous, I thought, but then again what I was considering to buy was more than just a piece of taxidermy, it was whatever experience this man had out in the woods, or out in the fields, with whatever hunting companions he may have fallen out of touch with. These were all included in the piece's value, and it raised the price to more than I could afford. I bought the pheasant instead, a wall mount with its wings spread and beak partially open. I got it for $20 and took it home, where I hung it over the entryway from my living room to the office/foyer (this was a small, small apartment). Friends pretended to admire it.[1]

The first piece of taxidermy—well, "taxidermy"—I ever owned was a miniature plastic moose head hung on the wall of my bedroom, probably around the time I was collecting baseball cards (which I did not out of an affinity for the game but rather because baseball cards seemed to have been what most of the neighborhood boys had graduated to, their Garbage Pail Kids cards' edges softening and

---

[1] I've since given the mounted pheasant away on Craigslist, offering it up for free. I had nearly three-dozen requests.

rounding at the bottom of neglected toy chests), and that I have truthfully forgotten all about the existence of this moose head until, truthfully, I started writing this chapter says something about either the effect this mounting had on my life or the extent of my mistrust of memory. Maybe both. But I used to retire and wake each day with a plastic moose presiding over my tiny sleeping self. It, too, was tiny, maybe not a Lilliputian moose but more like a Cabbage Patch one. One corner of his antlers was chipped off and missing. It belonged to my father at one point in his life, and one day, in coming across it in my grandparents' attic, I took it for my own and hung it on the wall as a kind of badge that read I AM MY FATHER'S SON. Just as I hung the plaque made of painted plaster of Paris celebrating the Pittsburgh Pirates' 1960 World Series win despite not being able to name a single Pittsburgh Pirate. All this the effluvia of a self-conscious boyhood's dying end. All this before the CD longboxes and the signed ticket stubs, the later trappings of a stumbled-upon adolescence whose mission suddenly became announcing to the world *I Am Not Anything Like My Father or My Mother or Anyone Else Who Has Ever Lived on This Stupid Planet.*

Like Moosehead Lager, my moose head came from Canada, it turns out, from a trip to Niagara Falls my father took with his parents and grandparents in the summer of 1955. It would have been July, during the one week that my pipe-fitter grandfather got each year to take his family someplace other than the rural hills of Pennsylvania's Monongahela Valley. Dad was eight and wanted to go to the Canadian side of the falls to give him something to brag about to the boys back home, and the group wandered into any souvenir shop, and there it was: a miniature moose head. "I knew I'd never get a real moose head, so I wanted it," he tells me. "I also got a miniature birch canoe." I'm on the phone with him, trying to figure out how this relic made its way to my bedroom, this faux head that's now almost talismanic in what it seems to have predicted about my adulthood. It's one of the longest conversations we've had in recent memory.

"But what attracted you to that moose head?" I ask. "Granddad never had any taxidermy in your house, did he?"

"No, but I was trying to decorate my room, okay? And I just thought it would look good. But now that I think about it, there was a guy down the street where I used to go as a kid." And then in almost a caricature of father-knows-best fashion my dad begins to explain to me how he had to walk a quarter of a mile each morning to wait for the school bus. "And there was no shelter or anything like that," he says. "Nothing to protect you from the snow or what-not. So instead of standing out in the cold, this lady who had a daughter in high school, her last name was Pigford, and there were a few Pigfords in the area. But this Pigford lady had one arm. I never did find out how she lost that arm, but she would let me sit in her parlor until the bus was ready to come. Her husband had a lot of taxidermy that I would look at. He had an owl, a pheasant, a deer, and a raccoon. The owl would sit on the newel post of the stairs."

My father had the sort of classic rural American boyhood I could map easily onto Carl Akeley's despite the shift in locale. The Maddens kept a few chickens but didn't have a quarter of the land the Akeleys had for a full-fledged farm. Still, my father spent most of his time outdoors, fishing, doing a little hunting ("I was just starting to hunt when I got that moose head. I know I had my first shotgun.") and a lot of trapping. He'd get muskrats mostly and stretch their skins out in the sun to dry, and he'd sell them to Sears, Roebuck ("or maybe Montgomery Ward; I can't remember") for fifty cents a pelt. Mink would go for two dollars. In the 1950s one could just show up some Sunday afternoon and hand these over, it seems—an enterprise that today seems ripe for some episode of *Jackass*.[2] But of

---

[2] In episode five of *Jackass*'s first season, the host, Johnny Knoxville, announces to the camera that "we're gonna walk into a taxidermy [*sic*] and see if they'll stuff and mount my grandmother." He brings the old woman, still alive, into a couple of shops in the valley and asks with all

all the pelts he won, he never kept one for himself. Ditto any animal he may have hunted, and ditto all the fish he's ever caught. The man has owned, in my lifetime, two fishing boats and has been out on the water more times than the Olivia Cruise Line. He's cast a rod more often than I've cracked open a book, and not once has he ever brought a fish home for anything other than a meal. Perhaps this is a testament to my father's poor performance with a rod and reel, but in truth it's a simple function of personality. My father is not a collector. Try as I might to set for him an ideological motivation behind his purchase of the moose head, I can't. Its purchase was utilitarian: he needed to decorate his room. He thought it would look good.

The preferred term for killing among zoologists, biologists, and other research scientists is collecting. No museum keeps live animals in cages or aquaria; museums collect and store study skins and boxes of skeletons in cabinets up in the back chambers the public doesn't usually get access to. Or they collect fish and amphibians and drop them with many other specimens in jars of a ten-percent-alcohol solution. This is often called a museum's wet collection. Carl Akeley went on collecting expeditions at each of the three museums he worked for, but the most famous trips he took were the five collecting expeditions to Africa for both the Field Museum (in 1896 and 1905) and the American Museum of Natural History (in 1909, 1921, and 1925), where he collected, which is to say he shot, 328 various forms of antelope (e.g., gazelles, elands, dik-diks, duikers, impalas, hartebeests, gemsboks), 103 rodents, 27 monkeys, 20 elephants, 16 lions, 13 warthogs, 12 jackals, 9 gorillas, 8 baboons, 6 buffalo, 6 zebras, 5 donkeys, 3 cheetahs, 3 hippos, 2 rhinoceroses, 2 giraffes, 2 leopards, and a porcupine. That's 566 animals, not counting hundreds and hun-

---

sincerity whether they could do it. One taxidermist gives a rough estimate of $20,000 for the job.

dreds of additional birds and reptiles, but yes counting the eight specimens of *Neotragus moschatus akeleyi*, a subspecies of the suni antelope
named for our hero. Carl Akeley shot, harvested, bagged, collected
them all.

But before he was famous, before the Akeley method was de ri-
gueur among museum taxidermists nationwide, Carl Akeley was just
a Field Museum staffer, capable enough at his job to be brought along
by the zoology curator, Daniel Elliot on the museum's first expedition
to Africa in 1896. It was the first such expedition taken by any museum in the country. Carl wasn't even head taxidermist. Delia was
immediately jealous. She had followed him to Chicago only to watch
him run off for quite literal greener pastures halfway around the world.

The game Akeley and Elliot sought were antelopes, chiefly. Neither man was able in that trip to shoot any of the classic "big five"
that white hunters in Africa go for with a kind of madness: lion,
elephant, buffalo, leopard, and rhino. Whether this was a factor of permits or expertise is unclear. Carl was self-professedly not a good shot
as far as hunting in Africa went, and during that first trip he and Elliot
were happy to shoot whatever was available. Place yourself for a minute in their carefully chosen safari boots—so much of Africa was
unknown in 1896. Most of the animals Carl saw running over the
landscape he'd seen only stuffed before, shipped in from around the
world to Ward's Natural Science Establishment. Some of them, like
the mountain gorilla, hadn't even been discovered yet. Hence "darkest Africa"—so little about the continent had been illuminated at
the end of the nineteenth century. That said, while Akeley and Elliot
were more beggars than choosers, the former got quite early in Africa
the kind of madness that sets in the collector's eye. Soon after arriving, he became remorseful and angry if at the end of a day's hunting
he came back to camp empty-handed. And this anger not only lost
him some prize specimens—how hard for the hotheaded to truly
aim a firearm—but it almost got him killed.

All Carl had wanted was an ostrich, for what a boon it would be to his collection: the tallest bird on the planet. And while the animal has found itself stuck with a reputation of almost cartoonish stupidity, popping its little saurian head synecdochically under the earth's surface, ostriches are, in fact, Carl quickly found, clever little geese. He'd spent, that first trip, two complete hot days wandering around the flat, empty grasslands of Somalia's Haud region looking for bulbous, feathery bodies set tripodically on the dry soil and found none. Ostriches saw him coming before he ever saw them, and they hid themselves behind errant bushes and scurried off to the horizon whenever he tried to take a shot. Ostriches are fast, and they leave no discernible trail that would have made tracking them a walk in the proverbial park. By the third day Carl must have been flat-out ornery about so much time with a gun in his hands and nothing to show for it that the first animal he came upon that morning he shot dead before even realizing whether he and Elliot needed a specimen. It was a hyena, and as he walked over to where the animal fell he crouched down and saw mottled fur and patchy, scabrous skin, and Carl knew that no amount of his growing expertise with a skin and some plaster could make this particular animal look attractive behind museum glass. He let the dead dog lie. Soon after, he and his mule and his gun boy came across a warthog, and Carl shot that, too, and he left it, too, rather than spend precious ostrich-finding hours skinning and cleaning the carcass. And after many long and hot hours the sun fell to the edge of the country and the light started to fall away with it, and Carl saw: here, again, another empty-handed day behind him. They headed back to the camp, deciding to stop by the warthog to pick up at least one prize, but instead of lying there, dead, rotting slowly, the warthog was now trotting off for the bush, swaying in the jaws of an advantageous and hungry hyena. Carl fired, again, but missed. Another trophy lost.

Desperate, Carl then headed back to that first diseased hyena, deciding that returning to camp with refuse in his hands was better than returning alone. By now the sun had fallen well below the horizon. Objects in the distance were all gradually flattening against the landscape, and little breezes picked up speed and blew out the day's swelter. Everything had gone grayer. While it was difficult for him to see, it was clear as he reached the creekbed where he'd shot that first hyena that it, too, was gone. He got closer and saw from the corner of his eye a long shadow dart into the bushes. Here was something. Here was a living animal. Carl shot, blindly, right into the bush.

In response came the high, angry snarl of a leopard, and Carl's gut sank. Leopards, he knew, loved a good fight, and yet this one as it ran from cover out into the open evening seemed to be running away from him. Carl fired anyway, and after three shots, he hit the leopard and she fell. Within seconds she was back on her feet and running straight at him.

Carl's gun was empty.

The best way for a leopard to kill you is with a two-pronged attack. First she sets her jaws on your throat, crushing your windpipe like it were a cannoli. Then, while you lose a lot of blood and the ability to breathe, she sets her hind paws at your chest, unsheathes her hooked claws, and starts digging. She stops long after your heart has. Among all the ways to go it must rank among the direst, the body afterward being not so much a body as a burst vessel. Carl, then, was fortunate that his reflex was to raise an arm, as though it held a shield, as the leopard sprang upon him. This arm caught the leopard's jaws before his throat could. He gripped her neck with his other hand while she bit into him. This kept her claws away from his body. He tried to pull his right arm free, but the leopard's jaws were too strong, so he was only able to slide the thing out to the right, inch by inch, as each time the leopard readjusted her fangs' grip on his arm. Then he'd pull a little more of his arm through, the whole time keeping her limbs at enough distance to claw only at the frantic air between them. Gradually, the leopard gnashed the whole length of

Carl's arm like a corncob, until she held just his fist in her mouth. Rather than try to pull his fist out of the leopard's mouth, Carl pushed inward, driving it right down her throat. He kept choking the leopard with his left hand and began cutting off her windpipe. Somehow he fell down to the ground and landed on top of her, using his knees and elbows to pin her limbs to the ground. The leopard got weaker, and Carl began to think he may actually survive. He drove his knees into her chest:

> To my surprise, I felt a rib go. I did it again. I felt her relax, a sort of letting go, although she was still struggling. At the same time I felt myself weakening similarly, and then it became a question as to which would give up first. Little by little her struggling ceased. My strength had outlasted hers.

All this is in Akeley's memoir, *In Brightest Africa*. It forms the bulk of chapter 5, "Leopards & Rhinos," about neither of which animal Carl has much good to report. Rhinos, he says, are dumb, suspicious animals whose piss-poor eyesight leads them to charge indiscriminately wherever they think they smell danger, and are thus too easy to hunt sportily. Leopards he just sort of hates. I mean, it doesn't take a psychoanalyst to point out the rape imagery latent in Carl's writing of the encounter. And yet Carl's prejudice seems to come from some personal sense of decorum. "In spite of their fighting qualities I have never got to like or respect leopards very much," he writes in his memoir. "I think it is because the leopard has always seemed to me a sneaking kind of animal, and also perhaps because he will eat carrion even down to a dead and diseased hyena." Carl's unable, or unwilling, to admit how clear it is that this initial encounter with a leopard colored his opinion of the animal for the rest of his life, despite the fact that sneaking through the bush while hunting for food and eating carrion when nothing else is available are simple animalistic matters of trying to stay alive. For Carl, all animals were collectible, but every collectible animal fell into two categories: disreputable or respectable. In that latter category elephants seemed to reign. He also knew good, sportsmanlike hunting and cheap, shameful hunting.[3] As a collector he didn't get to discriminate; he shot the animals that were needed, and as we've seen he shot many more. And despite the stories he told, despite the heroics, despite the fact that he'd reportedly decline to skin certain shot elephants if their tusks, upon closer inspection, weren't large enough for display (opting all the same to "content [him]self" with taking said puny tusks and selling them), despite the ease with which he seemed to sleep at night, Carl also reports not to ever really enjoy collecting. He loved Africa, but not necessarily the role these expeditions placed in him.

> While I have found but little enjoyment in shooting any kind of animal, I confess that in hunting elephants and lions under certain conditions I have always felt that the animal had sufficient chance in the game to make it something like a sporting proposition. On the other hand, much of the shooting that I have had to do in order to obtain specimens for museum collections has had none of this aspect at all and has made me feel a great deal like a murderer.

It's an interesting binary to fit all animals into: those who make their collection feel honorable and just, and those who render this experience as murderous. Some animals will kill you as needed and others

---

[3] A similar distinction is made by hunting researchers (yes, they exist) between nature hunting and sport hunting, which I'll return to in chapter 7.

will just try to run away, but neither's a match for the bullet. Wild donkeys and zebras, thus, were no fun. Shooting them "makes one uncomfortable," Carl wrote. Ditto rhinos. Delia seems not to have shared this trouble. On Carl's second trip to Africa for the Field Museum, in 1905, she was able to accompany him along with two other members of the zoology department (Elliot was on the outs), and the only designs behind her being there seem to be that she was Carl Akeley's wife with dreams of seeing more of the world than a museum staffer's wife traditionally could expect to. Early on in the trip she became bored staying at the camp while the men went out in the wild, and she started to venture out on little solo collection expeditions of her own, trapping insects with nets and such, until eventually this, too, became tiresome enough that she decided she would begin carrying a gun and heading out across the plains to hunt the big game her husband sought and shot and brought victoriously back to camp. One afternoon she took a gun and a gun boy and went out and shot down an eland—an *illegal* eland, Carl informed her on her triumphant return. She had to pay a $25 fine. This didn't begin to deter her.

Delia wrote her own book on her African adventures—two books, actually, *Jungle Portraits* being the longer and more substantial one, with a structure that very much follows Carl's African memoir. Carl's book has chapters titled "My Acquaintance with Lions" and "Hunting the African Buffalo," and Delia's got "Apes and Monkeys" and "Crocodiles." The point, it seems, was to spend whole chapters describing the exotic animals native to the continent for an audience of Westerners who'd have to wait decades before nature programs showed them what these animals looked like and how they lived their lives. It's hard to remember this wasn't common knowledge a hundred years ago. Even as late as 1925, when Carl's book was published, no one had ever fully observed the methods that lions use while hunting. Carl assumes it's the male who does the hunting for the pride. "I think that the zebra is thrown by the lion's spring and then killed by a bite in the back of the neck, but this impression is from deduction and not from observation," he writes. Back then, Carl's and Delia's books must have been page-turners, but to a contemporary audience, they're sluggish and nigh on unreadable in parts. This, I think, is due to the form each chapter takes: the hunting narrative. It has three parts: the animal is seen; the animal is tracked; the animal is shot at. The only variation is in the climax: whether or not the bullet hits the beast. If not, the hunting narrative simply continues and continues and continues until the animal falls. For a story, the plot's all too predictable. No one gets hurt or killed (save for the animal). No one reveals himself to be a long-lost relative. No one wakes up from a coma with some surprise evidence. No one eventually discovers that the hunter was in fact a huntress. All that happens is a delay of the inevitable, the moving from turning point to climax as sluggish as a two-day trek through the savanna.

Carl's run-in with the leopard is famous for this reason. It bucks the standard model. Someone does get hurt. The story really begins not with Carl seeking an ostrich, but with that leopard poised in the air, for here is the moment where everything has changed. This is why it's the story we all continue to tell about Carl well after he died. All this is to say that the best hunting stories involve pain or loss of limb (or life) on the part of the hunter. The reasons for this are maybe twofold.

One: we like a sense of danger.

Two: we like a sense of justice.

What comes to mind here is Travis Morrison's "Song for the Orca":

This song is for the orca
swimming round in circles at Sea World.
Someday you'll drown the dude with the clipboard, someday.
This song is for the gator
laying in the roadside cage in F.L.A.
You'll tear the cracker to shreds, someday.

We'll all read about you in *USA Today,*
and it feels so nice that the Lord made this day,
and it feels so right to know that justice will have its say.

Museum expeditions to Africa around the turn of the twentieth century followed the safari model, where the white hunter-collector was assisted by upward of a hundred native men, all of them known to the *bwana* ("master") as only "boy." Twenty-year-old men, thirtysomething men, men Akeley's age, men with children to feed on a collecting expedition for the easy money he could make carrying supplies. They were boys, suddenly. When out searching for *Panthera leo* or *Gazella thomsonii* or *Giraffa camelopardalis,* the white hunter-collector took the shot with his gun boy crouched at his side, a fresh-loaded gun at the ready. When the animal fell, it fell to the porters—the bottom of the safari totem pole—to skin and butcher the animal. Carl often helped with the skinning. Some jobs were too big, and some kills too important for Carl to trust to the hired boys. On his second trip for the Field Museum in 1905, Carl exceeded the number of elephants he could legally shoot, and he still needed more for the grand group he'd envisioned for the museum. It was up to Delia to shoot one for him, and once she did, Carl rolled up his sleeves and got to work.

First, before a single cut was made, the elephant—an adult male—got to pose, dead, for a long series of photographs. Carl yelled at the porters to prop up a leg here and fan out an ear there, and he got up close with a camera to capture the details it would be his job to capture back in Chicago, the wrinkles around the jowls and brisket, the folds in the haunches.[4] He blocked out distractions, working very quickly and very methodically. There were only so many day-

---

[4] Later, he would use a stereoscopic camera to capture these details in three dimensions, thus getting a better sense of an animal's contours.

light hours, even in the height of summer. Once he got the pictures he needed, he pulled from his bag a calipers and tape measure and got to work hefting the animal carcass in his own two hands, pawing the thing like a lecherous tailor. Eye to eye. Shoulder blade to shoulder blade. Shoulder to foot. Tip to the tusk to tip of the tusk and trunk to tail. He tweezed each toe between the calipers, the heel, the knee. At several strategic locations along the lengthy trunk, moving quickly, always quickly, getting a sense of the scale of his trophy when the animal, as Mary Jobe Akeley writes, still had "the warmth of life in its body." In his pants pocket he carried with him a small leather-bound notebook, every day, and here was each measurement—more than thirty overall—recorded in pencil. And then it was time to pull the whole hide off. Recall from Jumbo the thickness of an elephant's hide, about twelve inches in places. Removed from the body, the sum of it weighed almost a ton. As Carl and his gun boy, Bill, cut into the flesh, porters ran to and from the camp with as much salt as they could carry. Freshly sharpened knives helped to both remove the skin and pare it down. The fleshing process was, as always, the hardest part, winnowing that thick skin down to just about an inch—a thickness Carl could finally work with. It could take days, porters bringing wet blankets and erecting little tarps to block out the ruinous sun. When the skin was all thinned out, porters covered it in salt. Carpeted it, really, wall-to-wall, an even pouring like a fresh snowfall. Anything less and the hide would spoil in the weeks and sometimes months it could take to ship back to the States for final preparation. The full hide was split in manageable, carryable lengths and rolled up in canvas. Carl always took the skull, and, of course, the tusks. The rest of the carcass was left for the natives. Word would spread as soon as Carl took his first snapshot that an elephant had been felled. The flesh could feed a whole tribe for a month. Apparently, it tastes "stringy" or "gamey," like moose or elk meat does.

For the Akeleys, Africa was the place where their love for each other began to wane. Or maybe diffuse is the better verb. To hear them write about it, separately, one eight years after the other, you'd think the two had only occasionally glimpsed the other out in some near distance, like a quarry never met. In their memoirs, spousal references are fleeting and scattershot. "Mr. Akeley gave the necessary instructions." "The following morning an attack of malaria kept Mr. Akeley in camp." Delia gets rendered as little more than a direct object. "Cunninghame helped Mrs. Akeley up a convenient tree." "He told Mrs. Akeley he was not afraid for himself but was afraid for his *Bwana*." And yet Carl devotes an entire chapter to Bill, his devoted Kenyan gun boy. Bill, who was just thirteen when Carl first met him. Or: was just "a little, naked, thirteen-year-old 'Kuke' with great black eyes." Bill, who "never was and never will be completely tamed." Bill, who "was the best tracker as well as the most keen and alert hunter, black or white, that [Carl] had ever known." Bill, who rarely left Carl Akeley's side in the fifteen months of the second Field expedition and the more than twenty-two months of the ill-fated first AMNH expedition, the endless one that nearly killed Carl. It is the purpose of a gun boy in a safari to be a kind of supplicant, often literally bowing at the feet of the white hunter as the latter stands with a bead on an animal, the gun boy silent and close with a loaded gun at the ready to hand upward. Reverence is the desired affect, here. Big, trusting Bambi eyes. The gun boy then received the spent rifle and reloaded it as fast as he could, particularly if the animal shot at was a rhino now charging horn first at his *bwana*. It was a kind of safaric law that the gun boy, though always equipped with a gun, was never actually allowed to shoot that gun, unless the *bwana* was under fatal attack, and even then it was almost like he had to be given the greenlight to, okay, yes, please shoot the animal that is gnawing on my ribcage. Just once did Bill ever shoot without Carl's saying to, while the two men were stalking elephants and one ran off upon sighting Carl's head peeking out over some dense undergrowth. The elephant was running away from Carl, but Bill, who couldn't quite see, thought she was running toward, and he fired his backup rifle directly into the elephant's face. This caused the tusker she was standing near—Carl's prize in this situation—to run off out of sight. Carl wheeled around and slapped Bill, backhanded, right across the face. Bill and his rifle fell to the jungle floor.

Bill didn't fire blindly, Carl soon realized. He'd only been trying to protect his *bwana*. Immediately, he wished he could take that backhand back and apply it, perhaps, to himself. His words on the matter, in *In Brightest Africa*, are telling: "Bill's heart was broken, and my apologies were forthcoming and were as humble as the dignity of a white man would permit."

The ongoing Bill-Carl relationship is the exact sort of thing Leslie Fiedler would have been all over had it appeared not in history but in a novel—one written by Melville, say. Reading Carl Akeley's words on Africa, it's as though for him the continent were some grand territory he could light out for, eschewing the domestic and replacing the trappings of a marriage with the looseness and adventure of male camaraderie he found in Bill, much as Ishmael found in Queequeg and Huck in Jim. It's unclear whether Carl and Delia even shared the same tent.[5] No, I'm not trying to imply that in Africa Carl found his sexual release elsewhere, but inarguably Bill, whom everyone but Carl knew as Wimbia Gikungu, was so loyal in his job that such loyalty brought out in Carl a reflexive devotion and affection he hadn't planned on finding over there. At one point

---

[5] About their sex life, Penelope Bodry-Sanders is characteristically speculative. "Mickie was a passionate, loving woman. Carl, on the other hand, always focused more on his work than relationships. One senses in him a low libido, occasionally surfacing ravenously, but once satisfied, put safely [!!!] to rest for a time."

during Carl's second Field expedition, Bill was accused of stealing from another white hunter in the party, an accusation that Bill—whose loyalty, according to Carl, was matched only by his pride—got enraged by. He became belligerent upon needing to give up his things for inspection, and Carl, while admittedly on the side of his gun boy, was forced by safari conventions to give Bill up to the local authorities. He was put in jail, and the safari continued on. Carl thought he'd lost Bill forever. Weeks and weeks later Carl was on Mount Kenya, following the trail of an elephant. As he puts it, "I had been longing for Bill all morning because of certain trouble we were having with our boys."

> Just as we were about to leave the pit to continue our march up the mountain side I heard a voice behind me:
>
> "*Jambo, Bwana.*"
>
> I recognized Bill's voice. I turned and saw the most disreputable Bill that I had ever seen. His clothing was worn to shreds, his shoes were practically all gone, and the only thing about him that was perfectly all right was his grin. I wanted to hug him.

Bill was so skilled at tracking that once he'd been released from jail he'd been able to find the safari's trail and follow it right to Carl. Bill met up with Carl's expedition again in 1909, on the hunt for a whole group of elephants for the AMNH. Toward the end of the expedition Carl was often so hindered by illness that he couldn't leave his tent. (You'll soon understand why.) Some days found him in a hospital with blackwater fever brought on by an attack of malaria. He spent much of the time unconscious, but at one point he awoke and looked out his window, where he saw Bill, standing out on the porch, gazing back at him. "There . . . was Bill, like a faithful dog."

It seemed to me that he stood there for hours with tears in his eyes staring at his master. A few days later he was allowed to come to my room. He approached the foot of the bed with a low *"Jambo, Bwana."*

I said, "It is all right, Bill; I'll soon be well."

With a great gulping sob, he burst into tears and bolted from the room.

Or such is the way Carl keeps putting it. And while the bulk of *In Brightest Africa* is taken up by Akeley's love affairs with the elephant and with Bill, Delia starts her book with a loving if rather condescending account of "our primitive neighbors"—all of them always, it seems, described as "dusky"—and follows this chapter with her longest in the book: "Apes and Monkeys," revealing for us the objects she found in Africa toward which she could direct that passion of hers we keep reading about. Delia never says where this obsession with monkeys came from, and Bodry-Sanders doesn't bother to speculate, but at some point during her first trip to Africa (i.e., Carl's second, the 1905–1906 expedition), she began watching the baboons and wild monkeys hanging literally out in the vicinity of their camps and became such an expert amateur primatologist that she felt she could not only distinguish among the animals' inherent attractiveness ("Of all the African monkeys, the guezeras . . . are the handsomest"), but she could also, she once wrote, "converse . . . in monkey language as I heard them doing with one another."

It doesn't take an amateur primatologist to think that Delia must have been looking for some kind of companionship. She was reportedly baby-mad by the time she and Carl first arrived together in Nairobi, where, upon seeing Bill, she wanted to adopt him, and since Carl was completely disinterested in bringing a baby back to the States with them, she started to adopt monkeys. Adopt and defend them. For the 1909 AMNH expedition, the Akeleys were accompanied by, among other people, John T. McCutcheon, a cartoonist for the *Chicago Tribune,* and one day in camp McCutcheon and Akeley and some other men got to talking about collecting animals for museums versus caging them in zoos. The argument was put forth that monkeys were filthy animals, owing to the status of their cages. Such an insinuation made Delia stand up and take her Mickie out on all the men. They hadn't spent half the time watching monkeys as she had. They didn't know what she did, that the very monkeys she'd been spending all her time with while they were out shooting game were clean and loving animals, and if their zoo cages were dirty it was the fault of the humans that encaged the animals in the first place. She then resolved to prove this to them, by baiting a basket trap with some corn and capturing a young vervet monkey. "She was so pretty and saucy," Delia wrote later, "that when we left the Tana River camp a few days later, I decided to take the irresistible little creature with me."

Such is the way J. T. Jr., named for the doubting McCutcheon, came into the Akeleys' life. It would be years before she left it.

The relationship between Delia and J. T. is so odd and so unbelievable that it probably warrants a whole book of its own. Fortunately, Delia wrote such a book, *"J. T. Jr.": The Biography of an African Monkey,* published in 1928. It is, above all, a love story between Delia and a monkey, or, more specifically, between Delia's mother instincts and an animal that refused to play the part of a child. To study her quarry more closely Delia kept her tied to a post, but in the day's long heat the sun made J. T. cry and wail. Delia, "touched by her distress" hired Ali, her tent boy, to be J. T.'s caretaker. She bought Ali a khaki suit befitting his promotion, which he topped with a bright red fez. It must have been a darling little image for Delia. "Every morning Ali appeared at the door of my tent with J. T.'s breakfast," she wrote. "His round, happy, chocolate-brown face shone from a compulsory application of soap. It was a joy to see his lovely white teeth flash when he smiled and his big black eyes melt with childish delight under J. T.'s royal welcome."

J. T. got her own "compulsory application of soap" each afternoon at three, thereby rendering Delia's original cleanliness experiment bunk. She'd travel from campsite to campsite on Ali's tiny shoulders. Delia took dozens of photographs of J. T. In them, she looks a lot like Phyllis Diller in blackface. Delia began to set up play dates for J. T. and other toy monkeys on safari—particularly one belonging to a district commissioner's wife. Her name was Peggy. That is, the monkey's name was Peggy. She and J. T. didn't get along. Delia brought J. T. into her bed every night. *Her bed!* The monkey would lie with her head resting on Delia's shoulder, and jump up with a screech at any errant noise. Years after her death, Delia wrote that she could "almost feel her little velvety hand grasping my nose and shutting off my breath and her furry body, all moist and warm, pressing against my head."

Imagine waking up to this. Every morning. Imagine entering your wife's tent at night and seeing a monkey there in her cot, draped like a stole around her shoulders, glaring distrustfully at you. Could there have been a clearer sign to Carl that, no thanks, I'd rather not share my bed with you tonight? Or was it that J. T.'s installation in Delia's tent was more curative than prophylactic? Did it fill a hole Carl had already begun to carve out of their marriage?

What's clear is that Carl thought very little of Delia's taking a wild animal out of the wild and that Delia either wouldn't acknowledge this or couldn't. On a train across the African plain Delia carried J. T. into the coach room, and the animal, freaked way out by steam hissing from engines and shoes smacking cement and luggage clattering into racks, scrambled in Delia's arms and bit her on the hand. She didn't break the skin, but, as Delia wrote, "the pain brought tears to my eyes." Carl came in and read what had happened, his wife's face crumpled in willed self-composure, J. T. looking maniacally out the window. "You need to punish her," he said. "Or she's going to do it again." But Delia didn't move. She didn't even say a word. "It was then," she wrote later, "that I realized how little we understand captive animals. J. T. was like a frightened child and needed all our sympathy. Then and there I made the resolution never to punish her nor permit any one [sic] else to do so, no matter what she did, a resolution which I kept during the nine years she was with me."

She'd take no advice, hear no criticisms about this new venture of her life, this careless adoption of a vervet monkey that had no business living among people. J. T. wasn't of the jungle. She wasn't the responsibility of others. J. T. was Delia's now.

If the true subject of every collection is the collector himself, what does it say about the 1909 AMNH expedition that the only official quarry were elephants? Four of them, to be precise, to be mounted as a group—more than any other museum in the country at the time. After seeing all that Carl had done in Chicago—*The Four Seasons,* the duo of elephants mounted in attack and titled *The Charging Bulls*—AMNH President Henry Fairfield Osborn secured the money to steal Carl from the Field Museum and send him to Africa. He and Delia had $25,000 and all the time they needed. They had fellow safarists McCutcheon and Fred Stephenson, a big-game hunter from Minnesota. What they also had, though they may not have known it at the time, was Carl's total size queenery when it came to collecting. Here's a man whose first elephant mount was Jumbo, itself made larger than its already high sixteen-foot frame by Barnum's demands. Ten- or twelve-foot tuskers wouldn't do. Carl needed the largest on the continent.

Elephants, as animals, are distinguished by their hide, size, and tusks, but there are other large pachyderms out there, other animals with tusks, and so the true distinguishing feature of an elephant is its trunk. An elephant's trunk can curl around the waist of a grown man and throw him fifty yards or more. It can carefully strip the leaves from a high branch. An elephant's trunk can siphon up water and spray some down its throat, or over the body of another elephant. When in danger, or when danger is sensed, a herd of elephants—and elephants are great, happy herd animals—will raise their trunks like parasols to the sky, twirling them about, sniffing for whatever may be in the distance. You could be two football fields away from an elephant, three even, but if those were all upwind yards the elephant would run away from you, no matter how quiet you were. They are, one can imagine, notoriously tough to track and hunt. Should an elephant want to move past you in the jungle without making a sound, it could. Like a basketball, the foot of an elephant expands as it hits the ground and then compresses as it's lifted; thus can they travel fleetly through swamps without getting stuck. Should you find success in tracking an elephant, and should you bring that elephant down (and should that elephant be among a herd), it is possible that its comrades in the herd will stop running away from the noise your gun has made and will return to the fallen body, using tusks and trunks and their enormous shoulders—imagine the power needed to carry a one-ton skin around—to try to lift the elephant back on its feet and off to safety. Elephants have been recorded returning to the sites where loved ones have died, communing with bones in clear mourning.

Also: "There are elephants in Kenia [sic] that have never lain down for a hundred years," according to Carl Akeley. And elephants in a herd communicate pending danger using infrasonic tones we can't hear without machines. And elephants know that what makes them susceptible to danger is the valuable ivory of their tusks, Bodry-Sanders writes, and so they'll surround tuskers when they sense danger, making it hard even to see a tusk much less get a shot at the animal carrying one.

In Brightest Africa is full of all sorts of fun facts about elephants, which was undoubtedly the animal that most occupied the thoughts of Carl Akeley. If he loved Bill, he adored the elephant. "I have come to the conclusion that of all the wild animals on this earth now, the African elephant is the most fascinating," he wrote in 1923, even after his years of hunting gorillas. By my count he collected three for the Field Museum and a whopping fifteen for the AMNH while on that 1909 expedition. He shot and killed countless others. He was, by 1910, elephant mad. Having shot all four elephants his original permit allowed, he asked the Ugandan Chief Secretary for permission to shoot four more and to shoot in the preserves.[6] Permission was granted. He once made an eight-hour trek to track a bull whose tusks he liked, only to leave the animal dead upon seeing a tumor cluttering the side of his face. Carl wouldn't stop, and after McCutcheon had bagged the lion he'd been hoping for and returned with his skin back home, after Teddy Roosevelt and his son Kermit had met up with the Akeleys and gone back home, after the AMNH wired the couple to inform them that all funds had run out, and after Akeley had tried to sell his recently deceased father's farm back in Clarendon, Carl still had not collected his perfect tusker. Bodry-Sanders makes the call when she reads Akeley as Ahab, on the search for his elusive white whale.

Instead of a tusker, he'd contracted malaria and suffered bouts of fever and dysentery, but he was somehow able to make it to Nairobi to convince safari outfitters Newland & Tarlton to loan him money to continue the hunt. Delia dragged him to the Uasin Gishu plateau, out in western Kenya, where the climate helped Carl recover. "Then one day, in a reckless moment," she writes, "we decided to trek across Mt. Kenya and go to the top." The mountain had supposedly been the Akeleys' first love, and Delia tried to lessen the distance that had

---

[6] This is interesting given that a decade later a very different Carl Akeley would begin work on establishing a gorilla preserve in the Kivu Mountains.

grown between them by taking a trip to the mountain's peak. Carl, though feeble, was game, and for a few days took photographs of the bamboo forests high up on the mountain as field research for some planned dioramas. He took Bill and a handful of porters with him on what was to be a short four-day excursion, two days up and two back. At some point the first day, they all came across the trail of three bull elephants, and Carl couldn't resist abandoning something as pissantish as a photo safari for a chance at his dream bull, his golden tusker. It took two whole days to track the elephants down (the minute detailing of which is the exact sort of thing that makes *In Brightest Africa* damn near unreadable), and Carl was finally able to get near enough to make sure his guns were in working order. This was the morning of the third day. The air at that hour was cool and wet—they were more than nine thousand feet above sea level—and as he waited for a sign of the elephants, Carl hopped from foot to foot and rubbed his hands together. What happened next concerns one of those weird, almost paranormal phenomena that's hard to put down on paper. The way you can be sitting in a chair with a pair of headphones on playing ear-crunching, sound-drowning music and just sort of know that there's a person now standing right behind you. That chill you get sometimes running down your back when certain strangers pass closely by. We are creatures of mass and we are physically—as in like physics—attracted in varying degrees to one another, and when you are standing just inches away from an elephant's mass, if your back is turned and you haven't heard a thing you'll just suddenly know it. The electrons jumping microscopically out from your body will tell you.

Carl's electrons all fired at once, and Carl turned to face two enormous tusks curving at him like weaponry. Here he was: the perfect tusker. He tried to fire his rifle but the gun was jammed. Before he could try again, the elephant swung those tusks right at Carl's chest. By reflex, Carl grabbed one tusk with his left hand, another with his right, and swung himself through like a gymnast, landing on his back on the ground. The elephant weighed approximately one hundred times what Carl weighed.[7] At that point it was another law of physics at work: the elephant sank himself right down on Carl, hoping to crush him. By luck, its tusks got stuck in the dirt. By bad luck, the elephant was able to swing his trunk inward, breaking Carl's nose and—with the heavy bristles that cluster along the underside—tear open his cheek. The elephant then laid his trunk on top of Carl's chest and did what its body wasn't able to. "I heard a wheezy grunt as he plunged down," Carl wrote, "and then—oblivion."

Bill and the porters were long gone, fearing for their lives. Delia was back at camp, where she was holding daily clinics for nearby natives on Western medicine. By sundown on the third day since Carl had headed out, she saw Bill approach camp with another porter. Carl was not with them. "Tembo piga bwana," Bill is reported to have said. *Elephant has struck master.* The light was disappearing. The animals in the jungle that woke up at night began waking up and chattering in the trees. Delia wanted to leave immediately. She sent two runners to the "nearest white official," a day's journey from camp. She told Bill to ready twenty men. The natives were proverbially restless about going through the dark forests at night, glaring at her with "black looks" and murderous intent, and in desperation Delia bullied them all into heading out. It took them a whole day of marching through rain-flooded sinkholes and slick mountain inclines to find her husband, and she writes that her first task upon arriving at Carl's tent was first aid. One eye of Carl's was swollen shut, and the forehead was busted open and scabby. His nose was bent up, squashed against his face. She could see the pearls of his bicuspids through a gaping hole in his cheek. Every couple of minutes, Carl spit up blood. Delia got to work. "The fact that his wounds were cared for so promptly prevented infection," she writes, "and without doubt saved his life."

---

[7] Imagine three Humvees. Imagine them being dropped right on you.

These words were written after she and Carl divorced. After his death, even, at a time when the legacy of Carl Akeley was something handled in full by his second wife, Mary Jobe Akeley. Delia has so much riding on this account of Carl's elephant attack that concludes her book, *Jungle Portraits*. She needs not to be wiped out of the narrative of Carl's life, especially because Mary Jobe Akeley will, ten years later, enact just such an erasure in her own biography of Carl. Compare Delia's words, though, with Carl's, himself writing after his divorce from Delia: "I don't suppose I would have pulled through even with Mrs. Akeley's care if it hadn't been for the Scotch medical missionary who nearly ran himself to death coming to my rescue."

One year later, incredibly, Carl and Delia would still be in Africa, the former's madness infesting the latter. "Whenever I closed my eyes," Delia wrote, "an endless procession of elephants charged down upon me, with their trunks and legs all tangled up in a nightmare of tropical vines. My head, arms, and legs seemed to swell up until they were as enormous as elephants' trunks and legs. They *were* elephants' trunks and legs and they *were* distorted vines!" Carl began writing such lines in his journals as "I must kill a Tembo today." It is hard to imagine what Delia *did* that whole time, every day for a year watching her husband leave camp on the trail of a tusker and come back empty-handed, their companions gone, J. T. Jr. demanding her affections and attentions, the sun hitting the thick canvas of tent for more and more hours each day as the summer sun rose ever higher in the sky, the dust that daily coated her throat. Her temples throbbed and she lay still for hours. Only at sundown could she find the energy to move, to write frantic letters. "I don't think," she wrote, in one, "we'll ever see America again."

What is it that makes a collector? To figure this out, we may want to try to understand just what it is that turns one man's trash into another man's treasure. Put more literally, what are the parameters by which an object gains or loses value as it moves through the global marketplace? Any sort of object, from anywhere, can become a collectible. Modiglianis. Vintage American musical scores. Beer cans. Animals. Susan M. Pearce, a prolific theorist on museum and individual collections, lays out the world of collectible objects among two axes:

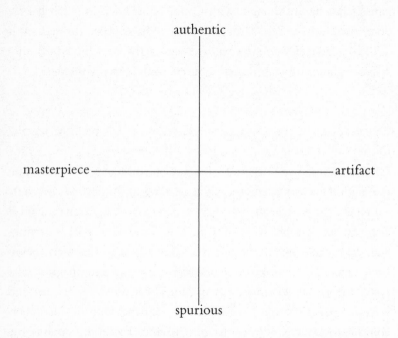

Starting in the top left quadrant (authentic masterpieces) and moving clockwise, what seems to happen is that the audience for each approach to collection decreases and specializes. That is, it's very easy for people to accept the need to collect and preserve authentic masterpieces—the *Mona Lisa,* Chartres, the original copy of the Declaration of Independence. As Pearce says, an authentic object "carries with it not only the notion of 'real' in the forensic sense, but also the feeling of 'genuine' in the emotional sense, of sincerity, honesty and truthfulness after its own kind. . . . Authenticity in material goods is the moral equivalent of lifelong friendship between people, the essence of honourable dealing." There's a kind of self-improvement we feel when we collect authentic masterpieces; we're surrounding ourselves with the best that has ever been made. Moving to authentic artifacts—aboriginal tools, John Wilkes Booth's revolver, *Antiques Roadshow* stuff—their history gives them value and makes them worth preserving. It's in the third quadrant, spurious artifacts, where people start asking questions. For here, history is gone, or at least it's drastically foreshortened, and these collectibles' mass-produced qualities remove any sense of authenticity from the object. So many of any given Wheaties box. So many Falstaff cans. "Collections made from commercially available artefacts [sic] are boring and tasteless," Pearce writes. "They fail to engage our deepest sympathies and lack the capacity to move us, unless . . . they have acquired human meaning." Thus, the audience for appreciating collections drops drastically as we move from the second to third quadrants. Indeed, in some collections of spurious artifacts, the only person capable of appreciation—the only person who can know the collection's value—is the collector.[8]

The final quadrant, spurious masterpieces, are those elements of kitsch or giftware that are just as mass-produced as those objects in quadrant 3, but which present themselves (spuriously) as one-of-a-kind, must-have items. "Collectibles" in other words. "Their kinship with fine art," Pearce writes, "rests in the fact that they too have no overt . . . functional or practical purpose." Whereas spurious artifacts begin their lives in some form of utility—transporting milk, containing a bag of flaked cereal—the *raison* for spurious masterpieces' *d'être* is to end up in a collection. Commemorative plates. Place-based spoons so tiny they can hold little more than one's mild

---

[8] My CD boxes—of albums only I loved in the aggregate—fit precisely in this quadrant.

admiration. These "unlovely" objects, as Pearce calls them, exist for, are sold to, and can only be appreciated by an audience of one. In this way they are like fetishes—resembling nothing we know from the worlds of nature, culture, or commerce but embodying an intense, idealized mythos.

Guess where Pearce puts taxidermized hunting trophies.

"The spurious essence of this kind of material rests in its intention to produce itself as 'important' when against traditional tests it is not," she writes. In other words, the hunting trophy is spurious because its value is assumed by the guy who shot it to be universal, museum ready. But while museum taxidermy might have universal value—not necessarily for its one-of-a-kind quality, but more for its authenticity as a representative of the species—trophies do not. They tell us nothing of an animal and are in no way authentic; indeed rarely do they include the animal in its entirety. A game head is to an authentic animal what for certain evangelical Christians the New Testament is to the word of God. You might think you've got the most important part, but there's a whole other half of the Bible missing.[9]

So to return to our question of what turns trash into treasure, the answer seems to lie in which quadrant of stuff a collector's got his or her eye on. Thus, it's somewhat spatial; trash in one place can become treasure through a simple change in locale. Witness Duchamp's urinal. But this isn't the only way that objects can be transformed. Time,

---

[9] Incidentally, the whole gamut of animal preservation can be mapped across Pearce's four quadrants. Museum-grade taxidermy, the stuff Carl Akeley made, as well as those award winners at the World Taxidermy Championships are taxidermy's authentic masterpieces, whereas skins and pelts, owing to their practical use, are authentic artifacts. Taxidermy's spurious artifact is without a doubt the lucky rabbit's foot, especially if it's connected to a little metal chain and made into a keyring. And sharing quadrant 4 with hunting trophies are jackalopes and any other form of novelty taxidermy—kittens in human clothing, frogs tending bar, etc.

Pearce argues, can make an unloved thing have value. This happens over the course of a single life, when "the humblest T-shirts and sweet wrappers can bring thoughts that lie too deep for tears if we find them while sorting out the belongings of the newly dead," but also over the course of history. Mass-produced or handmade, objects of little value today can become treasure tomorrow, leading Pearce to this rethinking of our original question: "this century's rubbish becomes the next century's meaningful artefact."

When I say that my father is not a collector, when I say that whatever collections I had as a child were few and soon abandoned, what exactly do I mean? Or, more specifically, *why* are father and son not collectors?[10] *Why,* given the same sort of emotional attachment to Camper Van Beethoven as any major fan, would I not even accept an old CD longbox of their album if it were offered to me for free? According to Pearce, only about a third of the population acquires objects for the purpose of collections—making it, statistically speaking, deviant behavior. Thus, there's been a whole mess of psychological study on what turns a person into a collector, and in the end even Pearce is unable to pin it down. "A combination of circumstance, accident and particular traits of personality means that for some people the qualities and possibilities which objects carry are particularly significant," she writes. "Collecting people have the capacity to bring their emotions and imaginations to bear on the world of objects, and are able to nourish these qualities by objects."

---

[10] I'm probably being disingenuous. There were the CD longboxes and the concert ticket stubs. The Garbage Pail Kids collection and the baseball cards. The editions of *Alice in Wonderland*. The crewelwork from the 1970s. I've collected, at varying times of my life, all of these, and that I still don't consider myself a collector says more about my poor sense of self-awareness than it does about the ethos of collecting.

Most of us, then, do not have this capacity, are not able to connect or root emotions in the world of objects. Does it follow that most taxidermists are the same? In considering the role of the hunting trophy, I want to consider the animal as object. I want to try to understand what makes an animal a thing to be hunted and what makes it a thing to be collected. And so the question follows: when do hunting and taxidermy become collecting pursuits? Take two different hunters: one goes out annually during his local deer season with some friends and family and over the years has collected one, maybe two deer he keeps on his wall as a tool for memory; the other goes on hunting trips across the globe, is a member of Safari Club International, keeps at least a mental if not printed checklist of animals he'd like to hunt, and has a whole room in his home full of game heads and thrilling stories behind the collection of each. Are these hunters different in kind or in degree?

Lee Dunekacke is a sixty-three-year-old farmer with a spread in Rising City, Nebraska, about a two-hours' drive due west from Omaha. His property, Dunekacke admits, is "very small," at least by Nebraska standards. Four hundred acres. In thirty-plus years those acres have been trod by hogs and cattle, turkeys and pheasants, and they've pushed up annual crops of corn, sorghum, soy, wheat, and milo. More wild rhubarb than Dunekacke knows what to do with. He's been hunting deer since he was seventeen and has, as he says, "every horn from every deer" he's ever shot. It's about twenty-five antlers, all told, some of them hung right up in the workshop behind his house. And the reason he has every horn from every deer he's ever shot is that every deer he's ever shot has been a buck. Every season, Dunekacke buys a permit and, if he's lucky, shoots one buck. "I have not shot a doe to this day," he says. "I just could not bring myself to do it."[11] This conversation happened on the phone

---

[11] He's also never encouraged anyone to hunt, not even his son, who came to it on his own. "I'm very protective of it," he says. "I know that if

one morning, and Dunekacke (say *doon*-uh-kak-ee) spoke with care throughout. It was like the man was handing over, bit by bit, his attitudes about hunting and deer conservation (he has personal interests in both), offering them to me to hold onto awhile. We'd met a few times before, face-to-face. I deejayed his daughter's wedding (that is, I stood behind the iTunes'd laptop at his daughter's wedding) and visited his farm out in Rising City one warm June evening before his daughter and son-in-law moved from Nebraska to Arkansas. Here I was shown the antlers in "The Shop" and the two mounted whitetail heads in "The Man Cave" attached to the shop's south side, a room with air conditioning where Dunekacke and his associates can relax with a beer. These comprise the alpha and omega of his animal collection: twenty-five antlers and just two heads. Only two?

The first has no particular story behind it. Was just a deer Dunekacke found, a "fairly decent" deer as he calls it, walking in the right field at the right time. He shot the buck and had it butchered into meat for the rest of the year. A friend of his was learning to be a taxidermist at the time and offered to mount it for free. As practice. It's a fine effort. As a taxidermy mount it presents all the parts of a deer's head in the right place, but no one would ever give the thing a ribbon. Carl Akeley would probably take one look at it and laugh, but Dunekacke's not interested in other people's awe or respect. He's interested in deer, in going out on a nice piece of land once a year and hunting a buck. Often with his son, who was there when Dunekacke shot the other deer he has mounted. "That day was so special," he says. "It was only my son and myself. I got pictures of him and me with our deer in a real special spot. And it's the best

---

everybody wanted to hunt, pretty soon there wouldn't be anything *to* hunt. And so my hunting that I do and I've done all my life is done on seasons and I only shoot one deer. Some people go out there and shoot as many as the game commission will allow."

deer I've ever taken in my life." An eleven-point buck: five tips on one side and six on the other. This time it was his son, Tom, who had a taxidermist friend. The mount hangs across the room from the first one, staring at it with the pride of a pretty girl.

So, again: why only two? And why is it that the idea to mount these two deer came from people other than Lee, the man who shot them? One answer lies in money. "It's quite costly to have one mounted," he says. "And I never did have a lot of money or funds." Is this true? It's hard to know whether Dunekacke's being sincere here, or whether this is a factor of some Great Plains humility when it comes to matters of money. It seems true. The Dunekacke spread is by all accounts a humble one, its house a modest four-bedroom ranch. And as most Nebraska transplants learn soon after they immigrate, these are trying times for the small family farmer. Dunekacke's four hundred acres of farmland are taxed each year, he tells me, at fifty dollars an acre. And yet he has an extensive gun collection, one he's both proud of and secretive about. "I won't tell you that," he says, when I ask how many guns he owns. "But I'll tell you that the oldest gun in my collection is a Winchester shotgun, from the late eighteen hundreds." No word on what he paid for it, if anything, but such a gun can run up to three thousand dollars. He could get a life-size bear mount for those prices. In other words, the money is there to fund the collection, but the costs are too much to spend on something as insignificant, to Dunekacke, as taxidermy.

Lee Dunekacke, then, is a collector, but not a collector of animals. And this provides us with another answer to why he's never gone out of his way to get a deer head mounted. "People mount deer heads because it shows some type of mark that they have achieved," he says. "Maybe the best you've gotten in your life." Dunekacke doesn't see shooting a deer as some kind of achievement. If he wants a trophy, he's got the antlers to hang. What other use could they have?

Richard Heinrich is a big-game hunter with little use for antlers that aren't large and attached to the animal's head—preferably one he's never shot before. His house in Hastings, Nebraska, is clad front to back in brick, and out by the front door he's got one elk antler set among his landscape's white rocks, lying there indiscriminately like some fallen branch. If it's a sign preparing visitors for their experience inside—*Here Be Monsters*—it falls a bit short. For how can a single elk antler prepare one for a life-size lion and lioness flanking the master bedroom's flat-screen television? For the gape-mouthed baboon head hung in the office near a display shelf of toy John Deeres? For the entertainment center's cabinet panels clad in zebra skin? While some hunters fashion themselves a trophy room, Heinrich has hunted on enough continents of the world to award himself a trophy house. There are game heads hung on the walls of just about every room: the great room that used to be a garage (what Heinrich calls the trophy room, because of its size I suppose), the sitting room off the front entryway, the office, the downstairs family room (which seems to get little use now that the great room's got a flat-screen).[12] I recognize very few of the animals. A porcupine mounted in the corner of the great room on top of the house's auxiliary fridge looks wilder and more unkempt than porcupines I've seen on television—quills splayed from its back half like the remnants of some explosion—and I'm told this is because it's an African brush-tailed porcupine. A rodent, technically, and much bigger than what you may be used to. I recognize the boar's head on a pillar behind the sofa and am told it's the head of a warthog. These corrections come not from Heinrich, but Mike Pebeck, his taxidermist and my guide through this house. Heinrich has so many animals he doesn't always identify them correctly. There's a caracal cat sitting on a side table in the living room, which Heinrich calls a

---

[12] I think the kitchen might be taxidermy free, but I visited Heinrich before his latest trip to Africa, so there's no telling what's hanging there now.

"carico cat" before Pebeck corrects him. It faces a lynx lying proudly on a wicker sofa with leopard-print cushions, looking like a pet about to be fed. The caracal is bigger than the lynx in a complicated way, sort of like how a basketball player is bigger than a wrestler. Its limbs are ganglier. Neither looks very real, but this is due more to the overall difficulty of mounting wild cats and the general shoddiness of catalog manikins than it is to any lack of taxidermy skills on Pebeck's part. I mean, witness the musk ox, its eyes glistening, its shaggy hair brushed and hanging sveltely like a prize Pekingese. Witness the tiny grysbok, the majestic and gorgeous red stags. "I like to get animals other people don't have," Heinrich says during my gawking, and if there were a fraternity of animal collectors (well, other than the Safari Club International) this would be its credo. *I like to get animals other people don't have.* Heinrich shows me, by way of example, his bushbuck, his blackbuck—the former a common antelope in South Africa, the latter a native of the Indian subcontinent and classified by the International Union for the Conservation of Nature and Natural Resources as "near threatened" (two clicks away from endangered). In other words: not so rare. His aoudad, however, is classified as "vulnerable," and on the floor near the television is a rug made from the skin of a mountain zebra, also vulnerable. "You can't hunt them anymore," Heinrich says, and there's if not pride in his voice then at least a kind of relief. *Just in time.*

I visit Heinrich's house just weeks before he, Pebeck, and four other men from the area are heading to southern Africa on another safari. There are 110 animals on the wish list for all six men, and they'll have two weeks to get them all. Heinrich wants an alligator ("crocodile," Pebeck corrects), a hippopotamus, a civet, a serval, and a klipspringer, among others. "He thinks he's shot everything in Africa," Pebeck tells me afterward on the drive back to his shop. "But he hasn't." Pebeck's referring specifically to the rarer animals, or the ones whose habitats are tough to access. The Lord Derby eland, he explains, costs $50,000 to shoot. The bongo can cost twice that much.[13] Heinrich has paid to shoot an elephant (which can cost upward of $10,000) but did not pay to ship the hide because a full-size elephant manikin itself costs another $10,000. Plus there's the problem of finding the space for a whole elephant in one's house. (And yet also the potential glee of being able to open fireside talks with "I think it's time we address the elephant in the room.") To compensate, Heinrich kept the tusks and had the ears made into wall paintings—one shows viewers a map of Africa and the other depicts naturalistic views of the "big five." Heinrich has his five, and in fact has as of this writing what's called the "dangerous seven": lion, leopard, elephant, rhino, buffalo, hippo, and crocodile. Black rhinoceroses are critically endangered, one step from extinction, and it's thus much harder, though not impossible, to get permits to hunt the animal. But a white rhinoceros can cost more than $100,000 to hunt, and so many hunters opt for what's called a "green hunt," where the rhino is shot with a tranquilizer dart and is out for the twenty to thirty minutes needed to take some measurements and pose for a photograph. This simulation costs around $8,000. "People pay for this?" I ask Pebeck.

"Rich paid for it," he says. "So many guys do it 'cause they need it for their 'big five,' see?" Then, he explains, if they want to show off their kill they can order a replication head from McKenzie or some other outfitter for another $3,000. You can do this, too. I can do it. We all could call up McKenzie and drop three grand and have shipped to our door a reproduction rhino head. We can hang it on our walls, but what we can't do is show off the photograph of us crouched down near the head of what only *looks* like a dead rhino.

---

[13] This money goes straight to the outfitter, the company a hunter is already paying to organize a whole safari. So add additional costs for permits, ammo, skinning, shipping, mounting, etc., and you've got for one trophy what can buy a whole house for most people.

We can't tell our fated, telic hunting narrative. Maybe every animal collection, every trophy room, is a collection of stories. A wall of heads linked hieroglyphically to one man's obsession. In this way is the taxidermist much like the author—or, better yet, the ghostwriter, taking the raw materials of an experience and fashioning it, through technique, into something legible.

Back at his shop I test this idea on Pebeck. Around us, like some kind of zoological panopticon observing our every move, are the results of his work and the work he has yet to do. The waterbuck, kudu, and elk he plans to take to the Nebraska State Taxidermists Association's annual competition in a couple weeks. Vacant fox and wolf skins hung up like scarves by their snouts. Dozens of antler racks strung up along the ceiling. He's got some vervet monkey skins in a freezer somewhere (cue Delia's subterranean about-face), and it's weird how none of this is weird to me. Just another collection waiting for a kind of display. I see the bird-fleshing wheel in the corner, and I know exactly what it's used for. I see the four power drills lined up along a wall, and I can imagine the parts they bore into. The work of the taxidermist. It's as thrilling as any old job. You get up; you go to work. You pick up things and do with them what you've been trained to do. You send it off when you're finished to whatever client or boss is expecting output. Except the taxidermist doesn't just have to please clients, he has to honor their memories. Most collections can simply be collected. You find the item, and you pay for it. But Heinrich's collection needs to be created for him, and with so many thousands of dollars spent on these animals, he has so much trust put into Pebeck to turn them back into the animals he saw in his sights as he pulled the trigger. How does a taxidermist know what to do with an animal skin he's never seen before? How can he be sure to justify the expense?

Pebeck doesn't romanticize his vocation. He never has and never will hang taxidermy in his own home, for instance. And so he shrugs when he answers me, baffled I'd even bother to ask. "I've mounted some of the most expensive animals on the planet," he says, "and I've mounted the cheapest animals on the planet. So it's all the same to me. Smoke and mirrors, is what it amounts to. Just smoke and mirrors."

SIX

And now we come, at last, to the jackalope. *Jack* as in the rabbit, *alope* as in the antelope. It is an animal as mythic as the chimera, the unicorn, the griffin, the Sasquatch. An animal seen only as a carcass and refuted by all as hokum, fiddle-faddle. And it is hokum. It's fiddle-faddle and poppycock all thrown together. The first, and quite possibly the only, animal myth invented by taxidermy. Oh, you can argue for the Feejee Mermaid, but what made Barnum's ugly little beast such a success were centuries of sea-born myths of lovely looking ladies with the flanks of a fish. Or maybe myths of great big fish with lady parts up top. Regardless, what I mean by all this is that mermaids donned the prows of ships long before some amateur taxidermist got a scheming, trickster's gleam in his eye. The jackalope, however, sprang Athena-like from the head of some gleaming-eyed, amateur taxidermist looking to make—mind the pun—an easy buck. And *then* came the mythology: a rabbit with antlers, roaming the countryside. Cowboys camping on the plains singing yodels by the fire and hearing jackalopes harmonize with them from a distance. It is a hunter's mythology, for anyone can shoot a plain rabbit. Rabbits—or hares, under which genus (*Lepus*) the jackrabbit technically falls—are a dime a dozen. They fuck, proverbially, like bunny rabbits, and a rabbit is an animal whose fur the furrier sews into shawls only in desperation. A fur for the forlorn. But a rabbit with a rack? Why, it's the difference between a poor little doe on your wall versus a proud old stag.

On a walk to dinner with a friend I hadn't seen in a while I mentioned I'd been spending some days thinking about jackalopes. "About what?" he asked, as though I'd made up a new word, and so it seems we have some uninitiated. For those who have maybe never seen a jackalope, much less heard of one, it's actually quite basic. A jackrabbit is to a rabbit what a stallion is to a shetland: larger, ropier, and far more ungainly than something kept in a hutch in the backyard. And while the desperate may go in for a rabbit fur coat, *no one* would pay for a jackrabbit coat, the hair coarser and suited in color less for looking pettable and more for blending into the desert rocks and high grasses, camo'd safely from the coyotes. And the ears! Rabbits are known for having big ears that flop over their heads like pigtails, but the ears that rise from the heads of jackrabbits look insectile, the antennae through which they can receive the signal of your mile-away footfalls. They are proportionate—surprise, surprise—to the horns of the pronghorn antelope, the horns of which shoot up simply from its head and curve slightly inward at the top, as though a giant beetle were emerging mandibles first from the brain. Like prongs, basically, as opposed to the baroque candelabras of the elk and the moose.[1] They're big enough to grab one's attention and small enough to sit right in front of some high jackrabbit ears.

Most jackalopes found around tourist traps and fraternity houses

---

[1] Confusingly, the pronghorn antelope is not an antelope, which like cows and sheep come from the *Bovidae* family. True antelopes have horns made of a keratinous sheath covering actual bone, which sheath stays put throughout the animal's life. Pronghorns shed this keratinous material annually, and then spring about the country with bare-naked bones for a while as new ones grow. This, of course, leads to a kind of horn surplus, and now we're beginning to understand the context in which an economy of cheap-and-easy jackalopes could arise.

and, reportedly, Ronald Reagan's Rancho del Cielo are made not from echt antelope horns but rather "spiked" deer antlers, the ones that fall annually off the heads of male deer too young for hunters to shoot. This, supposedly, was the magical combination that led Douglas Herrick, a taxidermist in Douglas, Wyoming, to come up with the idea to mount the world's first jackalope. As the story goes, it was 1932 and Doug and his brother Ralph came back to the former's taxidermy shop after a morning of hunting with nothing but a jackrabbit, which they tossed like rubbish onto the shop's floor. It landed next to a set of antlers. Douglas's eyes, so says his *New York Times* obituary, "brightened with inspiration." He sold the first one for $10. Douglas—the town in Wyoming, not the enterprising taxidermist who shares its name—is now the official Home of the Jackalope. It has a weekend festival, Jackalope Days, with a free pancake breakfast and something called the Hustle Street Dance that takes place in Jackalope Square. You can call the Douglas Chamber of Commerce up on the phone[2] and ask the folks there for an official jackalope hunting license, and some nice lady will answer the phone and take down your address and get one in the mail probably not that day but definitely the next morning. *For free!* Jackalope hunts are allowed in Wyoming only on 31 June.

I first learned of the jackalope as a kid watching the *America's Funniest Home Videos* spin-off show *America's Funniest People*, cohosted by Arleen Sorkin and Bob Saget's *Full House* comrade Dave Coulier. The show became a necessity once people started submitting to Saget's show videotapes that either had been staged and were just downright hammy—folks telling jokes right to the camera instead of participating in the unexpected caught-on-tape accidents and unrehearsed moments of preciousness that is the *AFV*'s bread and butter, and shortly after *America's Funniest People* premiered, the show began airing crudely taped sketches starring a jackalope. I remember only

---

[2] 877-WE-R-4-WYO.

that said jackalope would either terrorize the unsuspecting or run away from them. Very possibly both. It even had a catch phrase: "Fast as fast can be, you'll never catch me!" Most of it was shot from the animal's POV. It was another year or two before I realized the jackalope was not an invention of the show.

However the myth has grown from its origins, today the jackalope is synonymous with total goofballery. They fill the many rooms of the infamous South Dakota tourist trap Wall Drug almost as much as do "Free ice water!" signs—Ralph Herrick's son Jim supposedly delivers upward of twelve hundred jackalopes to Wall, South Dakota, each year. Ubuntu, the popular distribution of the Linux operating system, released a version titled Jaunty Jackalope— a nod, no doubt, to Apple's habit of naming its OSes after fierce cats. The Odessa Jackalopes of Odessa, Texas, are a team in the Central Hockey League, a double-A franchise that, like the jackalope itself, is decidedly more Western than Central. And there's even a Magic: The Gathering card depicting a jackalope herd. Summoning them costs three mana.

Did you know there's a species of hare in North America called the antelope jackrabbit? *Lepus alleni,* so named for the hind legs with which it can leap over the land like a gazelle. Chances are Douglas Herrick didn't know this, and chances are he also didn't know about the Shope papilloma virus, aka the cottontail rabbit papilloma virus (CRPV), which infects rabbits and hares, causing them to form keratinous growths—made of the same stuff as fingernails, hair, hoofs, and horns—on their faces or their heads. CRPV growing on the former can look grisly: a rabbit with warty fangs frowning at you. But CRPV growing on the latter, five-inch-long growths popping right out the top of the rabbit's head, can look quite jaunty indeed. Sort of like antlers. CRPV was discovered back in the 1930s, but it's been around maybe forever. The Germans have a long-standing mythology of their own involving a horned rabbit they call the *rasselbock* or *wolpertinger,* depending on how *Bayerisch* they are. The first appearance dates to the late eighteenth century, in a plate found in the seminal *Encyclopédie Méthodique*. So the question is: what really happened that late morning in 1932? Did Herrick create something new, or did he use available materials to fashion up a piece of hokum to sell to the public? In short: was he an artist or was he another P. T. Barnum?

Every time Carl Akeley came back from Africa he came back a changed man. Who wouldn't? On his first expedition in 1896 he grew a beard for the first time, the sort of raucous, slobby nest under the neck you see on some shoe-gazing indie rockers, and when he returned to that icy Chicago studio he probably ravished poor Delia with those same roughened hands that had brought a leopard to her death. In 1906 he'd come back the slayer of elephants, taught to be a white hunter by perhaps the most famous white hunter of his time: R. J. Cunninghame. It wasn't just the hunting, the killing, the collecting. It's not that Africa gave Akeley a heightened sense of power or self-worth. It's more like all that open space, all those empty months, gave him a dominion—however false, however temporary—in which to reign for a while as king. He was unloosed from the men of museum boards. By the looks of it he answered to no one but A. Blayney Percival, British East Africa's game warden. And even then, Carl found a way to work around him, collecting animals well beyond the legal limit.

In 1911 he returned from Africa having beat death for the second time, and having spent more than three months with nothing to do but lie bandaged in a tent and envision a hall for the American Museum to showcase the continent that nearly killed him. He returned with these monumental dreams as a grand success, a celebrity fêted at banquets, the guests full of questions about this big bull they'd read about in the papers, the one he eventually killed after having fully recovered. "Carl Akeley Bags Record Elephant," the *Chicago Daily Tri-*

bune had written in May. *The Washington Post* ran its own story in October: "Fight with Elephant." Standing eleven feet at the shoulder, Carl's tusker was smaller than Jumbo, but a front foot's circumference measured at sixty-seven inches. "This is by far the largest foot I have seen record of," Carl was quoted to have written in a letter to John T. McCutcheon. "The foot of Jumbo was only 61 inches."

The Akeleys stayed for a short time in a hotel suite overlooking Central Park, blocks from the American Museum of Natural History, and there they settled into married urban domesticity. Delia bought new dresses—bold rambunctions of sequin and bead—to wear to all the dinners they were invited to. Carl joined the sorts of clubs the professional, upwardly mobile man in those days was apt to join. The Explorers Club. The Adventurers Club. The New York Academy of Sciences. The Century Association. Even the Save the Redwoods League based in Berkeley, California.[3] The couple slept together, for a change, in one bed. An actual bed with a mattress under a ceiling no bugs could chew holes through.

In time they took up residence on one of the upper floors at 89th Street and Central Park West, a baroque sort of building, stuffed and trussed in the way a taxidermist would find satisfying. (It houses as of this writing a $30K-per-year private school.) Three bedrooms and maid's quarters—J. T. Jr. was given a room of her own. *Her own bedroom!* And for a while it was like some new kind of family they were starting. The three would sit down each morning to breakfast; J. T. preferred grapefruit, which Delia taught her to eat with a properly toothed spoon. At the bathroom sink, she'd sit on Carl's shoulder while he lathered his narrow jaw up with soap, her hand buried in his hair as though holding onto a wild animal. Once Carl's face was covered, J. T. would pick up the straight razor—ivory handled, naturally—and *proceed to shave his face for him.* Something right out of

---

[3] Carl joined up with the Freemasons back in Milwaukee, the Kilbourn Lodge No. 3, and would become a life member in 1922.

a horror film, this was their day-to-day life. At night they'd all go to bed, J. T. with her face pressed Narcissus-like against a hand mirror Delia had given her in the jungle.

Originally, J. T. was to live in the Bronx Zoo (run, at the time, by the Akeleys' friend William T. Hornaday), but every day when Delia would visit she couldn't bear to see locked in a cage what had now become for all purposes her adopted child. Here was the filthy animal that J. T.'s namesake had originally assumed all monkeys inherently were. Here was Delia's challenge rendered as a failure. But while a three-bedroom apartment on Central Park West was far more luxe than a cage in a zoo, the place was still a cage. J. T. was kept tethered on a leash when Delia couldn't (or wouldn't) play whatever reckless games of chase or peek-a-boo J. T. continually insisted on playing, and the hairy brat had to be shut in her bedroom when company came.

Stories of primates living in human families never end well, do they? Recall that *Friends* originally paired the perpetually solo science nerd Ross with a pet capuchin monkey named Marcel, who by just the end of the first season began humping Ross and the other Friends and all of their furniture to such an extent that it had to be sold to a zoo.[4] Travis, a chimpanzee who starred in several commercials, tore off a woman's face one afternoon in 2009 for reasons his owner, a seventy-year-old woman who treated Travis as her child, could never figure out. She stabbed Travis several times during the attack, and eventually he ran off and was shot down by the police. (The head of a paramedic crew that arrived on the scene was a one Captain Bill Ackley, for what it's worth.) Congress subsequently passed a bill barring the ownership of chimpanzees as pets.

---

[4] This, reportedly, is what also began happening on the set, though it didn't stop the monkey's meteoric path to stardom. Or, rather: monkeys'. Two capuchins played Marcel and then went on to star opposite Patrick Dempsey as "the host" in *Outbreak*.

Would that such a bill were in place back in the 1910s! In Africa, J. T. had, well, the open sky and the trees she'd known all her life, but more important she'd been given a paid Swahili boy to torment. In New York this luxury was gone, what with Carl spending full days in his studio and Delia trying to entertain visitors and call on her newfound friends. In retaliation, J. T. learned how to untie her leash and soon began having her run of the place. One day, Delia came home from lunch and found on her bedroom floor the scene of some sartorial disaster. J. T. had sneaked into her closet and ripped all the beads and sequins off one of her new dresses. Delia started to lock her closet and wardrobe but left the key in the hole, stupidly. How hard is it for a monkey that can shave a man's face to learn how to turn a key? Her next loss was an expensive hat embellished with a grand ostrich plume. J. T. annihilated it one lonely afternoon, and Delia began to lose her infinite patience. She got even by asking Carl for a leopard skin, which she hung in the wardrobe such that it was the first thing J. T. would see if she broke in. The trick worked—J. T. unlocked the door one morning and found herself face-to-face with a leopard. It was enough to send her shrieking to her bedroom, where she'd grab at the wallpaper's loose seams and tear long swaths of it down from the walls.

"It finally got to the point where I felt conscience-stricken whenever I had to leave her alone with the maid," Delia writes in *J. T. Jr.: The Biography of an African Monkey*. Not, to be clear, for what the maid would have to endure, but rather for what J. T. had to, "sitting as disconsolate as a lonely child with her monkey doll clasped in her arms." (It seems J. T. began to go through the same mothering instincts and anxieties that Delia did.) The thought of this, Delia writes, "spoiled my pleasure in any social affair I might have planned for the afternoon."

So Delia stayed home more and more, nervous to leave. And soon it was hard to get anyone to visit. Close friends began telling Delia that they were uncomfortable around this pet of hers that would jump suddenly onto their heads, or would run up and shriek at them if they did something as natural as laugh too loudly. Carl, too, began to suggest sending J. T. back to the zoo. "I was obliged to listen politely to dissertations on the danger of keeping her in an apartment," Delia wrote, but she dismissed all of it as the ignorance of "well-meaning friends who did not like monkeys nor approve of the personal sacrifices I was obliged to make in their behalf." *Personal sacrifices*. The tragedy of the whole J. T. affair is how willfully Delia pulled the ostrich plume, so to speak, over her own eyes. Her social life and her marriage were crumbling right before her, all because of her devotion to this animal that would never love her as a human might, that was never really hers the way her own child could be. And yet in all of her writing about J. T., she never seems to realize any of this. To Delia, the life she lived from J. T.'s capture to her death was a life of close, long-term zoological investigation. Mothering J. T. was never a feckless, futile effort to fill a void in her life; it was always simply a study. Her contribution to our understanding of animals.

Within just a year of living with J. T., Carl had practically moved into his studio, staying there later and later and arriving home after Delia (and more important, J. T.) fell asleep. They should have been happy together, landed and well off in a city that could make them both famous. But instead New York was where the nineteen-year marriage of Delia and Carl Akeley came to an end.

These days the AMNH takes up an entire block (though it's more like four blocks), bordered laterally by Central Park West and Columbus Avenue, and crosscut between 77th and 81st streets, and while from the inside the transitions feel pretty seamless, the museum is actually an amalgamation of more than twenty different buildings, erected at various moments throughout the museum's 132-year history. Back in 1912, however, these buildings numbered only two: a

Victorian Gothic building made of red brick in 1877 and a Roman-esque Revival façade on the south wing erected in 1900. At the time, there was no separate hall at the AMNH for its African collection, but rather a room in the building that was more of an ethnographic display than anything else, the sort of glass-cabinet-heavy corridor of weapons, artifacts, and native costumes inside which it's just like *torture* for field-tripping kids to slow down and spend time. When Carl was contracted to collect and mount four elephants for the AMNH the plan was to place the group in the middle of this room. Carl, while fighting death on Mount Kenya, had a better plan: a two-story hall lined with forty habitat dioramas, with a gallery on the second floor that could overlook the first, where his elephants would stand on a high pedestal—a stage, more like—free to the open air around them. They would be flanked fore and aft by smaller groups of white and black rhinoceroses,[5] right on the floor. Carl lay for weeks on his cot with bandages covering his face, unable to see anything but every small detail of every single diorama: the curl of a lioness's tongue as she licked her left forepaw, the rocks that surrounded the watering hole from which several species would be shown drinking, the cattle egret riding on the back of the bull buffalo.

The museum approved Carl's dream but for years did little to raise the funds to construct the building to contain it. There were even too few funds in 1912 for Carl to begin mounting his elephant skins. Quickly, he watched his returned-hero glory fade, and in his studio up in the Bronx with little else to do he built a scale model of his African Hall vision—a tiny diorama of Carl's own. The museum set it up in one of its hallways to get some of its more wealthy visitors excited, but no one took the bait. In the meantime, Carl took on

---

[5] Color has nothing to do with how the white and black rhinos got their names. Some say that "white" is a mistranslation of the Dutch *wijd,* meaning wide. The white rhino's nose is square and flat, whereas the black rhino's (named in response to his white cousin) is pointed.

contract work and began selling the museum some skulls and skins from his private collection—anything to make ends meet. The strange thing about Carl Akeley's time at the AMNH is that he was never in his seventeen years of working there a salaried employee.[6] All Carl's work for the museum was contracted, which is what he preferred. It was like Ward's all over again; Carl felt freer as a taxidermist to work on his own schedule, to refuse or accept contracts as they came, to avoid being stuck under institutional influence. Of course, it led to very little job stability—and he was almost fifty years old. He'd brought four complete elephant skins back with him from Africa, but these skins belonged to the museum, and without the funds to pay him there was nothing he could do but wait.

Carl kept returning again and again to a phrase he read in *Youth's Companion* back as a boy in Clarendon, one that stuck in his head all these years: "nothing but a taxidermist." This was his situation in a nutshell. He wasn't a museum administrator; he wasn't a hunter. Not really. He wasn't even much of a husband. All he could do was wait for people to bring him dead animals, and then he was able to put his mind to something. But to what: hunting trophies? Art is the sort of endeavor that needs to be done, he felt, in private. The visionary working solo, away from any distractions. But art has little value unless it can find an audience's appreciation. Without museum backing, what good was Carl's artistry? These years before the war, Carl found himself with many empty afternoons, and he started to take long solo walks in Central Park to pass the time, ending up

---

[6] The irony here is that when he was originally fired from Ward's for sleeping on the job, he applied to the AMNH for a taxidermy position. "I believe I can give you satisfaction in all classes of taxidermy and also on mounting small skeletons," Carl reportedly wrote to Joel Allen, the museum's first curator of birds and mammals. Allen turned him down. In his study on the history of the AMNH, Geoffrey Hellman notes that "Akeley is undoubtedly the only job applicant whom the Museum turned down and subsequently named a hall for."

more often than not at the Metropolitan Museum of Art. His favorite was the sculpture collection. There was a time when Carl was a boy that he wanted to be a sculptor. But it was just a fancy, he thought. "I could never contribute to that art what I could contribute to taxidermy," he wrote in *In Brightest Africa*. "So I turned away from sculpture." And in a sense, he turned away from art, for taxidermy, at least in the nineteenth century, at least before Carl got his hands on it, wasn't an art form. "It was in fact little better than a trade," he wrote. And so one way that Carl understood his life as a taxidermist was based on this turning away from sculpture, insisting that his "lesser trade"—this mounting of animal skins—could achieve the grandness and respect that sculpture enjoyed.[7]

In New York he saw it as his mission to open up the world of art to make room for the medium of taxidermy, and his African Hall was the only way he saw to accomplish this. But building African Hall required money, and money came from rich men, and rich men didn't just give their money away. Not to taxidermy. "It was a recognized thing to support art," Carl wrote. "Taxidermy had no such tradition." (It still doesn't.) Carl thought and thought about what to do, and he came upon a brilliant solution. If rich men didn't think taxidermy was an art, then he'd show them that a taxidermist could very well be an artist. And to do that he'd have to give them a medium they were far more familiar with. And so with nothing else to do Carl began to sculpt. The first piece he ever cast in bronze depicted two elephants trying to raise a third off the ground and carry him, in a sense, to safety. It told a story that Carl had watched in Africa, the aftermath of shooting his prize bull. The idea that elephants were such devoted herd animals with an all-for-one-and-one-for-all ethos moved him enough to try to replicate it here. He called the piece *The Wounded Comrade,* and it became his second-most-famous

---

[7] Incidentally, "sculptor" is what Carl perhaps aspirationally had listed on his passport as his occupation.

sculpture. The Brooklyn Museum owns one of the twenty-three casts Akeley had made.

In a way, Carl was right about his abilities. *The Wounded Comrade* did little for sculpture on the scale of what his muskrat diorama did for taxidermy. It's an unspectacular piece about which the best that can be said is that the subject is original and that Carl captured the massiveness of the elephants pretty well—especially given their 1/12 scale. Although to be fair, I should remember that in 1913 elephants weren't the known, familiar animals they are today. After all, the AMNH didn't even have one on display yet.

By the time the AMNH found the funds to begin work on the elephant group (secured from J. P. Morgan, who Akeley claims decided to fund the mounts after seeing a cast of *The Wounded Comrade*), it had been almost seven years since Carl had last mounted an elephant. This was the *Fighting Bulls* group he finished for the Field Museum in 1908. It was the work of a more naïve man than the one who got mauled on Mount Kenya, a man who thought he knew elephants but instead knew only what the public wanted. In all of his years studying elephants, Carl never once saw them fighting one another. They are, he wrote in his memoir, "at peace amongst themselves." But the Field Museum group shows two bulls in the thick of combat, one about to pierce its tusk through the heart of the other. It's as much a lie about the natural world as is the jackalope, and Carl knew this time around he had to try harder.

He envisioned four elephants in a tight cluster, which he'd title *The Alarm*. The conceit was that a viewer of the group would have just come within sight (or, more likely, smell) of the elephants, and Carl wanted to capture the animals at the moment before charging. He started with the big bull—his trophy, his darling. As he'd done with every mount in the past, he sculpted from clay a life-size manikin, looking at his photographic references and his field notes, using scrapers and modeling tools to replicate each fold of the skin. The end result was enormous. This bull was tall enough that standing next to the model Carl couldn't even touch the tusks if he'd jumped. There was simply no way to cast the whole hulking thing in plaster, and he dissembled the entire clay model and started over.

The problem, Carl realized, was that he'd been playing too much at being a sculptor. Maybe it was a more revered form of art, but this wasn't a piece of sculpture. It was a piece of taxidermy. He didn't need to build a monumental version of an animal already so monumental. He needed only to arrange the skin. Carl began to think of ways he could let the elephant's hide dictate the process; rather than use photographs as a reference in the modeling, couldn't he model directly from the skin somehow?

In time, Carl discovered he could. On a large angled platform, like the drafting table for a giant, he constructed a rudimentary elephant shape out of some wire cloth. A body part and two leg parts, nothing fancy. Then he added a layer of clay that would be sculpted and molded by hand, much the way a memory-foam mattress pad receives the contours of your sleeping body. Getting his model, then, was just a matter of draping the tanned skin over this clay layer and fancying himself a bit of a masseuse. Carl did a kind of deep-tissue massage, working all the skin's folds and wrinkles into the clay underneath, building up musculature where he knew he needed it.

Eventually he worked the whole segment over and was ready to make a cast.[8] With the skin adhered to the clay as it once was to flesh, Carl worried he might ruin all his modeling work if he tried to peel it off. So he didn't. It was a pachyderm, after all, with skin hardy

---

[8] Carl mounted elephants in four separate parts: the head was cut off around the neck and split right down the middle, bisecting the trunk to its tip, to make two head halves; the remainder of the body was split along the backbone and the breastbone, with slits running down each leg, to make the larger body halves.

enough to withstand some pressure—like, say, that from a layer of plaster. Imagine an elephant having broken its entire body and rushing to the emergency room: the end result was like this. A full-body cast. A Stay-Puft Marshmallow Elephant.

While Carl alone was responsible for figuring out a new, practical way to mount the elephant, he wasn't working alone. The AMNH had hired some assistants, Louis Jonas (from Jonas Brothers Taxidermy Supply in Denver), Raymond B. Potter (who according to Mary Jobe Akeley was the only person Carl ever wrote a letter of recommendation for), and a man named Fred Limekiller. This was fortunate, since once the plaster had hardened the whole section needed to be flipped over, and the men worked carefully to invert it without anything breaking. Because the plaster had dried, every swell and fold on the outside of the skin was preserved. So Carl removed the layers of wire cloth and clay from the inside, and then applied more plaster, sandwiching the skin between two layers. If he could let the skin dry like this it would become almost its own mold, ready not so much to be layered over a manikin, but more to have a manikin layered inside it.

To do so, Carl took the dry skin and coated the underside with his standby: papier-mâché. This he treated with shellac to make it impervious to moisture, and then he reinforced the whole thing with plywood, making a structure that replicated, to an extent, the animal's ribcage. And there he had it: a mounted elephant skin that was lighter and more durable than any he'd made before. He repeated the process with the three other segments; then it was time for assembly— the fun part, like putting together the world's most expensive toy.

Carl Akeley didn't make many sculptures. Fewer than a dozen, surely. He killed far more elephants than those he sculpted. But every time he sculpted an elephant he had in his artist's head a story to tell. One sculpture was called *Jungle Football* and depicted two young elephants—adorable—playing together—adorabler—with a ball of dirt made from a termite hill—*adorablest*! Based on a scene Akeley had watched in the wild, the message of the piece is clear: elephants play soccer, too. *Just like us!*

The sculpture of Carl Akeley is sentimental in ways he'd never allow his taxidermy to be. Sure: Akeley prayed devoutly at the altar of the family group. There were always baby animals in his dioramas. The dioramas couldn't be complete without baby animals. But this fabrication of the nuclear animal family had an educational or pedagogical basis that we can understand.[9] Most animals, mammals at least, have separate morphologies for the adult male and the adult female, and showing what the animals look like when young tells an efficient little story about growth and survival. Now, there's nothing false or zoologically inaccurate about Akeley's sculptures, but Akeley's sculptures are dramatized in ways his taxidermy is not. Put it this way: whereas his taxidermy is *The Four Seasons,* his sculpture is *Bambi.*

What sort of approach is this for a man who wanted taxidermy to be elevated to an art form? More to the point: what is it about sculpture that allowed Carl Akeley such sentimentality he didn't otherwise allow himself? One key difference between taxidermy and sculpture is, of course, the use of the actual parts in representing the animal. A taxidermist is beholden to that actual tanned skin, whereas the sculptor may use whatever materials he has on hand. It's a matter of abstraction: every sculpture asks of its viewer a suspension of disbelief. *Here is a panther,* the sculptor says. *Even though it's made of metal, imagine, please, that it is a panther. Can you see?* The taxidermist has no such luxury. The taxidermist presents a real hide and asks of us the

---

[9] It isn't that the animals Akeley mounted were in truth all solitary loners. They did form family groups, but these weren't, like, biblically limited to one father, one mother, and a brood of young.

impossible: *Please forget this animal is no longer living.* The sculptor needs only our imagination, whereas the taxidermist needs our trust. And so, freed from the burden of re-creating life, the sculptor can direct those energies toward capturing it, or even imagining it.

This division follows another in taxidermy between professional work and novelty pieces, which has to do with verisimilitude. Professional taxidermists[10] want to take animals that live in the world today and re-create them to a fanatical degree of realistic detail, right down to the eyelash. The professional taxidermist's vision is nature's vision—well it's *God's* vision, for most taxidermists. Novelty taxidermy has a vision, too, but it's a more playful one, with a verisimilitude of its own. Squirrels shooting pool still need to look like squirrels. Unicorns, jackalopes—they need to be recognizable. The difference is that novelty taxidermists, like sculptors, aren't beholden to zoology, and they, too, need only our imagination. Not our trust. Many taxidermists dismiss their work altogether. An Ohio taxidermist, Jim Tucker, told me once that he found these pieces insulting, not just to him as an artist but to the animals used therein. "Why kill jackrabbits to make jackalopes? Why have a deer's ass mounted with a face on it? The public thinks that people kill animals to make these stupid objects."

Tucker's referring to something called a swamp booger, an animal with a silly mythology of its own among hunters and another creature invented by taxidermy. The swamp booger is the answer to the question, *What are we supposed to do with all these posterior deer hides?* You take the ass skin of a deer, turn it upside down so the tail hangs to the floor, secure some glass eyes near the top, and fix an artificial bobcat jaw right where the anus used to be. *Et voila!* It's just the sort of thing certain men find hilarious—sitting somewhere on the classy-crassy continuum between WHO FARTED? T-shirts and actual public

---

[10] A lamentable term I'm going to have to use here by way of distinction; it's in no way to imply a lack of professionalism on the part of novelty taxidermists.

farting. Taxidermists can make easy money on swamp boogers and other novel uses of a deer's posterior. Dan Rinehart devotes a whole episode of his *Taxidermy for the Sportsman* series mounting a deer-rump bottle opener.[11] But not every taxidermist wants to go down this jokey road. Some cannot find a way to let the end justify the means of its creation, and it's easy to empathize with Tucker in his complaint. Animals had to die for *this*?

In many ways novelty taxidermy is a cartoon fantasy. It's what Walt Disney would have made had he been maybe more outdoorsy. As we've come over the centuries to be more scientifically knowledgeable about animals, we've wanted at the same time to romanticize and sentimentalize the creatures, and none wanted this more than the Victorians. *The Victorians!* Though born along a time span of more than sixty years, as a people they leave themselves ready for generalization and simplification. Type "how did the victorians" into Google's search window and it auto-suggests a list of oft-searched questions. *How did the Victorians celebrate Christmas? How did the Victorians dress? How did the Victorians wash their clothes? How did the Victorians keep warm? How did the Victorians speak?* It's as though the Victorians were merely a family with its own syndicated television show, rather than a whole swath of millions living at the apex of British imperialism. And yet when we ask (not necessarily of Google), How did the Victorians indulge their senses of whimsy while feeding a growing curiosity about the lives and bodies of animals? we find an answer in Walter Potter—easily the Walt Disney of his time. Potter was a self-taught taxidermist living in the south of England who, in the 1860s, opened his own museum of nature-cabinet displays, much along the lines of Charles Willson Peale's here in the States. The major difference was those cabinets' contents. Whereas Peale tried to display species naturalistically, with backdrops

---

[11] The video inevitably made its way to YouTube. "Talk about busting a cap in someone's ass," one commenter wrote.

painted to suggest their habitats, Potter wanted to tell stories, and he wanted those stories to be wildly untrue. So at Potter's museum in West Sussex, you found *The Kittens' Tea Party,* depicting some kittens sipping from little cups they hold in their paws, some passing trays of tiny biscuits. You found mechanical toads, each of them standing on hind legs around a little dioramic field, moving via unseen gears and sprockets as though in aerobic and gymnastic activity. In *A Friend in Need* you see rats using their forepaws to release another rat from a trap.

We've seen this sort of thing before, but the central difference between Potter's pieces and the sorts of moneymakers suggested in later booklets of J. W. Elwood's Northwestern School of Taxidermy is scale. These aren't shoebox dioramas, they're museum-scale pieces. Glass boxes the size of a Texas high school's trophy case—and no less cluttered. *The Kittens' Tea Party* puts no fewer than twelve taxidermized kittens around a table. *Kittens Wedding* maybe twice more. *The Rabbits' School—Class I, Writing* comprises thirteen such rabbits sitting among handcrafted dollhouse furniture. The museum's tour de force— and the cabinet that made him famous—was *The Original Death and Burial of Cock Robin,* which featured *ninety-eight* different species of birds in a rectangular glass case with a Grecian pediment on top. The scene—or "tableau," as most Potter enthusiasts call it—depicts the funeral proceedings of a robin, based on a popular nursery rhyme of the era, and for poor Cock Robin's burial it's like every bird he ever knew has come down from the heavens, each perched on a tree limb, its beak and eyes directed mourningly down (yes, there's a mourning dove among the ninety-eight) to just right of center, where a little coffin's cover is being laid over Cock Robin's corpse.[12]

The term for what can only be called Potter's mania with respect

---

[12] In 2003, Bonhams auctioned off every cabinet of Potter's museum, despite Damien Hirst's offer to buy the whole lot for a million pounds. *Cock Robin* fetched the highest price, at £23,500.

to animals is anthropomorphism. Like *taxidermy* the word stems from Greek: *anthropo* meaning "human" and *morph* meaning "form." The *OED* dates it to the mid–eighteenth century, when it referred to the "ascription of human forms and attributes to the Deity." In other words, man making God in his own image, rather than the other way around. It wasn't until the 1850s that the word's meaning got opened up to include placing human attributes on "anything impersonal or irrational"—i.e., animals. "We speak with large latitude of anthropomorphism when we speak of the 'vision' of these [mollusks]" is the *OED*'s quotation, attributed to the philosopher and critic George Henry Lewes. Though the word's meaning has altered since its conception, the solipsism has remained firmly in place. The anthropomorphing eye pulls the animal toward it. It looks at the animal and sees only itself. It's a kind of disregard, much like tolerating a gay person because he's "straight acting."

Potter has any number of stateside equivalents. Rick Nadeau is a taxidermist in Illinois whose Web site promises he "can mount any squirrel in just about any position or style you would like." He seems to specialize in "chest mounts" (think of a game head with arms on a plaque) of squirrels in little berets holding onto tiny automatic firearms. Another, Vito Marchino, died in the 1990s, but not before building a whole Potterian array of squirrels and chipmunks in motorized tableaux—including a "topless girlie show" with chipmunks in little grass skirts (and nothing else) walking rather like Egyptians on a plywood stage. Albino squirrels ride a Ferris wheel and some play basketball. All these tableaux exist in the basement of a funeral home in Wisconsin, where Marchino lived and worked (and, incidentally, taught Dan Rinehart's father everything he knew about taxidermy). The question behind Potter's work and others' is, *Why?* Why do we feel drawn toward posing animals' bodies into humanistic attitudes? Dressing them up and giving them props? Whence Spuds MacKenzie's appeal? Does it make animals more human, or does it restore in us some lost animal nature?

Harriet Ritvo, in her book *The Animal Estate*, argues that it does indeed restore something lost in us, but not our animal nature. When Darwin published *On the Origin of Species* in 1859, humans and animals were firmly linked—cousins, basically, sharing common ancestors. You'd think this would lead to a kind of empathy and identification, but instead, Ritvo argues, Darwin's theory only heightened humans' sense of superiority.

> Clearly, if people were animals, they were the top animals; and with God out of the picture, the source of human preeminence lay within. Ironically, by becoming animals, humans appropriated some attributes formerly reserved for the deity. And in the "struggle for life," as the subtitle of *On the Origin of Species* put it, the other animals were still ranked according to their relation to humanity.

In short: the Victorians in the time after Darwin became gods in their own right. This explains not only their (and our) fondness for dogs and horses—such loyal servants!—but also their interests in novelty taxidermy. For if manners and reason were what kept this particular animal separate from the beastly riffraff, what better fate for the lesser animals than becoming human? What better form of respect and admiration?

When the Victorians weren't seeing animals in their own godly image, they saw animals as objects for their own daily use. By this I mean not just as farm implements—cows, horses, oxen, sheep, and so on—but also as everyday household objects. As a result of the work of the taxidermist Rowland Ward, there was a craze in the Victorian era for furniture and other decorative items made from the parts of animals. His were so popular that he got the unofficial naming rights: "Wardian furniture" was the name generally given to any such object, much as we all Xerox things and use Band-Aids and Kleenex from time to time. Wardian furniture is pure classical kitsch. Picture a mounted bear standing on two legs with a tray of decanters fixed between its paws. Picture an occasional chair to sit in, the back of which is made from the torso of a giraffe, its forearms hugging your sides, its long head hovering inches above your own. Picture horse-hoof inkwells. Leopard-foot bookends. Ward (no relation to Akeley's boss) did them all. His company, Rowland Ward Ltd., was by the end of the Victorian era the largest and best-known taxidermist in Britain—the only shop with a Royal Warrant. With royalty and wealthy white hunters as its clients, Ward Ltd. preserved the bestial spoils of the British imperialist project. But after mounting a rich man's zebra head on a plaque, what's a taxidermist to do with all those left-over parts? There's so much of an elephant, but all anyone could handle was its head, trunk, and tusks. Furniture was the answer. Ward made elephant feet into any number of useful objects: stools, trashcans, and decanter stands were the most popular. And so in many ways Wardian furniture is the forefather to the swamp booger or any other act of taxidermic bricolage. A man's got to make a living somehow. And why limit one's memory of the hunt to something merely ornamental on a wall? As P. A. Morris puts it in his biography of Ward: "to Ward and his customers, shooting elephants for their ivory was normal practice . . . , so why waste the rest of the animal? By creating Ward-ian furniture, trophies could thus be mementoes and also be useful, quite apart from generating more taxidermy income from each animal shot."

It's what J. W. Elwood would exhort decades later: trophies could also be useful. And here, perhaps, is where all the divisions I've been drawing lie—utile or aesthetic? We can see animals either as re-sources for us to make varying uses of—food, industry, companion-ship, scientific record—or we can see animals as fellow creatures to be admired. Very likely we see them as both. Taxidermists cer-tainly do. Constructed as it is from animal parts, taxidermy sits right at this intersection of utility and aesthetics. We've seen all the ways taxidermy makes use of animals. Now I want to take a look at how (or even whether) taxidermy captures animals' beauty.

First, a question: what is it that makes animals beautiful? A frog and a butterfly. A leopard and a manta ray. How do we go about admiring these creatures? We can look to aesthetics, that branch of philosophy that deals with the nature of beauty, for answers. There are three models of nature appreciation currently *en vogue* among aestheticists. One is the object model, which considers the animal as a closed system. It looks at an animal as though it were a work of art, hung out of any context in a gallery. The animal is its own context, argues the object model.[13] Most taxidermy follows this philosophy: take just the head and put it on the wall. That's the way to best appreciate an animal's beauty.

But the problem with the object model is that animals are not works of art; they are works of creation, and to approach an appreciation of them with the same criteria we learn from art history 101 is to judge an animal through values not intrinsic to it. Fortunately there's the landscape model, which says to leave the animal be and admire it as part of the world it inhabits. After all, to fully appreciate a gazelle's grace, would you rather see one leap over a poured concrete floor or the wide, bright African plain? Museum dioramas adhere strictly to this model of animal beauty: see the animal among the plants and landscape. If there's a problem with this model it's that it tends to treat an environment, too, as though it were a work of art: something static and held within a frame. But, as Sheila Lintott points out in her summary of these arguments, environments are by their nature in a state of flux. Where, the question follows, does the natural environment for a gazelle end? Where does it even begin?

---

[13] This, for what it's worth, is a very modernist way of considering animals. It's like what would happen if T. S. Eliot wrote about aesthetics (which, of course, he did, siding pretty much with the object model).

Which brings us to the arousal model, so sexily named because it argues that the best way to appreciate nature and to see the beauty in animals is to let your subjective emotions guide you. We, as elements of nature ourselves, have instinctive reactions to animals that are valid and trustworthy. What the arousal model encourages the viewer to do is see the gazelle neither as an art object—all curves and soft colors—nor as one element within its natural environment. Instead, it encourages us to see the gazelle for its *gazelleness:* the qualities that make it distinct from any other species on the planet. This is what Paul Rhymer at the Smithsonian (itself following the object model devoutly in its new habitatless Mammal Hall) is talking about when he talks about the jizz of an animal. To capture it, to admire it, to love it—all it takes is a close, close look.

A big fan of the arousal model (though not necessarily identifying as such) was William Blake, who famously asked of the tiger, "What immortal hand or eye / Could frame thy fearful symmetry?" That perfect alignment of features that renders instantly for us a tiger's ferocity. Something about its nature broadcasts a warning and instills in us a fear mixed with awe—this is one way the tiger is beautiful. Do you remember all those studies of facial symmetry and beauty back in the 1990s? Magazine spreads with Denzel Washington's face laid out next to poor Lyle Lovett's? Guidelines and measurements to show the harmonious design and proportion in the former, the distortions of same in the latter? The idea was that symmetry was an indicator of robust health and thus a leading factor in our species' mate selection. Human or animal, we seem to want all the features in the right place.

Then again, Lyle Lovett won the heart of Julia Roberts, if only for a time, so nuts to this whole symmetry theory.

If philosophers and evolutionary biologists can't help us decide on animal beauty, we can always turn to artists: those guardians of the aesthetic. Animals have forever been the subject of our artistic endeavors, ever since the unknown prehistoric visionary (or visionaries) captured the bulls, horses, and stags on cave walls in Lascaux, France. Flat, brown. So often in motion, legs splayed and leaping fore and aft, running either from danger or toward it, danger being the little silhouetted matchstick men waiting with arrows nocked in bows. These scenes are more than fifteen thousand years old, made at a time, the art historian Kenneth Clark points out, before man learned to take dominion over animals. "Animals were in ascendan[ce]," he writes in his study of animals in art, "and distinguished from man less by their intellectual limitations than by their greater strength and speed." Clark believes the cave paintings show prehistoric man's admiration for animals. " 'This is what we want to be like,' they say, in unmistakeable accents; 'these are the most admirable of our kinsmen.' "

Gradually, of course, humans became ascendant and learned, for better or worse, to take dominion over animals, and still they remained the subjects of art, invoking in us the need for representation. Leonardo da Vinci sketched horses to an almost fanatical degree of detail. Albrecht Dürer created in 1502 what might be the *Mona Lisa* of animal art: *The Young Hare,* rendered so lifelike it almost makes you forget that photography won't be around for another 350 years.[14] And as the Enlightenment came along and brought natural science with it, animals became more sentimentalized and more personable. Eugène Delacroix's lions and Thomas Gainsborough's dogs are as alive and expressive as humans in Renaissance art once were. Or witness Sir Edwin Landseer's portraits of dogs, their eyes all wet and Disneyfied. Or Edward Hicks's Peaceable Kingdom paintings (ca. 1820), almost talismanic in their hope of eternal harmony between all God's creatures. The birds in John James Audubon's *Birds of America* (1840)

---

[14] The hare, Clark writes, "prompts the question, how did [Dürer] ever persuade a hare to sit still long enough for him to record all that detail?" Perhaps he knew a good taxidermist.

were all painted from models Audubon shot and stuffed and posed with wires—much like a taxidermist would. Here was natural science that read almost as a children's picture book, with all the birds going about their day-to-day lives in the richly foliaged places they call home. Here's where the anthropomorphism kicks in, culminating in perhaps everyone's favorite animal artwork: C. M. Coolidge's Dogs Playing Poker series (1906–34).

At some point in the twentieth century, animals became beautiful—or, at least, aesthetically interesting—when they stopped being "just" animals. Artists needed to transform animals, to make them less natural. Pablo Picasso preferred a bicycle seat and handlebars to an actual bull's-head trophy. Meret Oppenheim wanted neither a gazelle nor a teacup, but rather a teacup and saucer lined with a gazelle's fur. Max Ernst, in his *Elephant Celebes* (1921), wanted not an elephant so much as a boiler furnace. And the Victorians still loomed. We wanted not so much animals as other animal-like people. *The Wind in the Willows,* Walt Disney's singing mouse, Charles Schulz's Snoopy and Woodstock. And anthropomorphism still reigns. Coolidge's dogs playing poker are only a quick trot away from William Wegman's dogs playing dress-up.

In the past twenty years, there's been a fundamental change in the world of animal art. Whereas animals have always served as artists' subjects, they've never before served as artists' media. Now, however, it's like the art world has caught up with the taxidermy world—which has been using animals as its central medium for centuries. Witness Emily Valentine Bullock, an Australian artist who asserts, "Feathers are my paint," and uses bird feathers to create sculptures of the bizarre new animal species of her imagination. Or Nina Katchadourian, an American artist who has undergone what she calls "uninvited collaborations with nature." In one series of photographs, called *Natural Crossdressing* (2002), she poses with two caterpillars mustached on her upper lip. In *Quit Using Us* (2002), caterpillars are arranged (well, used, really) to spell out those titular words. Or of course the granddaddy of them all: Damien Hirst. His vivisectioned cows, pigs, and sheep in enormous tanks of formaldehyde aren't just *about* death and decay; they actively press the viewer to witness (and, thus, consider the ramifications of) animal death. *In and Out of Love* (1991) is a piece that hatched butterflies in a room of white canvases treated with sugar and paste; the butterflies land to feed and are stuck there forever. In *A Thousand Years* (1990), Hirst put a rotting cow's head at the floor of a glass case and a bug zapper up near the top. A white box serves as a place for maggots to become flies, feed off the rotting head, and then float up to their death in the zapper.[15]

Earlier animal art may have celebrated the life of animals, but Hirst celebrates their death. Or, more particularly, their transition through life's stages. Sure, his split animals in formaldehyde are only dead—though suspended and denied decay—but his early works show us eggs, larvae, pupae, adult insects and the death thereof. What insects will have over us any day of the week are sheer numbers (the Smithsonian has estimated that at any given moment there are 10 quintillion [10,000,000,000,000,000,000] insects alive on this planet; that's 1.6 billion insects for every human) and rapid gestation. As rapid as a single day for the mayfly. And in this rapidity Hirst finds something instructive.

Whence this shift? How has our relationship with animals become comfortable (or some could argue controlling) enough that we now put their bodies or body parts into our creative works? The art critic John Molyneux sees this as a reflection of the times. Writing specifically about Hirst's early work, he reads Hirst's use of animals as a way "to force a face to face confrontation with the brute fact of death on a blasé modern audience for whom images of death are superabun-

---

[15] While the original incarnation of *A Thousand Years* featured a rotting head, Hirst now employs the taxidermist Emily Mayer to make artificial heads for him.

dant while its reality becomes ever more removed and hidden. Short of exhibiting an actual human corpse this was about as far as Hirst could go."

Not to worry, John. Human corpses are now on exhibit all over the world, a bizarre phenomenon we'll look at in the next chapter.

Some of this new animal art isn't just commenting generally on humans and animals but specifically on taxidermy and its practices, and artists are learning all the techniques of traditional taxidermy to create their work. Berlinde de Bruyckere is a Belgian artist who drapes horsehides over presculpted forms, but the end result only suggests "horse"—their faces hidden shamefully from view. "Idiots" is the name given to the partnership of the Dutch artists Afke Golsteijn and Floris Bakker, who embellish works of taxidermy with man-made materials. *Industrial Evolution* (2007) attaches an embroidered wedding-gown train onto a bird's small tail, and *Ophelia* (2005) fuses the front half of a taxidermized lion with a spillage of golden ceramic orbs, very liquid looking.

In America, these artists have combined into loose confederation aligned with the Minnesota Association of Rogue Taxidermists. Yes, rogue taxidermists. It's an evocative concept: nomadic men and women hiding in the shadows of your backyard and pouncing on the squirrels that tip over the bird feeders, the moles under your garden, appearing at your doorstep days later with the animal mounted to your unpresumed liking. *The rogue taxidermist strikes again!* The reality is less heroic, perhaps. More arty. What makes this taxidermy so rogue is the appearance of the animal after the artist has gotten his hands on it. Whereas a professional taxidermist re-creates an animal toward its living nature, rogue taxidermists move toward fabulism, fantasy, and deconstruction. The name comes from a group of three artists—Scott Bibus, Sarina Brewer, and Robert Marbury—who found themselves independently working with animals and animal parts. They exhibited together for the first time in Minneapolis in

2004, founding the MART, which begat a Web site, which attracted other artists from around the country doing similar work.

A look at the art of the MART's founding members shows the breadth of work that can fall under rogue taxidermy. Bibus is the goremeister of the bunch. Sample titles include *Frog Eating a Human Toe* (2005), *Vomiting Frog* (2005), and *My Heart* (2010), which depicts a plaintive-looking squirrel holding its own heart out to the viewer, arteries and other viscera still connecting the shiny red thing back to the squirrel's torso. (This was an anniversary present for Bibus's wife.) Brewer is the MART's goth queen. Much of her work is on hybrid creatures—the griffin or the Feejee Mermaid, even an ant-lered squirrel she calls *Der Wolpertinger*—that mash up the parts of separate animals to make something new. There's a decided dark-ness to her mounts, a celebration of the macabre. It's like what Siouxsie Sioux would buy were she in the market for animal art. Both Bibus and Brewer are trained taxidermists, whereas Marbury is the self-professed vegan of the group. He works with plush-toy animals rather than dead ones. The sorts of things you'd buy a toddler. Marbury's "urban beasts" get new eyes and teeth and are staged in various poses and locations around cities, then captured on film in the style of nature photography. It's all a kind of visual pun on the idea of "stuffed animals," and the quasi-scientific names he assigns these new species play with taxidermy's attempts at re-creating nature with perfect accuracy.

Through the MART Web site, the organization has grown to more than two dozen members, all of whom have been indepen-dently doing similar deconstructive work with animals. Whereas among professional taxidermists women are few, they oddly make up the majority of rogue taxidermists. And whereas the majority of professional taxidermists are hunters, nearly every rogue taxidermist takes great pains to reveal the nonmurderous ways she finds her ma-terials. Brewer writes that "she utilizes animals that are roadkill, discarded livestock, destroyed nuisance animals, casualties of the pet trade, or animals that died of natural causes. None of the animals she uses are hunting trophies or were killed for the purpose of using them in her art." She's reported having dead animals delivered anonymously to her doorstep, to the point where she had to use her Web site to ask folks to stop. Rogues, then, are more gatherers than hunters; theirs is a kind of green taxidermy.[16]

While professional taxidermy seems destined—despite its artistry and mastery—for lowbrow status, rogue taxidermists have managed to blend the low and the high. Their work shows in galleries, not dens. In this way, we can read rogues as postmodern taxidermists. If professional taxidermy seeks representation with total fidelity to nature, rogues turn away from this, seeking instead to call our attention to the contradictions behind such representation, to the very techniques of the taxidermist's trade. They expose the lie behind conventional taxidermy. No wonder the two sides can't get along. Here's a professional quoted in an article on the novelty taxidermist Rick Nadeau:

> "Professionals think [rogues] give taxidermy an unprofessional look," explains Pete Sweitzer, president of the Illinois Taxidermist Association and an early mentor of Nadeau's.
>
> "Professionals consider themselves artists. A talented taxidermist will make a mount look so real that you can't tell it from a live animal. You can't recreate what God put on Earth, but you can get close."

This is a lie, make no mistake. No one on the planet is so unversed in what an animal is that he'll truly encounter a piece of taxidermy

---

[16] And they're not alone. Jack Fishwick, a leading British bird taxidermist who judges often at the World Taxidermy Championships, once said that "[t]here are so many natural causes for a bird to die of. No need for hunting, shooting, or maiming."

and not be able to tell it from a live animal. Live animals tend not to come as shoulders, necks, and heads hovering over some open space. They tend to keep their bodies intact. Also, they don't stick their heads through holes in walls. In short: taxidermy is always found in a context where animals aren't. So to say that professional taxidermy is somehow better, or that such a professional is more talented, is to tell a lie you hope no one calls you out on.

Whether rogue taxidermists have founded a lasting movement in the art world or have merely capitalized off a growing trend is still as of this writing to be decided (also to be decided: whether there's a difference), but to be sure, taxidermy in the waning years of G. W. Bush's tenure began to enjoy a kind of vogue among both high and low culture. In New York particularly it's been difficult to enter bars and restaurants without seeing a head hung somewhat ironically on the wall. In April of 2007, *New York* magazine ran a piece of this new direction in décor. "Once an art form confined to frat houses, Upper West Side beer bars, and *New Yorker* cartoons, taxidermy has made its way into restaurants all over town." Now-defunct design magazines such as *Domino, Blueprint,* and *Metropolitan Home* once featured rooms on their covers with exotic game heads hung over chaises and ultramodern sectionals. Balsa-wood and cardboard game-head replicas are available for the vegan or queasy devotee. Urban Outfitters carries them for as low as $28.

Not to be outdone, in late April of 2007 the *New York Times* covered this taxidermy-as-design boom in the Thursday Styles section. Many experts came up with many ideas on what it meant that the antler was ubiquitous now in fashion and design. Some saw it as a rebellion against the war and gloom of the Bush era. Others read it as a masculine assertion in a traditionally feminine world. Regardless of what it may mean, one line from the article seems telling:

"Design enthusiasts crave spaces and shapes that suggest a lived-in authenticity, as opposed to the stark coolness of modern design."

Taxidermy, then, may not be inherently authentic, but it can suggest authenticity, much the way trucker caps or a can of PBR seem to. For whatever reason, it's important to us now. There's a need to have around us some facet of the bestial. Perhaps the title to animal scientist Temple Grandin's recent book is right: animals make us human.

Carl Akeley had just began work on the second elephant in his group when Woodrow Wilson asked Congress to declare war on Germany. This was April 1917. Congress said will do. Back then, war declarations got followed by sincere forms of personal sacrifice. Food became rationed. Sauerkraut became liberty cabbage. Posters were raised on walls around the country. Carl felt that Uncle Sam wanted him, but Carl was "nothing but a taxidermist." He couldn't see a way to contribute to the war effort, but he saw such a contribution as vital. African Hall was no closer to fruition than when he'd dreamt of it back on the mountain, and while he was glad to actually be working on the elephant group he saw the fourth specimen as some looming specter of finality. The terror of completion: what next?

Carl needed a new direction, a new project. One more immediate, like the war. "I had to get into it," he wrote. "The only way to be happy was to get into it." So one evening after wetting down some blankets to cover up his elephant skins, he left the museum and walked the eight blocks homeward with his head trained on the ground. Practically scratching his chin the whole way. There was a conversation brewing in his head that he wanted to have with Delia. The past few years had been difficult, nothing like those times together in Milwaukee or Chicago. It seemed to Carl that he and Delia were closest when they shared a goal. *The Alarm* was the exact sort of thing they should have been working on together, like *The Four Seasons,* but Delia would never leave J. T. alone.

At home he found Delia in bed, lying underneath a quilt she'd brought out from the wardrobe. "Close the door," she said. "You're letting in a draft." Outside it had been a mild spring day, but here was his wife with a chill, the quilt pulled right up to her chin.

"Do you have a fever?" he asked. "Let me feel your forehead."

Delia batted his hand away. "I've never been ill a day in my life," she said. "You know that."

"Mickie," Carl said. "Mickie, I wanted to talk to you about something. About this war. Maybe—"

And here his wife winced, as though he'd hurt her, as though even a conversation between them was too much for her to bear. From the other side of the bed, he saw J. T. creep her head above the mattress like a prairie dog, her eyes long and wet and trained right on Delia.

"Why isn't she in bed?" Carl asked.

Delia turned her face toward the window. "Don't get angry," she said, "We had an accident."

"What kind of accident?"

"I got bit," Delia said. "On the ankle."

Carl stripped off the covers, and J. T. rushed back to the corner of the room, screeching. Up close he saw Delia's whole foot wrapped in a makeshift bandage that bloomed here and there with stains of her blood. The toes that peeked out the top were swollen dark and round—like an elephant's foot, he thought.

"I *told* you that animal needed to go!" he yelled. He stomped on the floor to keep J. T. at bay.

"Leave her alone!" Delia said. "It's not her fault. I tried to put her to bed, but she wanted to play. I gave her a little kick and. . . . It was stupid of me."

"It was her fault!" he said. "She did it to you, and believe me, Mickie, she'll do it again! That animal needs to be in a zoo."

When the doctor came, he indicated that the wound had been infected—J. T.'s fangs had sawlike edges on them that tore unevenly into Delia's flesh, nearly severing one of her tendons—and diagnosed sepsis, bacteria in the blood. Delia needed an operation, but she wouldn't leave J. T. And here Carl saw the situation for what it was: his wife would never leave that monkey. Not ever. Not for him. Not even to save her own life. Stubbornly, she demanded they bring a surgical nurse to perform the operation right there in the bedroom, and over the course of three months Delia slowly began to recover. It took two more bites, one on the shoulder, one on the wrist, for Delia finally to realize J. T. had to go. She made arrangements to ship the monkey to the Rock Creek Park Zoo in Washington, D.C. (now the Smithsonian's National Zoo), and felt immediately as empty and lost as Carl had been feeling since leaving Africa.

"Any one who has had to part with a child, an invalid, or a pet who has been a responsibility for many years, will understand how lost I felt," she wrote in *J. T. Jr.*, "for as I have said before, I had given up practically all my social life and many of my friends to devote myself to the care and study of this interesting little creature." And what, Delia, did you learn from this ongoing study? That monkeys are, indeed, clean when given regular access to bathtubs and freshly washed bedsheets? That they may enjoy living in captivity alongside humans for a time, but not forever? That without another creature to dote on your life had little meaning? The tragedy of Delia Akeley is that all her life she'd wanted escape and freedom, that all her life she'd never answered to anyone but herself, and that all her life she took on any dare or challenge that came her way, and yet all that this Mickieness ever got her was a new sort of cage, a new unhappy home to be trapped in. She'd wanted to run away and saw Carl as her ticket, but with Carl and his cohorts she had something to prove, and it ended up trapping her. And now here she was. Her marriage was in ruins, but she was free for the first time in years. She could go anywhere she wanted. Delia and Carl never did have that conversation about the war effort, but all the same Delia resolved to join up, to light out for some territories of her own. One night, as Carl tried to slip into bed without waking her, she declared that she was going to France to do relief work for the armed forces.

"I plan to sell those tusks to the museum," she said. "That'll get me enough for my berth."

"Mickie, wait. What about me? About us? We can finally be together now."

"I sail out this Saturday," she said and rolled onto her side away from him.

That was the end of their marriage. They wouldn't be officially divorced until 1922, and by then Carl would have already fallen in love with another woman. But that night he felt the irrevocable end and spent the next couple years alone, bitter and furious at Delia's desertion. Carl holed up in his studio, day after day, working on his sentimental little sculptures, African Hall nothing but a dream. A nifty little model gathering dust.

SEVEN

Human preservation comes in many forms—not one of them as lasting as good old mounted-skin taxidermy. Throughout our glorious past humans have been mummified and they have been embalmed, practices that, while they seem to lie along the lines of taxidermy, bear in the end little relation to our interests. Mummification drains a body and fills it with herbs and potions and wraps it up to dry, intact, for centuries. Embalmment replaces the cadaver's blood with certain chemicals to stave off, for a short time, the decaying process. Just enough time to get a good long look at a corpse before it's buried or burned. There is a third choice, and it is cryogenic freezing, like what Walt Disney reportedly did to his head, and while this is the least permanent of human-preservation options—provided, that is, that our science comes up with the technology of reanimation of frozen cells—it's nothing like taxidermy. Mummies are nothing like mounted animals. Embalmed corpses even less so. This is not to disparage mummies. Certainly a museum's acquisition of a new mummy makes far more headlines than its acquisition of a new dead animal. Mummies are unlike taxidermized animals not because taxidermy is some achievement beyond the ancient Egyptians' capabilities but because mummies are human, and to mount a human skin in a lifelike pose is an action we will not, as a species, put up with.

Imagine it. It takes only the smallest of moments for one to realize that paying thousands of dollars to preserve septuagenarian Aunt Alma as though caught in the midst of her favorite hobby (needlepoint, maybe, or calling her congressman) is a terrible idea. And not because of the costs. Not because of what happens to the skin of a human when you remove it from a corpse, cure it, and tan it. The leathering of a human hide. The things that happen to leather over time. We have so little hair to cover us up. It would be a full-on George Hamilton treatment for poor Aunt Alma, only much, much worse. And yet this, too, isn't it. This isn't why we don't, or probably even can't, taxidermize humans. It's their presence. Photographs of dead people we loved and still love and continue to miss are one thing, but their three-dimensional rendering is a separate thing altogether, this hard monument with plastic eyes that can look right at you, though only when you shift yourself into a specific position and never otherwise, no matter how much you might want them to. A body but a false body, never to speak, never to raise a hand hello, never to step toward you as you walk through the door, never to stand if sitting and never to sit if standing, never to fit itself into those easy rhythms of restful human breathing, never to sneeze or belch, never, never to nod the head, and never, of course, to speak. We can stomach it with animals. We may not like it, but we can stomach it. We can, however, afford no such treatment of each other. We can kill. We can torture. We can hack off limbs and rape one another in the foulest of ways. We humans can scalp a human, but who among us can have a go at the whole epidermis?

Edward Gein could. In 1957, police from Plainfield, Wisconsin, broke into Gein's house after he was suspected of killing a woman in town. What they found among the bottles, cans, and newspapers piled on the floor of his living room was a soup bowl made from a human skull. More skulls spiked on the bedposts. A chair seat made from human skin. And lampshades. Wastebaskets. All from tanned human hides. A bracelet of skin worn close on his own skin. Gein had a pull for the window shade decorated with a woman's lips and a belt made from a sewn-together string of nipples. And it gets worse. A box of noses and another box full of vaginas, each of which Gein carefully incised from the dug-up bodies of fresh corpses. One vagina he gilded in silver paint and topped off with a red ribbon—a present only he would want. In his confession to the murders and the grave robbing, Gein admitted to sometimes holding these vaginas over his own genitals in front of the mirror, and now we begin to see where Thomas Harris got his idea for Buffalo Bill in *Silence of the Lambs*. Gein seemed to have been making a woman suit that he could don, and by which he could transform. Police found leggings made from leg skin and a vest made from a woman's torso, breasts and all. He'd peeled the faces off the skulls of nine different women, hair still attached, and wore these around the house as masks. When asked whether he saw any resemblance between these women and his own mother, Gein replied, "Some."

Everything in Gein's house was some grim mix of hoarder and horror show except for his late mother's room, which was sealed up and kept in curatorial condition. Immaculate. Untouched for years. And now we begin to see where Robert Bloch—whose novel *Psycho* became the basis for Hitchcock's masterpiece—got his idea for Norman Bates. *My hobby is stuffing things. You know: taxidermy.* Gein could dress a deer (and I guess a person), but he was never a traditional taxidermist, and yet through this cinematic connection he's probably done more damage to our collective idea of The Taxidermist than anyone. The Taxidermist is troubled. The Taxidermist is deranged and not to be trusted. The Taxidermist does weird things to animals (or worse) because he cannot connect with people. And this notion continues well beyond Bates and Buffalo Bill (and Leatherface, the villain of *Texas Chainsaw Massacre,* another Ed Gein analogue). The taxidermist in the Hungarian filmmaker György Pálfi's *Taxidermia* mounts his own obese father and a handful of cats before embalming and decapitating himself. The title character in Matteo Garrone's

L'imbalsamatore is a short and ugly taxidermist fated (spoiler alert) to die. Never is a taxidermist just a guy with a job or a woman who goes to church and volunteers in the community—or, if they are, these are façades hiding dark and disturbing secrets. Taxidermists are villains, not heroes. They are characters who need to die at story's end.[1]

For Ed Gein, this process took a while. He died in a mental hospital in 1984—nearly thiry years after his skin work was found. Gein's corpse didn't receive the treatment his victims' did, but instead was buried in Wisconsin, topped with a gravestone that's inevitably become a target for serial-killer fans looking for tokens of their fandom. When it comes to serial killers it's always a shame that no one works to remember the names of their victims—quick, who did Jeffrey Dahmer (another Wisconsinite) dismember?—but Gein himself will always stay in the hearts and minds of a public eager to dabble, for a time, among such dark violence.

Easily the most famous "victim" of human preservation is Vladimir Lenin, who wanted to be buried in the ground but was deemed (by Stalin) too important to inter right away. On the evening of his death in 1924, the politburo decided to bring in embalmers to keep the body preserved for weeks so that Soviets could make pilgrimages to see the body of the man who had brought about the rise of communism in Russia. St. Petersburg had by this time been renamed to Leningrad, and the "Cult of Lenin" was powerful enough that after a month of public viewing visits to the body were still in demand. The embalmers decided to keep Lenin's corpse preserved indefinitely. And so they have, for more than eighty-five years. Twice a week, Lenin gets rubbed with a mixture of glycerin and potassium acetate

---

[1] A recent exception was seen in 2010's *Dinner for Schmucks*. Yes, the film's central schmuck is a taxidermist who makes little domestic dioramas of mice, but he's still alive by film's end and turns out to be pretty much the only character with a heart.

to keep his skin looking healthy—or, well, healthier than it other-wise would. Then, once every year, Lenin gets removed from his little case and is given the full-body treatment: the embalmers dis-robe him and remove the rubber bandages that cover the skin under his clothes, and then the body is drained. It's a lot like changing the oil in your car. Once clear, Lenin's veins and arteries are refilled with the glycerin mixture, and then the whole package soaks in a tub of the stuff. This is enough to restore the necessary elasticity to the skin. His viscera were removed long ago, but the bones are all still intact to preserve his body's shape. To keep the mouth together, his lips have been sewn shut, and glass eyes have been inserted under his eyelids. Otherwise you'd have a very ghastly Vladimir to gawk at.

Lenin's skin might look a lot like it once did when it was moving around the world on its own, but Lenin himself still looks dead. This is the goal of the mortician: to remind the living that the person ly-ing in the coffin is, yes, dead but that she looks all right, doesn't she? The hair, the makeup, the dress chosen by her relatives—it's like she's ready for a nice dinner. The motivation behind embalming humans before death is wishful thinking, the idea being that our own inevi-table death will be similarly pleasant. Death being only a certain kind of long sleep.

Or maybe the point of the embalmed corpse is simply representational—the corpse a better symbol of the life that once ani-mated it than any photograph or portrait could be. This was the mo-tivation behind history's other famous preserved body out there: Jeremy Bentham, the philosopher often credited for founding the school of utilitarianism—the belief that life should be read as an attempt to maximize the common good. "The greatest happiness for the greatest number of people," goes the central tenet, and as a utili-tarian through and through Bentham was optimistic that, even in death, he could be of some civic use. Years before his death he wrote plans in his will for his body to be preserved and put on display, "not out of affectation of singularity," he wrote, "but to the intent and with the desire that mankind may reap some small benefit in and by my decease."

In his will, Bentham called for a dissection lecture of his body, itself instrumental to his notions of use and public benefit. The point, he wrote, was "first to communicate curious interesting & highly important knowledge & secondly to show that the primitive horror at dissection originates in ignorance & is kept up by misconception and that the human body when dissected instead of being an object of disgust is as much more beautiful than any other piece of mechanism as it is more curious and wonderful."[2] For Bentham, then, a corpse wasn't so much a corpse as it was another human body available for study, one without a spirit to object to any prodding or slicing.

The utility, however, of the preserved body Bentham called his "Auto-Icon" is a little less clear. In what way does a man's inanimate body provide good to a great number of people? Bentham was no Vladimir Lenin. Bentham wanted his head dried similarly to the *Mokomokai*—a Maori rite of preserving the tattooed heads of family members, accomplished by removing the brains and eyes, sewing up all orifices, boiling the head and letting it dry. His close friend, Dr. Southwood Smith, tried to preserve the head through a slow extraction of fluids—sort of like what Don Franzen does when freeze-drying pets, though without such technological innovations as a vacuum drum—and the end result was a ghastly, blackened thing devoid of all expression. Even with the insertion of glass eyes in the sockets, Smith found it unsuitable for display as part of the Auto-Icon and ordered a wax head from a French sculptor. This was attached to Bentham's articulated skeleton, which was fit inside Bentham's clothes and stuffed with wool straw and hay to fill out his form. Then, like

---

[2] You'll forgive me for quoting Bentham everywhere I can. There's something so exotic and charged by the relentlessness of his run-ons.

a store manikin, he was posed. This was Bentham's wish, that his skeleton be "put together in such manner as that the whole figure may be seated in a Chair usually occupied by me when living in the attitude in which I am sitting when engaged in thought in the course of the time employed in writing." So it's a kind of action pose, for a man whose actions chiefly revolved around reading and writing. *The Thinker* rendered in the skin of the nineteenth-century gentleman: a flannel coat and cotton trousers.

It's a stretch to call the Auto-Icon (which sits even still in the corridors of University College, London) human taxidermy. No skin is used, for instance, so there goes "-dermy" right out the window.[3] But two things make me want to reconsider this needless distinction. One is the nature of Bentham's request, the importance, to him, that he be displayed "in a Chair usually occupied by me when living." He's even holding on to Dapple, the walking stick he favored so much he gave it a little name. And so the effect is clear: the Auto-Icon is meant to be seen as though you've just come across Bentham hard at work, though sitting in a little glass case. The illusion of life and animation so central to successful taxidermy is there. But more than its simple lifelikeness is the name Bentham chose for this project: Auto-Icon. In an unpublished pamphlet that spells out all his ideas for body preservation, Bentham calls the Auto-Icon a man who is his own image. In the end Bentham found his own best use could be as himself. His body not as an object or tool but as the best representative of himself, his soul even, that he could find.

For Bentham, then, a body without life isn't a corpse, or at least doesn't have to be. If the body is a kind of vessel, that doesn't change in its death. A body without life is a symbol of that life. An icon.

---

[3] The mummified head, gray hair and all, has since about 1975 been locked in a box and hidden uselessly away; turns out the head was a favorite thing to steal among prankster college kids. No one can view the head now, unless under "exceptional circumstances."

What can account for the overwhelming global success of the *Body Worlds* exhibit? Have you seen it, the exhibition of actual human body parts that have been "plastinated" so as never to decay? A liver. A set of lungs. A whole body that once pumped blood through miles of veins and arteries now turned into a gummy, rubbery thing you could touch—*if only they'd let you! Body Worlds* premiered in Tokyo in 1995 and has traveled just about everywhere in the world where there are people curious about the inner workings of this machine they've been carrying around all their workaday lives. In 2009, *Body Worlds* garnered its twenty-eight-millionth visitor. It's wildly popular despite the fact that for many of the world's earlier religions such a proud display of adulterated human bodies is nothing short of sacrilege. Genesis may allow us "dominion over the fish of the sea, and over the fowl of the air, and over the cattle, and over all the earth, and over every creeping thing that creepeth upon the earth," but Leviticus forbids . . . well, just about everything, I suppose, but specifically our making "any cuttings in [our] flesh" (circumcision being, I guess, one God-willed exception). And of course the New Testament insists our bodies "are the temple of God," and "if any man defile the temple of God, him shall God destroy; for the temple of God is holy." And yet gods be damned: here be a sacrilege of the body so compelling it's spawned at least two imitators.

For those unfamiliar, the bodies of *Body Worlds* are frozen by a process of plastination, wherein the process's inventor, Dr. Gunther von Hagens, vacuum pumps all the fluids out of a corpse and injects it with a certain chemical cocktail of his own design, which travels throughout the body and, like a new kind of Midas touch, turns every organic bit it encounters into something harder and artificial. The organic rendered inorganic and thus permanent. Or at least permanenter. Hagens can verify that every body he's ever laid his hands on was donated to him,[4] and at one point British tabloid the *Daily Mail* claimed he was in talks with the Jackson family about plastinating the late King of Pop (doing the moonwalk, perhaps, with beloved Bubbles mounted fawningly at his unfleshed, skeletal feet). All *Body Worlds* bodies are skinned, as a rule, so that the intricacies of musculature, viscera, and circulatory systems are exposed for scrutiny. It's actually very cool: the life-size version of those transparent human-body kits you can build at home. Except here before you is the real thing. Oh, and they're posed.

It seems to be important that they're posed. It seems important to the experience of seeing human body parts on display—static poses are perhaps too reminiscent of the death and decay these bodies have found a way to cheat. So you've got a man running. A guitar player sort of, like, *shredding* on some kind of stage, his torso all bent rockingly backward, a Fender Stratocaster in his hands. Three dudes playing poker like C. M. Coolidge's famous dogs—a display apparently solicited by the producers of the film *Casino Royale,* which features a scene set at the *Body Worlds* exhibit. There's even been a couple making out, the heterosexuality of which is made clear by the ratty golden-haired wig fixed to the exposed scalp of the woman. Here's where the absurdity kicks in. Stephen Colbert once joked that plastinated bodies "help science answer one of the most enduring questions: What would it look like if just nerves caught a football?"

The joke works because of the dubious nature of the exhibit. *Body Worlds* tends to find exhibition space in natural history museums, so there's the feel of science going on. And, sure, Hagens fills out the exhibition with "close up" displays of single organs or, say, the brain and spinal cord that do give visitors a clear idea of how

---

[4] It's unclear whether the bodies were donated for the sole purpose of being plastinated and put on absurdist display, or whether they were donated instead for the more general purpose of "scientific study," which on some level *Body Worlds* sort of is—scientific study as tourist attraction.

their bodies work. But when he starts exhibiting pieces called *The Sex Couple,* with a woman (dewigged now) riding a man in the pornography-centric reverse-cowgirl position, one can't help seeing the show as exploitative, or as a technological development by Hagens that is good for little more than a new kind of freak show.

A visit to *Body Worlds* is the sort of afternoon activity that I'd imagine would be a pretty hard sell to a group of tourists: *Who wants to see some deskinned, plastic body parts posed whimsically under spotlights? Anyone? They've got a couple having sex. . . .* And yet, as I've said, there are at least two imitation exhibits, one of which, titled *Bodies . . . The Exhibition,* has been reeling in audiences at Manhattan's South Street Seaport since 2005. To ease the gruesomeness of the experience, *Bodies* keeps the focus on education: "You will leave with a greater understanding of your own physical makeup and with a deeper respect for the machine that gives you the power of life," it promises. And I suppose this is true. In the hour or so I spend touring through its eight galleries, I learn that there are more than sixty thousand miles of blood vessels in the human body and that the human eyeball does not change in size from infancy to adulthood. I learn that, while a healthy penis may look a little like Florida, a penis with cancer looks more gnarled and flayed like the Scandinavian Peninsula, and that a penis in cross-section looks like a hog's pawprint.[5] I learn that some people are poor judges of the distance sound carries, or maybe that they just have little shame. "I like this," I overhear at one point the female half of a thirtysomething Jersey couple say to her bruiser of a boyfriend. "I like learning things. You'll probably maul me tonight because you know all these new access points." *New access points? Like what, the peripheral nervous system?* I'm standing maybe too close to this couple, notebook in hand, a glass case of some human brains between us, and I hope as

---

[5] I couldn't help noticing that said cross-section had been cut on the bias, like a zucchini, to make, I guess, the penis look a little girthier.

I write the conversation down that she means a mauling in her brain point—some Adorno after dinner, perhaps?—but from the way he snickers I know some baser access will be granted this evening, if not sooner.

There's much in *Bodies* that isn't easy to take a close look at. If there's anything to learn it's that our bodies aren't all beauty and wonder. For some reason the plastination process leaves fingernails intact, as well as eyebrows, eyelashes, and, well, the hair around the anus. The effect of noticing these on otherwise deskinned bodies is precisely like finding some pinfeathers stuck to a roasted chicken wing. And because of the lack of skin all the specimens are missing their scrotums, separating the poor testicles like opened drapes on either side of the penis. Also, *Bodies* is big on disease and the failures of the body. A large case sits on the floor right inside the entryway to the *Respiratory* Gallery, inviting visitors to "leave [their] cigarettes in this gallery and quit smoking now." Marlboros and Newports dominate the three-foot stack of offerings. For further encouragement, two lungs are on display, one from a lifelong smoker and another from a tuberculosis victim. Guess which one's blacker. There's a very fleshy specimen displaying "adipose (fat) tissue," and the fact that here, in our fifth gallery, is the first female specimen of the whole exhibition is a sadness that seems to have been lost on Premier Exhibitions of Atlanta, Georgia, the company that tours *Bodies* around the world. The penultimate gallery of the exhibition is dedicated to "fetal development," and visitors are asked to "pause a moment and consider if [they] wish to enter this gallery," where fetuses that died in utero are preserved at thirty-two, twenty-four, fourteen, and just nine weeks. The youngest fetus looks alien and disturbing, with limbs curled inward and a head and eyes composing easily sixty percent of its total mass. Thankfully they've spared the fetuses the goofy indignity of action poses. Instead, we see them floating in alcohol as though caught in the amnion. We see them inside a cross-section of a pregnant woman's torso or suffering (or well, having suffered) from spina bifida or conjoined as twins.[6] And despite all this questionable destruction/deployment of human bodies I hear and see little to no outrage. Everyone seems to have paused a moment to consider whether they want to see the fetuses and decided, okay, yes, let's see the fetuses. One of the final stops on the exhibition before we're invited to browse the gift shop is a table full of loose-leaf binders. "Please share your thoughts," a sign reads, and I take a minute to flip through some pages.

"I thought the tiny humans were awesome! I loved your wonderful mueseum [sic]!"

"In the room where you show babies, I like the nine weeks one. It's a tiny human! It looked so cool! You must work hard on these exhibits."

"I didn't see that many women here but owell [sic] it was still really cool. The babys [sic] exhibit was really sad and very interesting."

"My only complaint was that most of the displays were of men . . . why is that?"

It's a good question, another being: why do all the specimens have an Asiatic look to them? Another commenter ventures a guess. "I did notice a lack of women, which may be due to the fact that more men volunteered than women." Except that in the case of *Bodies . . . The Exhibition,* nobody volunteered. I found this out from the gallery educator who was sitting in a lab coat in the corner (she's a bona fide medical student, so the lab coat retained a kind of officialness) and

---

[6] Echoes of Chang and Eng, and easily *Bodies*'s most Barnumesque throwback.

who told me that the bodies and body parts I'd been looking at came from unclaimed corpses at Dalian Medical University in China, where an anatomist named Dr. Sui Hongjin once worked with Hagens on developing his plastination technique. This explains the apparent ethnicity of the specimens, but what about the lack of women? This I don't get any insight on until just before I leave the exhibit, when I happen to notice a little sign hung in the corner just inside the door. Incredibly easy to miss, here's what it says:

> This exhibit displays full body cadavers as well as human body parts, organs, fetuses and embryos that come from cadavers of Chinese citizens or residents. With respect to the human parts, organs, fetuses and embryos you are viewing, Premier relies solely on the representations of its Chinese partners and cannot independently verify that they do not belong to persons executed while incarcerated in Chinese prisons.

In other words, I just spent two hours and $26.50 to look at the skinned and plastinated bodies of executed Chinese prisoners. And their unborn fetuses. As of this writing, *Bodies* has been open at the South Street Seaport for more than five years, and not without some controversy. It began before *Bodies* even opened in the United States, which it did at the Tampa Museum of Science and Industry in August of 2005. A year earlier Hagens released a statement officially discriminating his *Body Worlds* exhibit from this new one from China, claiming that he didn't know whence Hongjin got his bodies. "Until I receive proof to the contrary," he wrote, "I personally am assuming that he obtained these bodies in accordance with the laws that apply in the People's Republic of China."[7] *Bodies* opened

---

[7] The controversy stems deeper and earlier than this, in that the German magazine *Der Spiegel* has published several articles linking Hagens to the

in New York in November of 2005, and different versions traveled throughout the country, with human rights advocates getting vocal about the unclear origins of these bodies. San Francisco passed an ordinance in September of that year amending the city's police code prohibiting the display of human corpses and body parts without written authorization from the deceased or the deceased's next of kin, essentially banning Premier Exhibitions from bringing its show to the city. Little notice was taken, however, until *20/20* produced a segment on *Bodies* in February of 2008 that uncovered the very apparent connections between *Bodies* and China's trade in human corpses. According to the report, Dalian Medical University claims never to have provided specimens to Premier Exhibitions, and the reporter, Brian Ross, took undercover cameras thirty miles away from Dalian, where Premier's body preparation was being done. What he found was a filthy mess of ramshackle buildings, the sort of vast, dark, abandoned spaces that tend to appear in the final acts of horror films. He also received photos from a former trafficker in human bodies that showed corpses lying on the snowy ground outside a research facility, their heads covered in plastic. The Chinese government executes more of its citizens than any other country in the world, upward of 1,700 each year according to an Amnesty International report, preferring a point-blank pistol shot to the back of the skull to get the job done. Hence the plastic bags.

The *20/20* segment admitted that no hard evidence exists that any of the more than 1,000 bodies and body parts on display at all of Premier's exhibits were taken from executed prisoners. And with this lack of evidence then New York State Attorney General Andrew M. Cuomo was able to do little more than get Premier to agree in a settlement to put up signs like the one I saw on my departure, with its slippery double negative. Those signs went up in May 2008,

---

same trafficking in Chinese prisoners from which the aforementioned press release tried to distance him.

after *Bodies*—in New York alone—had been seen by more than 1.5 million people. And the exhibition is still open to a public eager to see in plastic what once lived in flesh.

Bodies . . . The Exhibition has no animal bodies on display, but Hagens has plastinated a giraffe and an ostrich and a horse, among other creatures. I don't know why this is. I don't know why Hagens, once he figured out a way to do the things he's now famous for doing, went right for cadavers, but he must have known what would draw viewers. People have been flocking to this exhibit in numbers that far outrank every single visitor of every single World Taxidermy Championships ever held, and thus it seems to follow that we're happier or more comfortable or more eager and curious to look at a dead human than a dead animal. It's like my friend Heather. She's not a fan of film violence, but she'd much rather watch the cinematic slaying of a human character than an animal one. And if the character is an animal and if the animal is a dog and if that dog gets killed on the screen, Heather has been known to stand up and walk right out of the theater. It's a thing with which she'll have no truck.

Call her extreme, but if there's anything I've discovered in writing this book it's that people can have very extreme emotions when it comes to animals. And maybe this is just as good a place as any to get into the ongoing debates surrounding animal rights, for by its very nature taxidermy is an affront to those rights. At least, this is the stance taken by People for the Ethical Treatment of Animals. "If an animal dies of natural causes," Colleen O'Brien, PETA's director of communications, told me, "PETA would not be ethically opposed to his or her body being preserved by taxidermy, although it strikes us as disrespectful to put the animal on display. We'd never preserve and display a beloved *human* family member."

Indeed. PETA's ethos is a golden-rule variant: do not do unto animals what we would not do unto ourselves. This is the way taxidermy is disrespectful—we wouldn't allow it for one another. All the taxidermists I've talked with, naturally, disagree with PETA on this and just about every other issue (recall that acronym-revising T-shirt at the WTC). They see taxidermy as a chief form of respect for animals. What does it mean, also, that most taxidermists I've talked with are also hunters? Like Wendy Christensen-Senk, the chief taxidermist at the Milwaukee Public Museum, and the hunter who easily had the most patience while trying to talk with me about her passion. Which it is, a passion. Yes, she loves taxidermy, but it cannot compare to the act of bow hunting elk, her favorite quarry. It's not what most people think when they think of hunting. An arrow can go only a fraction of the distance of a bullet, and so it's not sitting up in a tree and listening for the footfalls of something tiny and precious. Elk are animals larger than most Volkswagens, and when they run it sounds like a fleet of horses at the finish line, and for Wendy the only way she's going to come out of this with a kill is to run right alongside these animals, all of them bugling their guttural squeals over the thundering of their hoofs. "There is literally nothing more exciting in the world," she says, likening it to a religious experience. There's such closeness, such direct access to the elk at its most animal. Of every kind of animal on the planet Wendy loves the elk the most. She tries to hunt one every year.

Like most contradictions, it's one we're uncomfortable with, and the one that characterizes what the environmental scholar Stephen R. Kellert calls "nature hunters": people who love and admire the animals they hunt, who do it for an "intense involvement with wild animals in their natural habitats." Nature hunters are distinguished from utilitarian hunters, who do it for the meat, and sport hunters, who do it for the mastery and competition.

> The nature hunter, more than any other hunter, felt [in Kellert's study] the need to rationalize the death of the animal. Motivated by genuine affection for wildlife, the nature hunter

faced the paradox of inflicting death on the object of his affection. In contrast, the utilitarian/meat and dominionistic/sport hunters revealed far less concern and affection for wildlife, and the kill could be more easily justified by satisfactions such as obtaining meat or displaying skill.

This study was done more than thirty years ago, and hunting has been much on the decline since then,[8] but Kellert found that most hunters (43.8 percent) were classified as utilitarian, with sport hunters falling in second place (38.5 percent). Nature hunters constituted only 17.7 percent of those surveyed, putting them very much in the minority. But it's a vital minority because this is the demographic that almost every taxidermist I spoke with would place himself or herself in. For what other reason than affection and admiration for wildlife would a person become a taxidermist? Certainly not the money. "I have an extreme love for wildlife," Wendy says. "I've always had one. When I was young it always bothered me to see animals all destroyed on the roadside. I thought, *What a waste. Why not try to make them look better and more lifelike?*"

Here, then, is a kind of respect for animals. Wendy sees taxidermy as a way to correct misfortunes wrought by nature—or by cars and bullets, which are different, newer facets of our nature. This animal was alive; then it died. Let's make it look alive again. One major element of taxidermy is the way it broadcasts human dominance. We can do this to animals, but they can't do this to us, which brings us back to PETA's original complaint. James Swan, in his *A Defense of Hunting,* gets quite smartly at the idea that the debate over animal rights is essentially an ongoing custody battle. "Down through the ages," he writes, "the concept of stewardship—that humans have a responsibility to care for the creatures that feed them—has been the

---

[8] Though of all hunters, the percentage of women who hunt has been on the rise.

law of the land and it has worked to the benefit of both." The question of course is who gets to decide what's best for animals, and what exactly does that entail? Even posing such a question, and certainly coming to an answer for it, implies that humans and animals—like parents and their children—are not equal. The liberator, historically, is never on common ground with the liberated.

If there's anyone on the planet best qualified to speak for animals it's the bioethicist Peter Singer, if only because he seems to have taken the most time to think about it. In his *Animal Liberation*—the PETA bible, in many ways—Singer lays out the case for the equal consideration of animals and the minimizing (if not the end) of animal suffering. Singer's approach is rational, not emotional. He admits early on to not being particularly interested in animals, or even loving them. He "simply want[s] them treated as the independent sentient beings that they are, and not as a means to human ends." Singer smartly avoids claiming that he knows what's best for animals. He just knows what's bad for humans and humans' ethical living. "Speciesism" is the term coined in Singer's book, referring to a prejudice toward members of one's own species and against those of another species. It's as ethically wrong as racism or sexism is Singer's overall claim, and because we would never sit back and allow suffering on other humans for any reason we should also reject the same kinds of suffering done to animals.

Singer's focus on suffering is where his ideas begin to overlap with hunting. "The conclusions argued for in this book flow from the principle of minimizing suffering alone," he writes.

> The idea that it is also wrong to kill animals painlessly gives some of these conclusions additional support that is welcome but strictly unnecessary. Interestingly enough, this is true even of the conclusion that we ought to become vegetarians, a conclusion that in the popular mind is generally based on some kind of absolute prohibition on killing.

But it's not, Singer says. The point of vegetarianism is all about changing one's diet to minimize animal suffering. Hence the book's investigative focus on factory farms:[9] here animals suffer all their lives in order to become cheap food or pretty coats. Is this really how we should treat them? And rare is the hunter who disregards animal suffering. Rare is the hunter who isn't concerned for the conservation and proliferation of game. And it's here that hunters and animal-rights activists have tons of basic, fundamental stuff in common, but what gets broadcast is "meat is murder" and "you'll pry my gun out of my cold, dead hands." What are we supposed to *do* with these creatures we share the planet with? How can we live together? Killing them without any regard seems wrong, but so does leaving them alone, which is PETA's preferred solution to the us-them problem. "In a perfect world," O'Brien says, "all animals would be free from human interference and free to live their lives the way nature intended. They would be part of the ecological scheme, as they were before humans domesticated them."

Animals in one corner, humans in another. Because, it seems, they can't play together nicely, PETA asks them not to play together at all.

Some weak confessions: I kill most spiders that make their way into my home, and I've hit fewer than five animals while driving. Never on purpose. I've killed betta fish through neglect, perhaps, and I once killed a very tiny garter snake that had a habit of hanging out on my patio. I took a shovel and brought it down about a dozen times on what I guess I could only call its "neck" until all the frantic whipping of its thin body stopped, and the relief I felt at no longer having

---

[9] It's PETA's focus, too, along with animal testing and animals used in entertainment (zoos, circuses, etc.). Despite what most hunters seem to believe, hunting, so says Colleen O'Brien, isn't really high on the list of PETA's priorities. "PETA opposes it," she says, but by the organization's reckoning "fewer than seven percent of Americans hunt."

to worry about a snake (or, let's be honest, "worry" about a "snake") lasted maybe minutes. Probably only seconds. Then the remorse kicked in, and I felt, like Akeley claimed to in Africa, like a murderer. This was two years ago, and I still feel awful about it. I'm not about to try to figure out what this says about me, but maybe it points to a disposition. Killing noninsect/nonarachnid animals is not for me. Sorry, folks. I'm just not cut out for it.

But despite maybe a short run in my misguided teenage years I've never felt much fury or even held any mild criticism toward hunters. I've also never understood the impulse. But what have I ever known about animals? What have I ever bothered to find out? I think that I get it, the hunting impulse. I know that the truth of this world is that our capacity for love, for this emotion we've always put a name to, is large enough to allow some room for animals, and yet this allowance isn't as warm as our love for other people. It's colder, darker, and full of bloodshed. In other words, not only can we humans feel a palpable love for an animal, but for many people this love has lots of capacity for cruelty. We keep our dogs in cages throughout the workday because, we rationalize, they enjoy having a small, tight space all their own. And when it comes time to sleep at night we do it pretty soundly. Likewise, many people go out in the wild and find animals to shoot and kill, and their nights are just as restful. They're not monsters. They don't lack empathetic skills. Or at least I can't believe that they do. Moral equivalence isn't anything I know much of. I'm not Singer. But increasingly these days, as I see more of the world and talk to new kinds of people, it's getting harder and harder to confidently call something out when I see it as "wrong" or "immoral." Maybe in the abstract, this kind of thing is easy, but to talk with Wendy and to think of her as a hypocrite is as impossible as imagining what it feels like to die.

I'm taking a lot of time to think about hunting in a book that's been meant to focus on taxidermy. And not just in this chapter. Throughout the book I've found myself shifting gears somewhere in

the middle of a chapter to try to come to certain terms with hunting, only to realize this was off topic and trash it all. Hunting is not
taxidermy. The latter can exist without the former. But more often
than not taxidermy is an outcome of hunting, and so it's seemed disingenuous all this time to talk so freely about taxidermy without ac-
knowledging its grisly, ethically murky cousin.

If it's true that hunting can be (but isn't necessarily always) a way
to honor an animal or that tangential to the act of hunting is a respect and love for the animal being hunted, then it follows to me
that taxidermy is probably the best way to broadcast this love to a
dubious audience. Because you can love deer all you want, but it seems
strange and self-defeating to act on that love by going out into the
wild and shooting the animal and leaving it there to rot and decay.
What kind of stewardship is that? But if you shoot the deer and dress
the carcass and butcher the meat to feed your family through the winter and take the skin and make something of it—especially if that
something is a monument to the very animal that once lived to provide you with all it has provided you—isn't this a form of honor, of
deferential respect?

We make icons of our idols, and we have done this since Lascaux.
It's why self-conscious eBay'd taxidermy is, in the end, such a drag
to find in people's houses. An animal had to die for this? To outfit a
TV room with a retro-chic vibe? And I say this and I ask these questions as a man who has purchased and hung self-conscious eBay'd
taxidermy. But no longer. Let this be a bit of advice for anyone looking to get a game head: don't just get the mount, get the story behind
the mount. Talk to the hunter and listen to the steps he took to track
down the animal and shoot it. Figure out what happened to the flesh,
the bones, the rest of the skin you're not seeing. Maybe it uncomfort-
ably reminds us that this thing we have decorating our homes had its
life taken from it, but more than anything it keeps taxidermy honest.
Every mount is an encounter, a chance to engage in an animal that
would have otherwise been a stranger to you. It's why we invented

epitaphs: none of us wants to be forgotten in death. We can't ever know whether animals feel the same way, but doesn't it seem respectful to assume so?

No one can ever guarantee he'll be remembered. For Carl Akeley, African Hall was his best shot, but by 1921—ten years after he returned with the skins—the elephant group hadn't even been completed. No money had been raised to break ground on the new wing. Carl was fifty-seven years old at a time when the average life expectancy was fifty-six. His first marriage had died. His second one was about to begin, but it wouldn't last long. He had killed hundreds of animals no one had ever seen. But up until 1921 he had never named one of them. He had never looked into the eyes of an animal he'd taken down and saw therein a personality, a personhood, to put a name to. Then, in the summer of 1921, he went with his lawyer and a handful of wealthy women to the Belgian Congo (once Zaire, now the Democratic Republic of the Congo) and shot his first gorilla. It was a long time coming. Back in 1910, wandering through German East Africa with Delia in search of his big tusker, Carl bought permits from the German government and secured the funds for a gorilla-hunting excursion. Then an elephant nearly tore off his face, and plans changed.[10]

Now, eleven years later, he followed a team of native guides up the side of Mount Mikeno (ca. 10,000 feet), the territory almost vertical in places and slick with mud from the constant rains. After two hours of slow climbing, Carl looked down on the trail and saw in the midst of

---

[10] For the record, Carl never fully recovered from his elephant mauling. Photographs of the man in Africa show him as hale and alive. He was never "built" like, say, Roosevelt, but he was strong. Carl's African body was that of a featherweight boxer's. The New York / wartime photographs, however, show a much weaker man. Sunken eyes and sagged skin.

a mud hole a gorilla's unmistakable fistprint. Knuckles like the roots of a tree. "There is no other track like this on earth," Carl wrote in *In Brightest Africa*. "There is no other hand in the world so large." Soon they caught up with the animal: a large adult male. A perfect specimen. The gorilla saw Carl and his men and let them know it. "The thrill of it! I had actually heard the roar of a bull gorilla!" Carl fixed himself against a four-inch-diameter sapling that grew hopefully out of the mountainside. Behind this tree: a two hundred-foot drop into a chasm. He braced himself and fired. The gorilla fell down the steep slope, landing just eight feet away. This Carl dubbed the Old Man of Mikeno. Some days later he shot a female, and her orphaned child was speared by one of his guides. Carl stayed awake through the night to skin the child, preserving the little body in formalin. He didn't bother to give the mother a name, but this young gorilla he named Clarence.

It's what Carl's short for.

Throughout his adult life, Carl's close friends called him Ake. It was the sort of manly, collegial nickname he would have encouraged. Everyone else called him Carl. He hadn't been Clarence since he left Clarendon, and so this was the person he named the dead gorilla after: the boy Akeley. The restless middle child. The boy who spent more time out of his mother's house than in it, following birds from tree to tree, looking so closely at the wildlife he hoped one day to capture.

Little dead Clarence. It's Carl Akeley's Rosebud. In the late, late years of his life he had gone for the fourth time to Africa as sick as he'd ever felt—blood-poisoned, twenty pounds lost in just three weeks—and there he killed some small part of himself. The hunter part. He returned in the fall of 1921 with a new resolve, a new shot at leaving his legacy on the world. He was going to start a gorilla preserve. He was going to make sure no more Clarences died by the hands of white hunters.

———

At the dawn of the twentieth century, gorillas were ferocious, man-eating creatures that nabbed women away from camps in the night and crushed gun barrels in their jaws. Which is to say, they were extremely misunderstood animals. After all, they'd only just been described in scientific literature—the more common western, or lowland, gorilla (*Gorilla gorilla*)[11] in 1847 and its cousin, the eastern, or mountain, gorilla (*Gorilla berengi*) in 1903. By the time Akeley shot Clarence, only a handful of people had even seen this latter species, which lives way up in the mountains in very dense jungle. Prince William of Sweden was one of them. He shot fourteen gorillas just days before Carl arrived in the Belgian Congo. In his preliminary notes for the 1921 expedition Carl already saw the need for preservation. He and his party would be hunting in the plateau joining the Mikeno, Karisimbi, and Bisoke mountains, and, he wrote, "I doubt if the entire gorilla population will exceed fifty individuals. It will be a very simple matter to exterminate them."

Gorillas are members of the *Hominidae* family, which also contains chimpanzees, orangutans, and humans, and almost a hundred years later the mountain gorilla is still near extinction—only about 680 are alive in the world today. The International Union for Conservation of Nature classifies the mountain gorilla as "endangered," meaning it faces a high risk of extinction in the wild. This puts it on par with the tiger, the giant panda, the blue whale, the sea otter, the whooping crane, the snow leopard, the Tasmanian devil, the mountain nyala, the northern abalone, and nearly 2,500 other animal species (to say nothing of those the IUCN classifies as "critically endangered"). Now: no one wants to play favorites in the Who Gets Saved? Game of Biological Extinction. Call me speciesist—or, well, familyist—but it's hard not to root for the hominids. Every

---

[11] One of a small number of animals with an echoic nomenclature. See also *Rattus rattus, Bison bison, Vulpes vulpes, Lynx lynx,* et al.

single species in that family is endangered, except for us. The IUCN, cheekily perhaps, classifies humans as species of "least concern."

After returning from his gorilla expedition in 1921, Carl traveled the States giving lectures on the gentility and endangerment of the gorilla. Lecturing was a task he normally hated.[12] But he was happy to put the mounting of the gorilla skins on hold to share what he'd learned about this otherwise misunderstood animal. He lectured wherever he could, even going out to Battle Creek, Michigan, at the request of the Corn Flakes inventor John Harvey Kellogg, where Carl informed the guests at Kellogg's sanitarium that the gorilla was, like them, vegetarian. Akeley's remarks on the gorilla formed the basis for his chapter in *In Brightest Africa* titled "Is the Gorilla Almost a Man?" and the similarities among the *Gorilla* and *Homo* genera seemed to dwell on the man almost daily in the last six years of his life. Witness the naming of baby Clarence. Witness also this confession,

---

[12] Throughout his career at the American Museum of Natural History he was asked to give lectures, and by all accounts Carl never relished standing in front of a podium. He also hated writing down his stories, preferring instead to talk extemporaneously to a small group, pipe in hand. From a typed manuscript of Carl's on his elephant mauling: "Upon returning from the summit of Kenya to the shambas at the edge of the forest I went back again to the bamboos to make the photographic studies for the background and gather materials for accessories of the group. While thus engaged I met a bull elephant who left me much the worse for the experience and necessitated my return to the base camp on a stretcher." However, when writing in his diaries in the field, hours after the events, Carl's able to relax, and the writing becomes quite good. Here he is on a tribal lion spearing he witnessed: "Tragedy was at-hand when—the circle of warriors complete round the raging devil in his lair—every man suddenly crouched low behind his shield like a runner tense for the start—the long keen lances flashing white fire in the sun, the lion, with mane erect, fangs simply foaming defiance—his great muscles rippling neath his great loins—and his tail lashing his flanks as he turned this way and that—with short snarling roars—seeking in vain a channel of escape."

about the Old Man of Mikeno: "I am really fonder of him than I am of myself." In 1924, Carl took this inspiration and worked it into his sculpture. The piece, depicting a man with windswept hair and hypernoble brow emerging out of the shrugged-off cloak of a gorilla skin, he called *The Chrysalis*, and its evolutionary undertones were altogether unsubtle enough to warrant not even being called undertones. Dr. John Roach Stratton, a Baptist pastor who made a name for himself in the 1920s by taking on evolution in general and the American Museum of Natural History's Hall of the Age of Man (now The Anne and Bernard Spitzer Hall of Human Origins) in specific, called Carl's sculpture "the complete crystallized negation of Bible teaching" and lamented it as evidence of "the wave of animalism that is sweeping the country and degrading American youth." Carl submitted the sculpture for an exhibition of the National Academy of Design, who, fearing controversy, rejected the piece.

Carl was unfazed, continuing his lecture series and promoting his book. He left, in these years between gorilla trips, a whole mess of papers, notes, and diaries. Much of it the AMNH secretary Dorothy Greene formed into chapters that would become his memoir, but much of it never saw print. Much of it ended up, as so many manuscripts do, in drawers and boxes, and then, at some point in the eighty-plus years since Carl's sudden death, it all got to the climate-controlled archives of the AMNH, where you can schedule a visit to pore over the pages at a wide wooden table under the watchful eyes of people paid to ensure these documents stick around for many more years than Carl himself did. And amid all the materials, in one of the folders among all the folders in one of the boxes among all the boxes, there's this piece of paper, in Akeley's scratchy illegible hand, detailing some thoughts of his regarding that first gorilla expedition:

> The story of the complete success of the expedition has
> been told—how the gorillas were found in a region perfectly
> healthy and in a region so beautiful that almost anyone

would be willing to ~~live there~~ leave their bones there if necessary.

We can't ever know the impetus for Carl's spooky and prescient revision here, but it's almost as though he knew. He knew: he'd never be able to live, really live, among the gorillas he found at the tops of mountains, so he'd have to the do the next best thing. He'd have to die among them.

Mary Jobe made for herself a life of adventure long before she let Carl Akeley enter into it. A masters degree from Columbia University, a fellowship in the Royal Geographic Society in London. Throughout the 1910s she'd made numerous explorations through the mountainous regions of British Columbia, sometimes with a male companion whom she slept with out of wedlock and had no qualms thereover. But more often Mary Jobe ventured forth solo, and received from the U.S. press the erroneous distinction of having been the first white woman to feast eyes upon the exotic native peoples of northern British Columbia. "Red Men Probably Never Have Seen a White Woman," read one subhead of the *New York Herald,* "but She Expects Little Trouble." And she found little trouble, little she couldn't handle. In 1914 she made it to the top of an uncharted peak of the Canadian Rockies 150 miles northwest of Mount Robson, and the Canadian government named the mountain in her honor: Mount Jobe, altitude around 11,000 feet.[13]

And now this man, this little taxidermist she couldn't help falling in love with, despite his marriage to another woman. British Columbia, was, yes, far, but Africa was farther, wasn't it? Mary bided

---

[13] Not everyone was impressed. The Vancouver *Sun* wrote that, "We have so many little mounds about that altitude that it is possible one may have been overlooked."

her time for six years before Carl made an honest woman out of her, remaining the mistress at home while he ran off to Africa with the Bradleys to hunt gorillas. In 1924 she and Carl were finally married, and in 1925 Carl railed up to Rochester for a weekend to meet with George Eastman, the founder of Kodak, to ask for money so that work on African Hall could be started in earnest. This was in August, and Mary was sitting in their apartment on East 37th Street with a book and her fingers crossed. Any hope of beginning work on African Hall hinged on Eastman's support; the AMNH had made it clear there was no money in the budget for another expedition. She hadn't expected Carl to be this late, and when he came through the door just after nine o'clock, he tossed his hat through the air and kicked up his heels. "We got it, Mary!" he said. "He's in for six groups." And he laughed and capered about like a schoolboy, her sixty-one-year-old husband looking for the first time like the man she'd always imagined, the young adventurer who lived his life to the fullest long before she'd ever met him.

The expedition would leave in January of 1926, and in the coming months Carl not only had to hire fellow taxidermists and scene painters to accompany him, but the AMNH president, Henry Fairfield Osborn, requested that he mount a kind of miniexhibition, a preview of what visitors to the completed hall might experience, in order to drum up some public funds for its construction. African Hall had been approved for thirteen years, and the only thing to show for it was Carl's mounted bull elephant. He now had merely three months to put together some small version of his forty-group vision. The hall opened in December of 1925. Carl had managed, in his fevered excitement about his pending expedition, to mount five gorillas, the remaining three elephants from his 1909 expedition, and a group of lions, the skins of which the museum happened to have on hand. For this latter group he hired a painter to make a rudimentary backdrop. The hall was filled out with Carl's near-life-size sculptures of the Nandi spearmen he watched slay a lion back in 1910. The total effect was to his dream of African Hall what corpse parts were to Dr. Frankenstein's mad project: a hasty assembly, still lacking the spark of life.

Mary was proud. She stood the whole evening by the Nandi spearmen and watched Carl show off his crude little lion diorama like a kid at show-and-tell. At the end of the evening they were at home and Carl surprised her with a new question, "Would you like to go with me? Would you go to Africa?"

The plan had been for her to stay in New York for the duration of the winter and then spend the warmer months in Mystic, Connecticut, preparing the camp she helped run for another summer season. It was a saddening plan; the expedition would take sixteen months, and she'd only been married to Carl for fifteen. Was it, she worried, an inauspicious honeymoon? There in their bedroom she stopped unlacing her boots and looked up at him.

"We haven't found anyone to manage the books, the personnel," Carl explained. "We don't even have a driver. It wouldn't be terribly thrilling work, but it would be hard work. And I hope it would be heartening work."

She mentioned the camp. Her speaking engagements already lined up for the year. The home they'd just begun to make.

"I know it, Mary," he said. "I'm asking you to give it up, for a time. I'm asking you to work with me."

What choice did she have? This man was no longer her companion, her lover; he was her husband, and this was a marriage. A partnership. It's what she signed up for, wasn't it? Whatever life she'd been making for herself stateside would have to be put on hold.

Before she knew it, Mary had left the snows of New York for the hot summer sun of British East Africa, the sky deep and blue and everywhere overhead. Her husband gone every day in the field, back after sunset to sleep in a separate tent. And after watching klipspringers bounce among the kopjes and fall to her husband's sure aim, after the weeks-long hunt for a bull giraffe tall enough to suit Carl, after the heat, after the typhoid fevers both she and her husband caught, after the nine wild dogs Carl shot indiscriminately from the passenger (shotgun) seat while she drove aimlessly over the African plains, after reaching camp that night and watching her husband run off after dinner to skin nine dog carcasses, and after smelling the funk of same, Mary Jobe Akeley found herself racing a rickety old truck over craggy dirt roads to Nairobi, her husband blanketed on a cot in the back, his mind reeling with fever and delirium, the closest hospital no fewer than three hundred miles away.

His body at expedition's start had been so sporty, so hale. That first klipspringer he brought down he'd brought to Mary's tent, the dead animal slung around his narrow shoulders. Hanging there, it was no bigger than a scarf, really, but she was charmed by the image. Her own circus strongman, showing off. He skinned all four klipspringers himself, all nine dogs, working most days from 4 A.M. until long after sundown, George Eastman out gallivanting on his own shopping spree. And then days after finishing with the dogs, Carl's fever returned, this time to a temperature of 103, and for seven days he couldn't even leave his tent, wouldn't take any offered food. Mary had had to make the decision to get him to a hospital. Carl raged at any plans that would steer him off course, and every member of the staff stayed out of what had suddenly become an ongoing quarrel between spouses. She asked his assistants, Robert Rockwell and Richard Raddatz, to help Carl into a cot and to fix the cot in the back of the truck, and all the while Carl ranted and shouted at them. He called her a worrywart, a fussy hen. She felt like a jailer taking him off to prison. This, Mary thought, was the reward he left for her loyalty. This rage. This fever, these sweats, this dysentery and lack of appetite. Carl had just turned sixty-two. What kind of sixty-two-year-old man works such long hours, refuses so much help?

The man she married, she realized. The man she fell in love with for this exact reason.

She drove on, Carl drifting in and out of sleep despite the bumpiness of the terrain. After a few hours the sky darkened and opened up, rain falling all about them. In no time at all the dusty roads turned to muddy roads, and then swampy roads, and soon there was nothing for the truck's wheels to hold on to. They'd have to make camp here, in the middle of the jungle.

Bill was with her, old Bill now, Carl's devoted gun boy all grown up. He'd just appeared one day at their door after they originally arrived in Nairobi, somewhat like a genie, and that morning when Mary had been introduced to this man—Carl beaming as though here before her was his own flesh and blood—she'd noticed a hesitation, a darkening of his eyes. It was clear she was not what he'd expected. It was clear he thought fondly of that other woman, the one who had ruined Carl's life. But that flicker of unrecognition, of regret, lasted seconds, and from that point on Bill had been nothing but devoted to them both. Now, as the rains increased, Bill pitched the tent over the truck's bed, getting *bwana* dry, and Mary found wood to make a fire near enough to the truck for Carl to be warmed by it. There the two sat as the day got darker. The heat made the wet air miserable, and Carl's fever would not go down.

Mary sat and stared into the blackness of the trees that marked the edge of the bush, and there she saw a lioness watching them. It was at too far a distance to see others, but not so far that she couldn't hear them, a whole pride of big cats growling as though airing their displeasure at all this mud, all this rain. She pointed out this lioness to Bill, and he simply nodded. She knew lions didn't attack humans unless provoked. Weeks earlier she'd shot her first lion—her first animal—at Carl's urging, and throughout the whole miserable experience the animal had just stood there and stared at her, curious about the long object she held up calmly to her eye. Carl had whooped when he fell, and she turned to him and said, in as clear and pleasant a voice as she could muster, "Thank you, Carl, but I don't think I'll be doing any more hunting."

Mary got maybe an hour of sleep that night. Maybe less. As the rains slowly abated and the night stretched infinitely the lions' roars only got louder and more continuous. Could they smell Carl's illness? She hoped he had better success sleeping, but in the morning, when she got up to check on him in the tent, he was wide awake and smiling at her. "Mary," he said. "The lions gave us a farewell concert last night."

Three days later they were in Nairobi. Carl's face as they carried him into the Kenya Nursing Home was slack and gray like that of an embalmed corpse. Mary stayed up through the night as they treated his fever, and in the morning a nurse stopped by to report he was doing better. "I can't believe it, quite frankly," she said. "When you came yesterday, I had no idea he could live through the night."

Carl stayed twenty-one days in Nairobi, visited by everyone he knew in Africa. Eastman, hot on the trail of exciting game, failed to stop by.[14] Mary made the decision, against the doctor's suggestions, to release Carl. She'd hoped that getting back on his feet and working toward his goals would bring him out of his sickness. There was so much more to do. There were wooden cases to build in which to ship the collection home, and there were greater kudu to collect out near Kilimanjaro, but Carl told her to scrap all that. He wanted to

---

[14] He famously filmed a rhinoceros charging right at the camera, not calling for the shot until it was a mere twenty feet away. It was a film he showed just about everyone back home who'd indulge him, and the resulting calls of "Bad business, George!" and "Terrible!" were maybe his favorite trophies from the whole trip.

head straight from Nairobi to the Kivu Mountains. It was time to visit the gorillas.

Nairobi is a mountain town. It sits more than 6,000 feet above sea level between Mount Kenya to the north (where Carl got up-close and too personal with an elephant) and Mount Kilimanjaro to the south (the famous snows of which are said to be fast disappearing). To the west of the city spreads the East African Rift, a long valley that cuts down through the middle of the continent, where its tectonic plates rub perpetually against one another. Nairobi, then, is not immune to earthquakes. Nor does it have any gorillas in the vicinity. Those were more than five hundred miles to the west, across the East African Rift and past Lake Victoria to the Lake Kivu region that sits right at the borders of Uganda, Rwanda, and the Democratic Republic of the Congo. To drive from Nairobi to Lake Kivu is a lot like driving from Salt Lake City to Lake Tahoe—on dirt roads. It took Mary and Carl more than a week to get there. On 18 October 1926, they celebrated their two-year anniversary together. The couple spent it with Ugandan royalty, making camp at the palace of a native king who claimed to have more than seven thousand subjects. Carl was alert and happy. In Uganda the air was warm but breezy, and as Mary sat on the ground and beheld the gifts of smoked fish and great green plantain chandeliers the tribesman offered she could tell her husband was at last breathing clearly and fully, and she knew she'd been right to urge him out of that hospital and back on the trail.

And yet, wasn't there throughout the journey to the Congo an air of decadence swelling around them? Mary felt as though she could smell it in the humidity, and soon she was able to see it. At one point en route to Uganda, they'd come to the top of a steep incline and saw stretched on the plains before them a whole little town dropped in the middle of nowhere. Carl had stopped and spit and glared at the scene. "It's been just fifteen years, Mary," he said. "Fifteen years since I hunted lions here with Colonel Roosevelt, and there wasn't a single house here back then. Just plains, filled with herds of antelope and zebra and plenty of lions. In three hundred miles we've not seen a dozen animals. Now it's desolation!" Bill had looked back at him, seeming to share in Carl's grief and rage, and Mary saw that there was more between them than she could ever know. They'd crafted an Africa of their own together, one where the rules of sportsmanship and *bwana* / boy loyalty were supposed to have spared them from any fault. This desolation Carl railed against wasn't his own doing, nor had he helped keep these animals as abundant as they'd been before he ever saw this country.

This is why she was so proud of the work he'd done since 1921 to start the *Parc National Albert*, keeping hunters and poachers from entering the chief habitat of the mountain gorilla. It was, she knew, a form of atonement. Whereas African Hall was a testament to the animals that died in Africa by his hand, the *Parc National Albert* would be a testament to those that would live. And this is why she shared Carl's sense of urgency that they go there directly: to see the gorilla, man's closest cousin of all the primates, in its natural habitat. To take in the mountains' panoramas framed by the gray moss and green vines that hung like theater curtains from the trees, the massive fern fronds that spread everywhere, the ubiquitous wild celery's herby leaves. It all had to happen now, when the cold rains that fell daily on the mountain would take hours to clear, setting the atmosphere just right for William Leigh, the painter Carl hired for the expedition, to capture the soft purples and yellows of the sun beaming on the landscape. Here, at the top of a mountain on the other side of the world, was her husband's most cherished spot, the place he'd make his home if he could. She wanted to live there with him, if only for a time.

To get there, Carl had to be carried up the mountainside. Just a couple hours into the climb, Mary had come upon him sitting with his head hung down between his knees, his breathing as jagged as the hillside. "I feel very strange," he'd said. "Very dizzy. I need to think about what to do next." He wanted to keep going after a short rest, but Mary wouldn't allow it. Bill and Raddatz fashioned a cot, and their progress the rest of the day was considerably slower, though for Mary it flew by, her mind not on the trail or the mountain but on the life that seemed to be leaking out of her husband the higher they went. Why hadn't they brought a doctor with them? What good was a taxidermist when a man's body was ailing?

What good a mountain climber, for that matter? Mary had some expertise here, she knew, and now she tried to use it. On the hillside, she visored her brow and made an estimate on how much farther they'd have to travel, and she made a guess at three days. It took five. The rains that they'd been expecting had indeed come on time, but they had not stopped after the brief showers Carl had described. The rains came on that second day and then continued, the air getting colder and colder the higher they went. Carl wanted to make camp in the same place where in 1921 he'd gone gorilla hunting and by the time they reached the spot they were at 11,000 feet and soaked and miserable. Carl was put in his tent immediately, and he told Mary she should pitch hers just outside the camp's perimeter. "For noise, dear," he said. "I don't want your sleep disturbed."

Thus began their final days together. The next morning Carl woke late and felt nauseated and wouldn't eat. His fever was back at 103. Raddatz tried to find plant specimens to collect, from which he could make artificial leaves and flowers for the diorama. Leigh sketched trees and mountains in the distance. Jean Derscheid, a Belgian zoologist sent to help establish the Parc National Albert, tried to survey the landscape. Mary sat in Carl's tent, replacing one cool rag on his forehead with another. She tried to breathe deeply and calmly, to steady herself for him, but the air this high was so thin that one deep breath could barely fill her lungs. How, she wondered, was Carl getting the air he needed? Carl just slept, and then he couldn't sleep. Outside, the rain turned to sleet and then snow, and Carl's fever got worse. He'd been suffering for days from dysentery, and despite his lack of food intake his bowels emptied themselves over the bedsheets every few hours. Mary, dutifully, bathed and changed her sick husband each time, his eyes following her ministrations wordlessly, pitifully. She knew that if anything was killing this man it was such incapacity. She sat with him when he needed her to, and while he slept she caught what sleep she could in her own tent. The next day he said one thing to her: "I feel as if I were boiling." His cheek was cold and clammy. She sent one of their native guides for a doctor—a six-day trip there and back. The next day Carl awoke having slept well. He and Raddatz spent hours in the tent talking, man to man, and Mary laid on her own cot way out of earshot. She guessed she'd just wait her turn. She had no idea what could have been so important at this stage. What did they have to talk about? How could her husband still want to work after all this suffering? What could Raddatz do for him that she, his own wife, could not? In those long hours that last day she grew to hate this place Carl loved. The air too thin. The ground too wet. This was no place for newlyweds. This kind of adventure was not ever what she'd signed on for. Yes, she had married a sixty-year-old man, but was that something she had to be punished for? She wanted to go home. She wanted to go with her husband back home. She wanted to go to his tent right now and lift him over her shoulder and carry him down this mountain, drive him the five hundred miles back to Nairobi, catch the train to Mombasa and there board a ship through the Suez Canal and then on to London and then on, at last, to New York. It could take less than two months. It could be the happiest two months of their lives.

All that day and the next she looked in on Carl in his tent, and every time she saw he was asleep. A good sign, she felt. A sign of progress. And then around four thirty she was just sitting in her tent with nothing on her mind, nothing to do to pass the time but wait, and she looked up to see Derscheid's face in the tent's opening. "Mary," he said, and it was all he had to say. It was all he had to do to make her old body collapse, the wind sucked right out of her lungs.

Clarence Ethan Akeley died on Wednesday, 17 November 1926, and every major newspaper in the country carried his obituary. Well, they carried the Associated Press wire, dateline 30 November, which is how long it took Mary's wire to reach the AMNH. The obituary states that the museum had earlier denied reports of a nervous breakdown, which nervous breakdown both George Eastman and his physician, Dr. Audley Stewart, went on record to confirm. "We left him at Nairobi apparently recovering from a nervous breakdown," Eastman told the AP. It's everywhere in the literature of Carl's death: *breakdown*. It was the world's first shot at writing this man's history, and who knows whether they got it right. The obit claimed he was "the first in this country to make taxidermy a fine art," forgetting any of the work done by Hornaday, Webster, Lucas, and other Society of American Taxidermists forefathers. Another AP story focused on his time in Rochester and spoke with some unnamed Ward's employees about Akeley's tenure there. "It is recalled," the story passively asserts, "that young Akeley's first attempt, mounting a zebra by moulding a papier-mâché framework over a plaster coat, failed and was discarded." The narrative was being set down so soon: the artist in perpetual struggle with his abilities, his mental capacities. *The Washington Post* was among the few that printed a photo, and lord only knows where the hell it came from. In it, Carl looks costumed. Made up. The sinister stooge to a noir villain, standing in the shadowed corner of a basement room, awaiting instructions. His hat is worn so low on his head that, in the photo, you can't make out his eyes, and his jaw hangs loose enough that his thin lips are split as if in a stupor. It would be wrong to say he looked cadaverous, dressed up as he is in a hat, suit, and heavy wool overcoat, but the lines that run down his jaw and neck—wormy, rigid—suggest aging far beyond his sixty-two years.

A life lived, if not roughly, then forcefully. A man whose home, after so many trips to "brightest Africa," must have become a dark and foreign place—the people there pale and sweaty. A world of strangers shuffling about on two dumb legs.

To hear of it, everyone loved Carl Akeley. Everyone. Even George Eastman, who found space in his heart to say in the obituary that Carl was "an interesting companion and a remarkable man." On 21 December 1926, AMNH President Osborn held a meeting in the museum's auditorium to remember Carl's life. Kermit Roosevelt said a few words, as did the Belgian ambassador. It took ten more years to collect the specimens and build the dioramas for African Hall, and whereas Carl had intended to name the place for his hero, Theodore Roosevelt, the museum proclaimed on 12 May 1936 that the hall would be named for Carl.[15] The Field Museum had already done this to its Hall of African Mammals back in 1927 (though by now the name has been unofficially decommissioned).

Carl E. Akeley Memorial African Hall opened on 19 May 1936—what would have been Carl's seventy-second birthday. It is Carl Akeley's legacy, and it's not his, comprising just twenty-eight dioramas to his planned forty, all but a few mounted by other taxidermists. Despite everything Carl tried to claim about Africa, it's the darkest hall in the museum. Darkest African Hall. If you enter from the Roosevelt Rotunda and make an immediate left, the first diorama you find is the gorilla group. Staring right at you, up on its hind legs and beating his chest as though animated in some Holly-

---

[15] Way back in October of 1927, Akeley freshly buried, the *Boston Traveler* reported that the hall would be named in the honor of "Mrs. Mary L. Jobe Akeley, African explorer, who is recognized as an authority in her sphere." To add to the overall wrongness of this bit of news, the story was printed alongside a photograph of Delia.

wood B-movie, is the Old Man of Mikeno. In his notes, Carl wrote that he didn't see how the gorilla group could depict much action:

> It may be legitimate to have one animal, perhaps one of the old males, standing nearly upright with his hands against his chest as though in the act of beating his chest. We have heard much of this performance on the part of enraged gorillas, but that it is necessarily the performance of an enraged gorilla I very much doubt. . . . I do not think it is ligitimate [sic] to mount a gorilla standing full upright as is frequently done to show his enormous size.

Needless to say, the Old Man of Mikeno is mounted standing fully upright, beating his chest. His mouth is partially open, but thankfully no teeth are being bared. Before him sits the adult female who never got a name, a piece of leaf hanging yokel-like from her lips, and baby Clarence staring into the near distance, as though bored and lost.

Other adulterations of Carl Akeley's vision were put in place. When building his model of African Hall and when selling the wealthy men of pre–World War I America on the idea of funding a whole new wing, Akeley had imagined bas-relief sculptures on the walls above each diorama that would depict the lives of the native peoples of Africa—a kind of symbiosis of land, animal, and man. The sculptures today show in flattened 3-D the animals featured in full below. The sculptures of the Nandi hunters that Carl had Mary show off during the trial run of African Hall are now in the museum's basement. You walk past them when looking for a place to grab some food or when wading through field-tripping tots on your way to the bathrooms. You wonder about New York's required ratio of chaperones to schoolkids and decide that whatever it might be it's altogether too low, and then suddenly looking you in the eye is a five-feet-tall figure of a man with a spear that seems incredibly familiar. Who wants to look at a piece of anthropological sculpture in the basement corridor of a natural history museum?

Every natural history museum has these places. Every natural history museum is very old and every natural history museum feels the pressure of novelty to reattract through its doors the people who came last year, or when their first kid hit toddler age but not their second or third, and so in come the animatronics and the interactive panels and the new wings holding four-story IMAX theaters and out go the sentimental bronzes of Africans made by a white man suffering some complex form of homesickness. Out go the glass cases of native birds mounted on little fake branches. This is progress, and I write that without heavy-lidded irony; I write it without any feelings whatever toward generations newer than mine, MTV'd or otherwise. It simply is the form that progression takes in the natural history museum, and it's not only a form of progression Carl Akeley would welcome were he alive today but also a form of progression he helped establish. The habitat diorama as he came to know it is above all a reaction against earlier museum-display models. The habitat diorama did a better job of educating the public on the lives and habits of certain exotic and everyday animals, but the habitat diorama is a step, not the conclusion, of some long progression. It has had, in the seventy-five years since African Hall's opening, to compete with cinema in the task of depicting animals in their natural habitats. Why look at a fake animal standing among fake plants in front of a fake backdrop when you can watch a movie of living, breathing animals in their real habitats moving and making noises like we real animals do?

Here's an answer: the camera keeps its requisite distance. Here's another one: movies, screened as they are in wide, dark auditoriums, envision for themselves a mass audience. There's only so much space to stand in front of a diorama, and that animal can look you right in the eye for as long as you need it to. I could talk to you about the value of an authentic animal hide, and we could weigh its deadness, its stillness, against the animation of a cinematic capturing of said hide in the wild. But more important is this idea of audience. One of the wonders of a diorama is the way its smallness can be packaged as completely *for you,* despite the generations of visitors who have passed it by.

There's an obvious trick to making something monumental: you get it off the ground. James Madison was reportedly five feet and four inches tall but you wouldn't know it from visiting the statue of him that sits in the Library of Congress. It's where we get the idiom of putting someone on a pedestal. We need to look up to the representations of people we look up to. The African elephant when fully grown already soars over the heads of even the tallest among us, but this wasn't any reason to deny the animal a more monumental scale. African Hall is a vast space, about three basketball courts laid side-by-side, anchored by an enormous pedestal holding eight mounted elephants five feet off the ground. The group is menacing. They, these eight, are meant to tower over viewers and they are meant in their facing the east entrance to greet visitors to African Hall as a challenge. A threat. *Here Be Monsters.* We visitors do our part to imagine life glimmering in those big glass eyes, and we play the role of African adventurer caught on the cusp of a charge. We don't play the part very well, for what's beheld, what's made awe-ful before our eyes, not the illusion of eight charging elephants but rather this taxidermy's epic scale. We're not, after all, in the jungle; we're on the Upper West Side, and no amount of theatrics and no careful Akeley methods will enable us to forget it. And yet. And still: nothing like this massive group exists on the planet.

The Alarm in its magnitude and its immensity turns African Hall into a kind of stage. A kind of theater-in-the-round with the twenty-eight dioramas that surround the group acting as opera boxes for the continent's bestial elite. Or, no, this is not the case, exactly. For the glass changes everything. Opera boxes are open and serve as stages of their own. Dioramas close and contain what they hold, and so the effect here is darker, more sinister. African Hall as a pervy coin-op peep show, each group of animals looking wantonly out at the largest among them, the trunks lengthy and with such heft, the hard tusks twinned and perky, raised buoyantly up to the heavens. It doesn't help that their booths are lit from the inside, the whole of the stage between them kept dark, the lights brought down as though before the start of a show. Here are long, harsh German expressionist shadows of bamboo stalks that slash across the bongo diorama. Here are the antelopes' barrel trunks, thin white lines painted bleedingly down their brown sides as though by a calligraphist. Their creeping postures in the scene as they climb a slight hill, one with a wall of glass at its crest and a man coated head to toe in cut fabrics just beyond. Here's another way the glass protects us from them: from the observer being himself observed, like at a police-station suspect lineup. Of course, being dead, the bongos can't observe anything. Compare this to the gemsbok group, five of which are lined right up in front of the glass and stare at you—*stare right at you*. An eerie, still quintet along the lines of something some hapless protagonist would encounter in a Kubrick film. The silent, uncurious gaze of the unfamiliar. "Their flesh is tasty," reads a nearby plaque, "and their thick, tough skin makes good leather." Is, now, good leather. Their ribbed horns, two of them, in a V, reach high over their horsey faces like the midworship arms of pagans around a fire. The fire is you.

It's such a rare experience to be acknowledged by an animal, to be truly looked at, eye to eye. To be looked at by a dead animal mounted behind glass is to enter into a staring contest you could never win. Try it with the greater kudu, just two scenes down from the creepy gemsbok. Here the buck is mounted on an incline, his head with its corkscrew horns a good three feet above your own head. Four or five if you're young. The head is turned youward. The buck looks down on you like a god would, a disappointed parent. Stare into its eyes. It's so easy to get highfalutin, but the difference between looking at a stuffed animal behind glass and going to the zoo to see something live is that with a diorama you're caught directly in this eye-to-eye encounter, instead of standing there like a fool trying to be a voyeur on the animal's day-to-day misery, hoping and praying that it turns its slow head and acknowledges you, there, with the camera and the waving. Diorama animals are looking right at us and are wholly unaware of us. If they were human this would be terrifying and awful, sitting for so long in front of one now-dead person's gaze. But they're just animal. They're fake, and this helps.

And this is what walking through African Hall comes down to. It's all fake. You reject this artifice as a sham, a shame, a waste of animal life or you embrace it. You embrace the fakeness of these effects, of your reactions and emotions. Everything you claim to feel. The background for the klipspringer group, depicting the Lukenia Hills in Kenya. The wide vista backing the gorilla group. It seems to look over the Virunga Mountains. It does not. *Ceci n'est pas une vue du mont.* The vines that reach from treetop to ground reach actually from ceiling to floor, and they, too, are fake, made of plastics and waxes through processes Akeley himself patented back in Chicago. Embrace it. The fakeness of the Old Man of Mikeno, standing up on two legs and beating his chest. No judge would award it a ribbon, not in a million years. The tree trunk felled in the okapi diorama, covered in wet green moss, its hollow core filled with mushrooms. It looks so real but it's fake and you know it's fake. Nothing lives forever. Nothing real avoids decay. The okapi themselves: squat-legged, squat-necked, squat-horned ungulates—like short and phony giraffes. And more vines here, an artificial forest canopy painted on the ceiling. You can see it, if you crouch close and crane your neck: fake treetops. There's a fake little Hitler face sketched on the front wall of the Upper Nile diorama, which diorama is backdropped with a flat

2-D painting of the river. It's nothing you could ever see, Hitler, not without smashing your face through the glass. The white rhinoceroses posed in perfect profile to the viewer, their verso sides painted an artificial white to better reflect light and prevent very real shadows from rendering the diorama more fake than it inherently is. Every diorama is an illusion. Every illusion requires fakery. It's a kind of faith we sign on for. We know the drool that hangs infantilely from the lips of the big bull buffalo is fake, made of a clear acrylic; we know that the zebra and antelope grazing in the distance from the pride of lions are made of pigment on plaster; we know the lions themselves are fake, seeing nothing, never again hungry for flesh. We know it and we don't want to know it, and we don't want to know that we know it. We look and try to see something real, and it never happens in African Hall, not once. We come close in the filthy and bloody hyena-jackal-vulture diorama, where, in the back there, a zebra carcass lies still and dead while being picked apart by several mad vultures. I mean: "a zebra carcass." I mean: "lies." I mean "dead" and "picked apart" and "mad." Which is more real, a dead animal's skin draped and mounted so as to enclose something living or the same piece of dead skin posed as though dead? Or, rather, which tells the better lie? Which constructed end—fake dead animal or fake living animal—best justifies the murderous means, the hunting, the slaying, the skinning?

I say neither. I say the answer is neither. We kill animals for all kinds of bullshit reasons. The juiced-up rottweiler torn open and panting on a cement floor, shot in the head after her first loss and of course her last one. The chicken slammed by hand against a concrete wall, its face smashed under a work-boot heel while Madonna's "Like a Prayer" plays on a nearby radio. The McNuggets and Crispy Strips that result. The mouse you find prone on the countertop, its neck laterally snapped and its tiny tongue still touching that dab of peanut butter. The snake's neck I split in two with a shovel on the patio. A raccoon at the edge of the woods shot from a speeding car's window one warm night. And we shoot horses, don't we? Yes, but now with tranquilizers strong enough to make a horse sleep himself to death. This was the end for Barbaro, a hero of a horse whose hoofs eventually failed on him. Lesser horses get less dignified treatments. Lesser horses get the rendering plant. The ant farm left to rot on a high shelf. The Sea-Monkeys crudding the bottom of a plastic tank. The giraffe made plastic by injected chemicals. The fourteen-foot tiger shark hunted by an Austrian and sold to Damien Hirst, who dunked the fish in 4,260 gallons of formaldehyde and made himself world famous. The piece has a title we're all good to note: *The Physical Impossibility of Death in the Mind of Someone Living.* The slow asphyxiation of a houseful of cockroaches as regrettable procedure and not as unbearable telos. Our desires to live near animals but not actually *with* them. (Our instinctive understanding of the bestiality taboo.) The distances we keep. The whitetail we smack with our fenders, the squirrels crushed under a tire, the aim we seem to take lest we swerve off the road and harm ourselves. Our self-protection. Our murderous self-preservation. Every single *dzzt* and *pop* of every backyard bug zapper. All those satisfying pyrotechnics.

Killed animals clutter up the gutters of our collective history. The extinctions we've accrued, like notches on a bedpost. The conquests. African Hall is a record of such conquest, and it's up to you whether you want to see it as a monument to killing or a monument to those that were killed. Because while we may kill animals for all kinds of bullshit reasons, we kill them for honorable ones, too, and then we make art out of it. We make our schoolkids read *The Yearling* and *Old Yeller,* and we use this art to remember the animal. And behind each click of those literary triggers was a young heart bursting with love. A taxidermized animal is a remembered animal, a memorialized animal, and something memorialized is something loved. Open your heart. We are not animals, we are given them.

Notes on Source Material

Having been born more than fifty years after his death, I never knew Carl Akeley, and so in building a life for him in these pages I've had to rely on the work of others—specifically Carl himself, whose *In Brightest Africa* (1923) laid the groundwork for the life narrative I sketch here. To fill in the gaps, I made much use of the archives at the American Museum of Natural History in New York, the Field Museum in Chicago, and the Milwaukee Public Museum. Mary Jobe Akeley's *The Wilderness Lives Again* (1940) has several flaws (the name Delia Akeley does not appear once in its pages, for instance), but it provided many insights on Akeley's early life and final months in Africa. Penelope Bodry-Sanders's *Carl Akeley: Africa's Collector, Africa's Savior* (1991) is a masterfully researched book I'm wholly indebted to. In 1927, the AMNH published its March-April issue of *Natural History* (volume 27, number 2) as a memorial to Akeley, which is full of stories and details by men who knew Akeley personally. It led to much hero worship, as did Roy Chapman Andrews's chapter on Akeley in *Beyond Adventure: The Lives of Three Explorers* (1962), but all the same as a researcher I found these records useful and fascinating.

Throughout the book I've done my best to write only details of Akeley's life I could find documented. In the interests of narrative

I've taken some liberties in giving my characters lines of dialogue to speak and inventing some setting details—always with an eye on extrapolating from what has been documented in the above sources and elsewhere. In doing this, I realize that I complicate the myth of Carl Akeley more than I sort it out, but such is the curse (or the gift?) of biography.

For chapter 1, I was lucky to find David Sturges Copeland's *History of Clarendon: From 1810 to 1888* (1889), which gave me a sense of life in Clarendon, New York, at the time Akeley lived there. Lewis Akeley, Carl's older brother, wrote a brief manuscript, "Early Life of Carl Akeley," for Mary Jobe Akeley (now in the AMNH archives), which gave me much insight into the Akeley family and Carl's boyhood. Details on the dogs exhibited at Tring come from Kim Dennis-Bryan and Juliet Clutton-Brock's *Dogs of the Last Hundred Years at the British Museum (Natural History)* (1988).

All the information I was able to find on J. W. Elwood's Northwestern School of Taxidermy came from the set of instruction booklets I mention buying at an old antique store, as well as any number of ads for the school I found digging through back issues of *Field and Stream*. Special thanks to Stephen Rogers (here, elsewhere, everywhere, really) for discovering Elwood's relentless borrowing from William T. Hornaday's *Taxidermy and Zoological Collecting* (1894) and Oliver Davie's *Methods in the Art of Taxidermy* (1894)—a close investigation of each of these texts revealed the extent to which Elwood piggybacked off those before him.

I used T. H. White's *The Bestiary: A Book of Beasts* (1960), including the introduction by Kenneth L. Frazier, to get a historical, literary, and visual sense of what these early attempts at classification were like. A general history of taxonomy was given to me in correspondence with Dr. John Janovy, and other sources—such as Michael Boylan's article, "Aristotle's Biology," from the University of Tennessee at Martin's *Internet Encyclopedia of Philosophy* and Erik Nordenskiöld *The History of Biology: A Survey* (1928)—filled in the details.

The good old *Encyclopædia Britannica* gave me what I needed on Carolus Linnaeus and his *Systema Naturae*. In uncovering early methods of animal preservation, I was helped greatly by the work of Fernando Marte, Amandine Péquignot, and David W. von Endt in their paper, "Arsenic in Taxidermy Collections: History, Detection, and Management," from the journal *Collection Forum* (2006). Christopher Frost's *A History of British Taxidermy* (1987) provided additional information on arsenic soap and its effects (or lack thereof) on taxidermists of the time. When it comes to the story and history of the Lisbon rhinoceros, I'm indebted to many sources, despite not having come away with any definite answers. Foremost thanks go to Silvio Bedini's *The Pope's Elephant* (2000) for a thorough account of the life of this rhino. Also L. C. Rookmaaker's article, "Specimens of Rhinoceros in European Collections before 1778," from the 1999 yearbook of the Swedish Linnaeus Society, helped both to illuminate and complicate the story. As it says in chapter 3, the best source I could trace this misconception to is a footnote in R. W. Shufeldt's article, "Scientific Taxidermy for Museums," found in the 1892 *Annual Report of the Board of Regents of the Smithsonian Institution,* and the only explanation I can think of for this myth's creation is a misunderstanding on George Brown Goode's part regarding another pachyderm (this one a hippopotamus) on exhibit in Florence that dates to the eighteenth century. See Liv Emma Thorsen's "The Hippopotamus in Florentine Zoological Museum 'La Specola': A Discussion of Stuffed Animals as Sources of Cultural History," from *Museologia scientifica* (2004) for further information. (And additional thanks here to Stephen Rogers and John Janelli for their illumination on the issue of the rhino.) The material on Ole Worm and the *Kunstkammer* comes from *The King's Kunstkammer* Web site produced by The National Museum of Denmark (www.kunstkammer.dk), as well as Ken Arnold's book, *Cabinets for the Curious: Looking Back at Early English Museums* (2006). Karen Wonders's book, *Habitat Dioramas: Illusions of Wilderness in Museums of Natural History* (1993), was one of the earliest sources of information on taxidermy I ever got my hands on, and it probably could have been mentioned earlier in these notes, but here in particular her exhaustively researched book gave me much insight on the history of taxidermic displays in Europe and the United States. Additional information on Charles Willson Peale came from Charles Coleman Sellers's biography, *Mr. Peale's Museum: Charles Wilson Peale and the First Popular Museum of Natural Science and Art* (1980); George Gaylord Simpson and H. Tobien's article, "The Rediscovery of Peale's Mastodon," from the 1954 *Proceedings of the American Philosophical Society*; as well as the book, *Mermaids, Mummies, and Mastodons: The Emergence of the American Museum* (1992), edited by William T. Alderson. These sources (Sellers in particular) had a little to say about P. T. Barnum in his dealings with the Peale family, but much of what I used came from James W. Cook's *The Arts of Deception: Playing with Fraud in the Age of Barnum* (2001), and Bluford Adams's *E Pluribus Barnum: The Great Showman and the Making of U.S. Popular Culture* (1997). Though very little of the account made its way into the final manuscript, I also learned much about the fire at Barnum's American Museum from its coverage in the *New York Times* from 14 July 1865. (My favorite line: "In a corner of the room was a pretty little kangaroo, but he too has gone, he can-go-roond no more.") Insight into the life of the young Delia Akeley came from Elizabeth Fagg Olds's chapter on Delia in *Women of the Four Winds* (1985), and for information on the beginnings of the Milwaukee Public Museum I went to Nancy Oestreich Lurie's *A Special Style: The Milwaukee Public Museum, 1882–1982*. Details on the donation and hunting history of Kenneth E. Behring came from Tim Golden's article, "Big-Game Hunter's Gift Roils the Smithsonian," from the 17 March 1999 *New York Times*.

Details surrounding the mountain lion appearances outside Omaha came from AP articles in the *Lincoln Journal Star* and coverage throughout November 2005 in the *Omaha World-Herald* by Abe Winter, Jennifer Gref, and Marion Rhodes. The *Nebraskaland* article on Todd Kranau I refer to was written by Doug Carroll and appeared in the

December 2002 issue of the magazine. While little of all that I found inside made it into the book, Colomon Jonas's *From "Stuffing" to Sculpturdermy: The Jonas Story* (1983) was a great resource not only on the beginnings of Jonas Brothers Taxidermy in particular but also on the early days of the U.S. taxidermy industry in general. Some of the history I provide on the Society of American Taxidermists comes from Hornaday's article "Masterpieces of American Taxidermy" from the July 1922 issue of *Scribner's* magazine, but I definitely owe much of what I learned on the SAT (and Hornaday's lordly role within) from Mary Ann Andrei's excellent article, *"Breathing New Life into Stuffed Animals:* The Society of American Taxidermists, 1880–1885" (2004), published in the journal *Collections*. Mark Alvey, the administrative coordinator at the Field Museum (and the author of a great piece on the movie camera Carl Akeley invented), was the first to inform me of the use of beet sugar as the snowy floor of the winter diorama in Akeley's *Four Seasons,* and in general Alvey was a great help throughout this project on Akeley's years in Chicago. That article, "Giving Away World Titles?" defending the World Taxidermy Championships's practice of withholding Best in World awards, appeared in *Breakthrough's* fall 2007 issue.

Data on the animals Carl Akeley collected for the Field Museum and American Museum of Natural History come from those museums' online collection databases. Most of the information here and in chapter 6 on J. T. Jr. comes from Delia Akeley's book *"J. T. Jr.": The Biography of an African Monkey* (1928), with extra details filled in by Bodry-Sanders. For contextual and historical information on safari hunting in British East Africa at the turn of the twentieth century, I found Brian Herne's *White Hunters: The Golden Age of African Safaris* (1999) extremely useful. Susan M. Pearce has written several books on the culture and history of collecting, but her *On Collecting: An Investigation into Collecting in the European Tradition* (1995) gave me the dual-axis array I borrow toward the end of chapter 5.

The story on the jackalope's invention came from Douglas Martin's obituary of Douglas Herrick from the 15 January 2003 issue of the *New York Times,* with additional information on jackalope lore and the Shope papillomavirus from Chuck Holliday and Dan Japuntich's research published on Holliday's Web site at Lafayette College. The tragic story of Travis the chimpanzee made numerous headlines nationwide the winter of 2009; I used Andy Newman and Anahad O'Connor's 17 February 2009 article in the *New York Times* for much of my details. I went to Geoffrey Hellman's *Bankers, Bones, & Beetles* (1969) for the history of the AMNH—specifically the buildings' erection dates and the weird factoid about Carl Akeley's one-time application for a job. Details on Walter Potter and his wacky tableaux came from Pat Morris's article, "Animal Magic," from the 7 December 2007 issue of the *Guardian,* as well as Frost's *History of British Taxidermy.* Rick Nadeau has a great Web site of his own (thesquirrelshole.com), and the newspaper article on his work I mention later in the chapter is Aimee Levitt's 12 August 2009 article, "Mount My Squirrel!" from the St. Louis *Riverfront Times.* Vito Marchino's tableaux came to my attention through numerous friends' forwarded e-mails and blog posts; RoadsideAmerica.com had the best photographs and history, and a phone call to the Cress Funeral Home in Madison, Wisconsin, verified that, yes, the squirrels are still available for viewing, but the funeral home asks that interested parties call the morning of their planned visits, in case there are any actual funerals going on that day, making the tittering of a bunch of silly novelty-taxidermy fans rather inappropriate. Harriet Ritvo's *The Animal Estate: The English and Other Creatures of the Victorian Age* (1987) not only has one of the better titles among all the sources I consulted but also gave me much insight on attitudes toward animals in Victorian England. Pat Morris's *Rowland Ward: Taxidermist to the World* (2003) filled in whatever narrow gaps Ritvo's book left on the Victorians in general and Wardian furniture in specific. Many thanks to Sheila Lintott's article, "Adjudicating the Debate Over Two Models of Nature Appreciation," from the *Journal of Aesthetic Education* (Autumn

2004), for laying out a summary of the object, landscape, and arousal models in terms legible to the nonaestheticist. William Blake's question of the tiger comes from his poem "The Tyger," published in *Songs of Experience* (1794). Thanks also to Kenneth Clark's *Animals and Men: Their Relationship as Reflected in Western Art from Prehistory to the Present Day* (1977) for its detailed account of the many forms animals have taken in the history of Western art. I got Emily Valentine Bullock's quote about animals being paint from her Web site: emilyvalentine.com.au, the factoid about the global insect population from the Smithsonian's *Encyclopedia Smithsonian,* and the quotation about Damien Hirst's use of animal parts being a forced confrontation with death from the summer 1998 issue of *International Socialism.* The information I use on the Minnesota Association of Rogue Taxidermists came from a variety of sources: the 7 February 2005 issue of U.S. checkout-line tabloid *Sun,* Joel Topcik's article on the MART in the 3 January 2005 issue of the *New York Times,* and personal correspondence with Robert Marbury. Jack Fishwick's quotation on hunting not needing to be an element of taxidermy comes from the BBC documentary *Taxidermy: Stuff the World* (2005). *New York* magazine's coverage of the emerging use of taxidermy in décor appeared in the 2 April 2007 issue, as a pop quiz titled "Stuffed." The *New York Times*'s article on the same was in a 26 April 2007 article titled "If There's a Buck in It Somewhere," written by Eric Wilson.

The details on Ed Gein's crimes came from Harold Schechter's *Deviant: The Shocking True Story of the Original "Psycho"* (1989), and the details on Lenin's embalming came from Ilya Zbarsky and Samuel Hutchinson's *Lenin's Embalmers* (1998), translated by Barbara Bray. (Zbarsky's father, Boris, was one of the original embalmers, and for what it's worth by the end of his book Ilya comes out as being pro-interment for Lenin's corpse, arguing that "embalming is a barbaric and anachronistic practice, alien to the cultures of Western societies.") Information on Jeremy Bentham and his Auto-Icon came from numerous sources: C. F. A. Marmoy's article "The 'Auto-Icon' of Jeremy

Bentham at University College, London," from a 1958 issue of *Medical History*; the online materials from University College, London's Bentham Project; and Bentham himself, whose unpublished pamphlet, "Auto-Icon; Further Uses of the Dead to the Living," I found in *Bentham's Auto-Icon and Related Writings* (2002), edited by James E. Crimmins. Ditto for the stuff on *Body Worlds* and its imitator, *Bodies . . . The Exhibition*—many valuable sources came to my aid in piecing together the mysteries around these strange shows. Much of the factual details on the process of plastination came from the *Body Worlds* Web site, and additional information on Dr. Gunther von Hagens, particularly his attempts to distance himself from allegations connecting his show to the Chinese corpse trade, came from press releases found on his site. Those allegations came from the 19 January 2004 issue of *Der Spiegel,* in an article, "Händler des Todes," written by Sven Roebel and Andreas Wasserman. The *London Telegraph* picked up the story on 25 January 2004, with an article that quotes the Amnesty International figure I use on China's annual number of executions. The *Daily Mail* piece on Hagens's interest in plastinating Michael Jackson ran on 26 June 2009. San Francisco's law essentially banning Premier Exhibitions from bringing its show to the city can be found in Article 11.1 of the San Francisco Police Code, amended on 6 September 2005. The *20/20* segment on *Bodies . . . The Exhibition* aired on 15 February 2008, and further action taken on the part of New York City was detailed in the *New York Times* on 29 May 2008 in an article titled " 'Bodies' Show Must Put Up Warnings." Stephen Colbert made his joke about *Bodies* on the 14 July 2009 episode of *The Colbert Report*. I first discovered Stephen R. Kellert's research on hunters in James A. Swan's book, *In Defense of Hunting* (1995), and the former's article, "Attitudes and Characteristics of Hunters and Antihunters," from *Transactions of the Forty-third North American Wildlife and Natural Resources Conference* (1978), filled in whatever details Swan left out. Peter Singer's *Animal Liberation* (1975) turns out to be a pretty good read, even if much of the information it provides is now, much to Singer's and PETA's credit, common knowledge. That data on life expectancy in 1921 came from the Centers for Disease Control. Regarding Clarence, the young gorilla Carl Akeley shot and named after some version of himself, I could find no information in the AMNH archives or other writing on Carl to corroborate Bodry-Sanders's account. Ditto Ake's line that he was fonder of the Old Man of Mikeno than he was of himself. Given Bodry-Sanders's longtime role in the AMNH as an archivist, I'm happy to take her word for it. Those quotations from John Roach Stratton on Akeley's *The Chrysalis* come from the 17 March 1924 and 9 April 1924 issues of the *Brooklyn Eagle*. That snarky line about Mary Jobe's mountain discovery appeared in the 21 September 1914 issue of the *Vancouver Sun*. Information on George Eastman's doings while in Africa comes from Elizabeth Brayer's *George Eastman: A Biography* (1996). The two articles run by the Associated Press after Akeley's death were datelined "Nairobi, British East Africa, Nov. 30" and "Rochester, N.Y. Nov. 30." *The Washington Post*'s photo, printed in its 1 December 1926 edition, has to be seen to be believed. Thanks to Stephen Quinn, whose *Windows on Nature: The Great Habitat Dioramas of the American Museum of Natural History* (2006) provided much inside information on the dioramas of African Hall, including the whitewashed rhinoceroses and the existence of the little Hitler caricature, dated 1939, on the inside wall of the Upper Nile diorama. Finally, the little detail about Madonna's "Like a Prayer" as background music in chicken slaughterhouses came from a video PETA distributed in 2004 showing workplace practices at a Pilgrim's Pride Corporation facility in Moorefield, West Virginia.

Acknowledgments

This book would have gone nowhere if it weren't for the knowledge and assistance of the many taxidermists patient enough to answer an ignorant kid's silly questions; Mike Pebeck, Todd Kranau, Don Franzen, Randy Holler, and Dan Rinehart deserve more recognition than I'm afraid I can give them here, and extra special thanks should be directed to the kind folks at the Taxidermy.net forums, specifically John Janelli and George Roof. Thanks to the good people behind this country's museum collections, including Trish Freeman, Todd Labedz, Suzanne McLaren, Stephen Rogers, Wendy Christensen-Senk, Mark Alvey, Paul Rhymer, Darrin Lunde, and the incredible Barbara Mathe, the archivist and head of library special collections for the American Museum of Natural History. Larry Blomquist and Skip Skidmore were extremely accommodating during my visit to the World Taxidermy Championships, as were the many judges I bothered. Thanks to all the hunters and artists I spoke and met with, especially Lee Dunekacke, Richard Heinrich, Robert Marbury, and Natalie Stevens. I owe a great debt to the Maude Hammond Fling estate for financial assistance during the research and early writing stages, as well as the University of Nebraska Office of Graduate Studies for selecting my proposal for the fellowship. Thanks also to Pamela and Theodore Madden for their patience and participation throughout this long process. Early versions of the manuscript were greatly improved by the input of many gracious people, including Tyrone Jaeger, Heather Green, Bryan DiSalvatore, John Janovy, and Sean Wilsey. I'm permanently indebted to Adam Peterson for his close, close reading of the book, and to the impeccable Katie Joseph for double-checking much of the animal facts I use. This book would be a rickety little thing without their help. And it would be nothing were it not for the early faith Gail Hochman and Jody Klein had in the book, as well as the encouragement and advocacy I received from Michael Flamini and everyone at St. Martin's. Finally, everything I was while writing this book I owe to Neal Nuttbrock, whose dismay at what I was spending much of my time thinking about was matched only by his belief in what I only hoped I could do. Thank you, Neal, for everything always.